MURDER
IN THE
HINDU
KUSH

MURDER
IN THE
HINDU
KUSH

GEORGE
HAYWARD
AND THE
GREAT
GAME

TIM HANNIGAN

The
History
Press

Front cover image: The only known photograph of George Hayward, *c.* 1870. (Image courtesy of the Royal Geographical Society (with IBG))

First published 2011
This paperback edition published 2019

The History Press
97 St George's Place
Cheltenham, GL50 3QB
www.thehistorypress.co.uk

British Library Cataloguing in Publication Data.
A catalogue record for this book is available from the British Library.

ISBN 978 0 7509 9205 3

Typesetting and origination by The History Press
Printed and bound in Great Britain by TJ International Ltd.

CONTENTS

MAPS

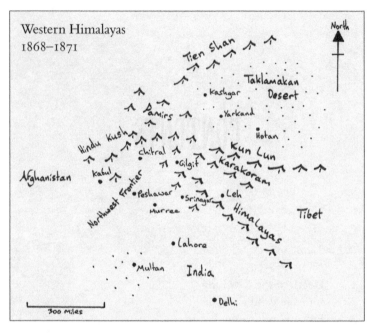

Western Himalayas
1868–1871

North

Tien Shan

Taklamakan
Desert

• Kashgar

• Yarkand

Pamirs

Hotan

Hindu Kush

Chitral

Kun Lun

Afghanistan

• Gilgit

Karakoram

• Kabul

Northwest Frontier

• Peshawar

• Srinagar

• Leh

• Murree

Himalayas

Tibet

• Lahore

• Multan

India

• Delhi

300 Miles

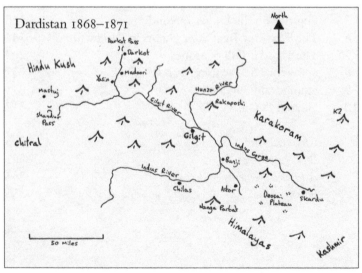

Dardistan 1868–1871

North

Hindu Kush

Darkot Pass

• Darkot

• Madoori

• Yasin

Hunza River

• Mastuj

Gilgit River

• Rakaposhi

Karakoram

K2

Shandur
Pass

Chitral

• Gilgit

Indus Gorge

Indus River

• Bunji

• Chilas

• Astor

Deosai
Plateau

• Skardu

Nanga Parbat

Himalayas

Kashmir

50 Miles

Eastern Turkestan
1868–1871

North

Tien Shan

Taklamakan

Kashgar

Pamirs

Yarkand River

Yarkand

Karghilik

Tashkurgan

Hunza

Shahidulla

Karakash River

Hotan

Gilgit

K2

Kun Lun

Karakoram
Pass

Lingzi
Thung

Kashmir

Karakoram

Srinagar

Leh

Pangong Lake

Himalayas

150 Miles

1

DEATH IN THE MORNING

The man had not slept all night. It was summer, but 9,000ft up in the high mountains of the Hindu Kush it had been cold during the hours of darkness. Now in the first blue-grey light before dawn, exhausted and hungry, he shivered. It was 18 July 1870.

He had arrived at this high campground the previous afternoon with his little party of servants and a group of surly local porters. For two days he had been moving slowly up this narrowing, steep-walled valley, with many a nervous backwards glance: he had left Yasin, the main village, on bad terms and these mountains were lawless and violent. He was far from any government or authority that could protect him, and he knew only too well that in this cold, rocky valley he was stripped of the privileges his nationality would afford him elsewhere. He was an Englishman – the first ever to reach this wild and stupendously remote spot, far beyond British territory, beyond even the troubled western frontier of Kashmir.

Only as he had moved further from Yasin the previous day had his mood lightened: the temperature had risen and a yellow haze softened the sharp edges of the vast peaks that towered over the valley. Though he was not moving at the scorching pace that he usually maintained, no one seemed to have followed him. No one had delayed his progress, and now, finally, he seemed on the brink of leaving all his recent troubles behind; tomorrow he would cross the high pass at the head of the valley and be gone from this troublesome territory. What was more, once he had passed that watershed he would at last be within striking distance of the very place he had been trying to reach for the previous two years: the High Pamirs; the Roof of the World; the unknown upland wilderness at the locked heart of Central Asia.

The valley was beautiful in a raw, almost violent way – this was a landscape of extremes. In the narrow bed there was green amongst the tumbled boulders, little terraces and patches of goat-cropped grass. The watercourses were lined with thickets of willow, in full leaf at this time of year, and there were ranks of slender poplar trees, bending and whispering in the running breeze. As the little party had pressed on upwards they passed occasional small villages of rough stone walls and flat roofs, stepped up the brown hillsides in uneven tiers. Sometimes the smell of wood smoke and pine sap or the sound of voices and the calls of goats drifted across the valley, and there were figures – broad-shouldered women in heavy skirts and bright skullcaps – at work in the little fields. Beyond that the land soared upwards, first through patches of threadbare pasture, and then into a vertical wasteland of fractured red-brown rock and scree. The great mountain walls towered higher and higher, into wind-scoured black buttresses and onwards into steep faces of permanent snow, glittering icy yellow and blue in the midday sunlight.

By late afternoon, when he pitched his rough canvas tent on a hillside below a stand of trees, the man had begun to relax. The day had passed without incident; he looked forward to the steep climb to the pass and anticipated the summit's great swelling view to the new country beyond. The local porters had downed their loads and wandered off bad-temperedly, but the man was unconcerned: he could find new men to carry his baggage in the morning. From here the journey would be physically tough but, he hoped, things would be less politically fraught.

Yet as the light lengthened down the valley, flaring the high peaks with gold and dropping slabs of blue shadow on to the lower slopes, one of his servants brought alarming news from the nearby hamlet of Darkot: he had been followed. A large group of armed men had trailed him all the way up the valley from Yasin. They had told the villagers that they had come to accompany the man over the pass, but they did not join his little camp nor even try to contact him. They were out of sight, hiding somewhere in the thick, scrubby forest, and the man was sure that they had sinister intentions.

The apprehension of the past days came rushing back, all the more intense now after the calm interlude. With a feeling of hollow nausea in the pit of his stomach the man realised the hopeless vulnerability of his position. There was no longer a chance for a quick about-turn back into less dangerous country.

Light fades very quickly after sunset in the high mountains, and in the heavy, blue stillness as the sky pales behind the ridges, sound carries a long way. Broken voices in the village; goats bleating as they were hurried down from the high pastures; and the noise of the stream, busy with meltwater from the curving glacier to the west, drifted up the valley to the lonely little campsite. Great smears of stars began to show in the rough-edged patch of sky. The man could hear his own heart beating.

He had no appetite and he declined his servants' offer of food. The five men who accompanied him – four servants and a munshi, or secretary – must have felt every bit as nervous, and all the more powerless, for they had simply followed him to this exposed place. Far from home, he had made their decisions. They were Kashmiris and Pashtuns, hard men from the lawless hills of the North-West Frontier, but this was not their country and they had good reason to be afraid. As the darkness came down, thick and heavy, the little group prepared for a miserable and lonely night, knowing that somewhere out of sight, somewhere on the hillsides or among the trees, men were watching them.

The man knew that he must not sleep. In the hours of darkness the rules change: awful things happen and men do deeds they would never do in the hard, judgemental glare of daylight. If evil was to befall him, the man was sure, it would do so before dawn. If all was well at sunrise, there would be hope. Anyone wishing to do him harm might hesitate then, and if he pressed quickly onwards with the same brash confidence with which he had left Yasin village perhaps it would carry him unscathed to the pass and beyond. What mattered now, more than anything, was that he must not sleep.

It was a long night. The man had loaded his rifles, taken his pistol in his left hand and sat in the doorway of his tent, his finger greasy with sweat on the trigger despite the cold. But you cannot sit alert like that for long after a day of hard uphill walking in the high mountains, no matter how pressing the need. Soon tiredness began to claw its way into the edges of his vision, his head swaying on weary shoulders. But he must not sleep!

The man took pen and paper, and lit a candle. He began to write, sitting at his collapsible camp table, simply for something to concentrate on, something to keep him alert. His left hand still firmly clasped the pistol. The single, lonely light flickered in the high, blank darkness – and the night rolled on. Cold air crept down from the glacier and the snow peaks, and a chill breeze moved through the poplars. The man wrote, on and on, long past midnight.

No one knows what he scribbled in those bleak hours, the pen scratching urgently in a spidery scrawl over the thin blue paper. When it came to making practical accounts of his previous journeys he had been a consummate professional, recording altitudes and route marches with military precision. In other moments he had proven himself capable of penning sharp passages of sarcastic humour, and also of impassioned and unrestrained indignation. Indeed, he had reason to suspect that it was an outburst of the

latter that had led him to his precarious vigil on this very mountainside. But whatever it was that he was writing that night, it
served its purpose: he did not sleep.

The tone of the darkness deepened; the wind dropped to nothing and the stars faded behind the peaks. Somewhere far to the
east, beyond the serried ranks of hills, morning was creeping out of
India. But the man had not stopped his writing, nor had he taken
his hand away from the revolver. When the morning light reached
him, the shapes of the valley formed like a photograph and were
clear in the bloodless light before dawn. The high crags were grey
and the branches of the trees hung limply in the cool air.

Finally, the man put down his pen and stepped out of the tent.
Everything was very still, and where the evening air had carried
sounds clearly and sharply, now the distant calls of sheep and goats
seemed deadened and muffled. His legs, arms and back ached
from sitting on the hard camp chair all night, and hunger gnawed
deep in his belly. He shivered, hugging himself in the chill grey air
as he glanced about the camp. There was no movement, no sound.
No sinister shadows flickered in the trees, no ominous party of
tribesmen loitered on the edge of the clearing. Perhaps the danger
had passed, or perhaps there had never been any danger at all. The
man wondered for a moment whether his long, sleepless vigil had
been an outburst of absurd panic over nothing. After all, there
had been other occasions when he had openly predicted his own
imminent demise and been proved wrong. Whatever the case, it
didn't matter; the night was over and he was exhausted.

Warming yellow sunshine began to seep over the eastern ridges.
Squatting down and still shivering, he kindled a small fire and boiled
water for tea. He drank it looking out over the valley. Goatherds
were beginning to move up the slopes with their flocks, and the
noise of the stream was reasserting itself after the false silence of first
light. All seemed well, and now the burden of extreme tiredness was
weighing ever more heavily; sleep was irresistible. He went back
into the tent and lay down, intending to catch a brief rest before
starting the day's journey. Unconsciousness came almost instantly,

waves of fatigue sweeping over him as he stretched out, bearing him down into a leaden sleep.

He did not see the single figure creeping across the clearing, flinching expectantly, but growing more confident as no pistol shot came, edging forward, peering into the tent and hurrying away with the news that the Englishman was finally asleep. He did not see the party of armed men in loose, rough clothes hurrying through the trees on the steep slope above the camp, then making their way swiftly, silently, down towards the tent. He did not see one of the Pashtuns challenging the intruders, and so deep was his sleep that he did not wake at the noise of the servant being overpowered.

The first thing he became aware of was a rough hand as it grasped him by the throat. He was dragged upwards from his camp bed, gagging and staggering. Perhaps in those moments of confusion he struggled to remember where he was, and by the time he had come fully to his senses a length of rough rope had been noosed around his neck and his hands were tightly bound behind him. He was dragged outside, blinking and squinting in the hard morning sunlight – for it was already about eight o'clock by now.

They pulled him away across the clearing, stumbling and tripping, and he saw that his servants and munshi had also been captured and bound and dragged off in other directions. As they hauled him uphill to the east, into the dense thicket of trees, he understood the ominous nature of what was happening: they were taking him away from the village, away from witnesses. He had already proved himself a brave man, but this was no time for stoical dignity: he begged; he pleaded with them; he offered to bargain. The captors paid no attention, ducking beneath low branches and hurriedly dragging him deeper into the thicket. They were lean men with fair skin burnt and creased by the harsh mountain climate. They wore twists of coarse turban-cloth or flat, roll-edged felt caps on their heads.

He would pay them off, the man said; they could take everything he had, all the gifts and equipment in the boxes back at his camp. The men scoffed at him. Had he not noticed his current circumstances? All that property was already theirs to take as they pleased. Very well, he said; then he would make sure that a ransom, a huge sum more than they could dream of, would be sent from his own people, the English who ruled India. But the men were not stupid; they knew that this was an empty offer and they paid him no heed. Desperate now, he said that he would send back down the valley to the Kashmiri frontier post at Gilgit; the governor there would provide the money if only they would release him. They were making a terrible mistake. If they would just send for his munshi everything could be arranged.

But they only jeered, enjoying his frantic attempts to bargain.

They were deep in the forest now, a mile from the village, and abruptly they came to a halt. The man stumbled to his knees on the rough ground and one of the captors reached out behind him and tore the ring from the finger of his bound hands. This, quite clearly, was it; the man understood that. And maybe too, in one sharp instant, he understood that he had been moving irresistibly towards this moment for many years, perhaps all his life. He began, desperately, to pray.

They hacked off his head with a sword.

The murderers half-buried the body under a pile of loose rocks, leaving the pale, limp hands sticking out into the mountain air. Then they went back to the clearing, killed the servants and looted the camp.

In the middle years of the nineteenth century it could take a long time for news to seep out of the high mountains west of Gilgit. It was almost a fortnight before word of the death reached the first Kashmiri garrison and began to make its way eastwards towards India, picking up stray threads of conjecture and bazaar gossip in the mountain villages along the way. By the end of August,

Kashmir and the towns where the rich Punjabi plains meet the foothills of the Himalayas were rife with rumours that an Englishman had been murdered somewhere in the Hindu Kush. For the British authorities then governing India, this was the worst possible news. Travelling Englishmen were not a common phenomenon in the high mountains beyond the frontier; if the rumour was true then the victim could only be one man – a controversial figure already well known to the government. And if he really had come to grief then his death would prove highly and politically inconvenient, having occurred on the fringes of the territory of the Maharaja of Kashmir.

Of the independent kingdoms (recognising ultimate British suzerainty) that made up much of India, Kashmir, with its ill-defined and contentious western border, was one of the largest. It was also by far the most strategically important. The maharaja was a difficult man who had to be handled with the most delicate of diplomatic skill. For some years there had been grumblings about his misrule – from both his own subjects and from visiting British citizens – and there had been a good deal of recent controversy about the actions of his troops in the more remote parts of the mountain kingdom. If the rumours of murder proved true they would cause a severe diplomatic headache.

In 1870 the British Raj was approaching its zenith. The 'Mutiny' – a bloody uprising by local Indian soldiers in 1857 – had brought to an end the old haphazard empire of the Honourable East India Company. India was now under the rule of the British crown, which covered the patchwork of acquiescent indigenous kingdoms and directly administered territories spanning a huge swathe from the Afghan border to the Bay of Bengal. On the map of the world India was entirely red. There would be no more great wars of conquest in the subcontinent, only border skirmishes and punitive raids.

The British, finding in Indian caste an echo of their own rigid Victorian class system, had established themselves at the very pinnacle of south Asian society. Nowhere, it was said, was an Englishman's life more sacred than in the subcontinent. In the unthinkable event of a white man's death at the hands of 'the natives', vengeance was essential, a duty in fact, to maintain respect if nothing else. But avenging the lonely death of a footloose Englishman in some wild and inhospitable upland valley beyond the River Indus would prove extremely difficult, no matter how necessary. And if, as the sizzling gossip was now beginning to suggest, the Maharaja of Kashmir himself was implicated in the death, then the connotations could prove catastrophic.

At first the authorities did their best to keep the rumours quiet. The identity of the dead man, obvious as it was, had not been confirmed, and conflicting reports about who was behind the murder were now pouring out of the mountains like spring meltwater. But by the beginning of September the news was so widespread in bazaars and teashops across north-west India that it could no longer be suppressed. On 9 September the viceroy, Lord Mayo, the supreme British authority in India, telegraphed the home government in London telling them of the rumour. The story quickly reached the Fellows of the Royal Geographical Society, for their vice-president, Sir Henry Rawlinson, was also a member of the government's India Council. As word spread among the venerable old geographers in the oak-panelled chambers of the society's London headquarters, there would have been a sense of bitter disappointment; they too would quickly have realised who the dead man must be. By the end of the month it was confirmed.

The victim's identity might now have been known, but little else about the murder was clear. Rumours continued to emerge from the mountains, new twists, assertions and allegations making their way down on to the plains on an almost daily basis. 'There are some very queer stories afloat,' wrote the viceroy in a confidential memo. Untangling the threads of misinformation would prove a troublesome task, not least given the remote and evidently hazardous nature of the crime scene. Indeed, the viceroy wondered, if the truth had the potential to prove so politically explosive, might it not be best if the waters remained muddy?

Still, on 3 October, two and a half months after the event, the news was finally made public in the British press: the 'distinguished traveller' Mr George Hayward, aged 32, Central Asian explorer par excellence and honoured holder of the Gold Medal of the Royal Geographical Society, was dead, assassinated on his journey to explore the Pamir Steppe.

2

INTO THE WILD

In the last months of the twentieth century it could still take a long time for news to seep out of the high mountains west of Gilgit – or more precisely, it could still take a long time for news to seep *in*.

On the morning of 12 October 1999 my father and I stopped to buy some bottled water and snacks from the Gilgit bazaar. The sky hung low and grim, seeming to rest on the jagged peaks of the mountains that locked the town into its bowl of grey-brown stone. Gilgit had grown from the lonely outpost of the mid-nineteenth century to become the principal town of Pakistan's far north, but it was still spectacularly remote. And lying in the belly of the world's highest mountain ranges, at the very point where the few precarious roads through the Western Himalayas meet, it still had a wild frontier feel. Ominous rifle shots crackled up on the stark slopes above the town from time to time, and the rough and dusty bazaar was full of smuggled goods from China. The faces of the men on the streets – and they were all men – showed that this was the meeting point, the hub of the mountains. There were Baltis with broad, wind-reddened Tibetan faces, and Uighurs and Kirghiz who looked like they had descended from the hordes of Genghis Khan. There were dark, smooth-skinned

Punjabis up from the plains; Pashtuns with great beaked noses and hollow cheeks; and here and there a scattering of freckles, a shock of red or blonde hair, and a pair of jade-green or lapis-blue eyes.

We loaded the water and food into the back of the jeep – driven by a large, gentle man of imperturbable calmness named Yusuf Mohammed – and headed west, winding out of town through narrow streets riddled with potholes, overhung with tangles of loose wire and lined with dark, jerry-built shops. The tarmac ran out not far beyond Gilgit, and the electricity cables soon after that. But the cloud cleared too and we rattled on between stands of tall poplars, copper-coloured by autumn, under an intense blue sky.

Beyond the edge of the mountains in Islamabad, 150 miles to the south, the plates were beginning to shift. Within a few hours events would unfold that would have a dramatic effect on the politics of Pakistan, and on developments in the region in the turbulent years to come. But we, making our way along the banks of the Gilgit River towards the Shandur Pass and onwards to Chitral, would hear nothing of it for the next three days. News did indeed travel slowly in those mountains.

I was 18 years old, and a few weeks earlier I had known almost nothing of Pakistan beyond a clutch of vague images of camels and turbans, confused with the more tropical exotica of India. I had only been out of Britain once (a week in Spain two years earlier), and though I desperately wanted to travel I had been brought up on the surfers' shore of Cornwall and was only interested in tropical places with good waves and beautiful women. I had dawdled through some ill-chosen A-levels and a year of a chef's apprenticeship, and I was already plotting trips to warm beaches in Bali, Australia and Hawaii. And then, at very short notice, came a completely unexpected chance to join my father for a month in the high mountains of northern Pakistan. It would never, ever have occurred to me to go to such a place – mainly because it was so far from the sea. I knew nothing of south Asian history, had only the vaguest notions about Islam and had never even heard of the Hindu Kush. But now here I was, bouncing around in the back of a stripped-down jeep, waving to village children in the stony fields and heading into the mountains along the same road that the explorer George Hayward took on his own final, fateful journey – though of course, I had never heard of him. It was the most gut-achingly beautiful place I had ever seen.

We spent the first night at Gupis, the very spot where Hayward turned off north into the Yasin Valley. We slept in a government inspection bungalow – a crumbling, British-built cottage of bare rooms and creaking furniture kept by an ancient, doddering care-taker. He slaughtered a chicken for our dinner, wringing its neck in the garden and half-muttering a prayer to make it halal, and we sat eating by lamplight in the humming darkness.

The next day we continued towards Shandur (leaving Hayward behind at the junction of Yasin). The road was rougher and wilder, and the country around us all the more stunning. The track fol-lowed the southern flank of a long valley, walled in by soaring snow-peaks. There were villages where small children with sun-burnished hair ran cheering after the jeep and women in embroidered blue skullcaps watched us shyly from the fields. Little terraces of winter wheat lined the hillsides and the streams and watercourses were marked by stands of willow and poplar, turn-ing to intense metallic reds and golds in the fading year. The sky was a brilliant aquamarine, and the river, bouncing and tumbling over boulders, matched its colour. Above us the barren mountain-sides were dusted with new snow. It was cold at night, but in the daytime you could still feel the warmth of the sun pressing on the back of your neck.

In Islamabad all political hell had broken loose, but there was no television and no radio up here, and as we stopped for a second night in another dusty inspection bungalow at Phundar, looking out over the higher reaches of the valley, we knew nothing about it.

It was difficult to imagine a more wonderfully remote place. The next day we crossed the high watershed of the Shandur Pass, a broad, grassy saddle flanked by sharp peaks and scoured by a biting wind, and began to drop into the northern fringes of the North-West Frontier Province. The mountains were taller and rougher here, and the valleys more ragged and stark. We rolled back on to cracked tarmac at dusk and came to the mountain bazaar of Chitral, a wild-edged township in a locked valley, long after dark.

The next morning, from a scruffy little office in the market, we called home on a crackling line. My mother, understandably, was concerned for our safety, worried that we had been caught up in recent events. We were at first puzzled, then startled, then finally highly amused as she explained – from a Cornish farmhouse thousands of miles away – that during our journey from Gilgit to Chitral the Government of Pakistan had been overthrown in a dramatic military coup. And we had known nothing about it.

In 1999 Pakistan was coming to the end of one of its troubled periods of civilian democracy. During the course of recent years, government corruption had reached orgiastic levels, and the nation's only consistently stable institution, the army, was beginning to grumble. The incumbent prime minister, Nawaz Sharif, and the then leader of the opposition, Benazir Bhutto, had spent the 1990s trading periods of inept and woefully corrupt government. Nervously aware of Pakistan's military default mode, on 12 October 1999 Sharif decided to dismiss the head of the army, Pervez Musharraf, while he was out of the country at a conference in Sri Lanka, replacing him with a tame general of his own choosing. Musharraf – a seemingly earnest man of a rather different mould from the bristling Sandhurst style of most south Asian generals – leapt aboard a commercial flight home while battalions across the country turned rapidly against the civilian government.

Desperate to keep Musharraf at arm's length, Nawaz Sharif ordered his plane diverted to a remote desert outpost. The plane – full of civilian passengers – circled; but air traffic controllers under Sharif's orders refused permission to land and fuel supplies dwindled. In response the army came on to the streets of Karachi, the airport was seized, and Musharraf touched down with, it was said, only seven minutes' worth of fuel to spare. Nawaz Sharif was later charged with hijacking. Meanwhile, in Islamabad, those civilian politicians who had any sense were busily shredding documents, disguising themselves as women and bolting over the garden wall. By the time my father and I reached Chitral late on 14 October Pakistan was, for the third time in its fifty-year history, a military dictatorship.

Because of these events, and because of the place where we had been so blissfully unaware of them, I came to associate the high mountains between Gilgit and Chitral with momentous happenings long before I knew anything of Victorian geopolitics, George Hayward and the Great Game.

When we left Pakistan at the end of October I was immensely impressed and grateful to have seen such a staggeringly beautiful place. But as the battered black and yellow taxi carried us through the morning rush hour to Islamabad airport I distinctly remember thinking that it was unlikely that I would ever return.

Three months later I was back on my appointed path, on the north shore of Oahu, Hawaii. It was hot and humid, the water was warm, the surf was good and there were palm trees and women in tiny bikinis. But each evening after I had made my barefooted way back to the hostel, sunburnt and shaken by the monstrous waves of the north Pacific, I lay reading on my sand-scattered bunk. The books I read were not of surf and sunshine, but of the high mountains of Asia and of journeys made there by Nick Danziger and Wilfred Thesiger.

The next September I was back in Pakistan, alone this time, dressed in a *pakol* and *shalwaar kamis*, and travelling by the cheapest means possible. The dusty backpack that I slung on to bus roofs and lugged through seething bazaars was full of books. They were books of history and adventure, and I consumed them as hungrily as I consumed the kebabs and *karahis* from the *chaikhannas* where

I ate. I read travel classics; I read of the violence of the partition of the subcontinent; of the trauma of Kashmir; of the mujahidin war against the Soviets in Afghanistan; and of epic mountaineering expeditions. But above all I read of the Europeans in the nineteenth century who had travelled in the mountains which now belong to Pakistan and the central Asian states. They were wildly romantic figures; men who were half-explorer, half-spy, travelling incognito and meeting grisly ends among hostile tribes, or bringing back explosive news of new passes, valleys and ranges – all of them were players of the Great Game.

At the beginning of the nineteenth century some 2,000 miles of mountains, deserts and unstable Muslim potentates separated Britain's Indian territories from the southern frontier of the Russian Empire. A hundred years later these same borders were only a few miles apart (just beyond the very pass that Hayward had been trying to cross when he was murdered). The Great Game was the cold war of intrigue, exploration and exploitation that the two mighty empires played for a century or more in the turbulent and ever contracting space between.

For much of the nineteenth century the political classes of Britain – particularly those involved with India – were obsessed with 'the Russian Threat' in a way that makes today's fretting about Islamist terrorism seem petty by comparison. It was Napoleon Bonaparte who started it off. In 1807, at the height of his pan-European rampage – and before he developed his own designs on Russia – the diminutive Corsican had suggested to Tsar Alexander I a joint Franco-Russian project to invade India and wrest it from nascent British control. India, with its impenetrable mysteries and untold riches, had always been the 'jewel in the crown' for would-be expansionists from the north and west. In voicing this ambition Napoleon was following a tradition that ran back at least as far as Alexander the Great. But in the early nineteenth century they were entering the modern era of global geopolitics. The British got wind of the plot with its talk of troops sweeping through the Khyber Pass – and went berserk, prompting a hysterical diplomatic crisis.

The planned invasion came to nothing of course. It was wildly impractical and beyond even Napoleon's mighty capabilities. But the damage was done: the idea of an invasion of India from the north was firmly planted in the British consciousness, and in popular and political imagination the Russian Threat loomed over the buxom bounties of the Raj like a rapacious Cossack raider for the rest of the century. And as Britain's Indian empire expanded ever westwards – from its initial tenuous toehold of mud, malaria and warehouses on the Ganges Delta to take in Sind, then the Punjab, and finally to nudge up against the fringes of Afghanistan – events in such outlandish places as Samarkand, Kashgar and Chitral were no longer the irrelevancies they had once been. The Game was in play.

The term 'Great Game' was coined by a British explorer who eventually met a sticky end at the hands of the Emir of Bokhara in modern-day Uzbekistan, but it was popularised by that laureate of empire, Rudyard Kipling. It was the coldest of cold wars – often quite literally so, in the icy heights of the Western Himalayas. There were no military engagements between British and Russian troops; players from the two sides only ever came face to face in the wilds of Central Asia on a handful of occasions. In fact, there was very little large-scale military action at all. The Great Game was instead a phenomenon where minor skirmishes in remote mountain fiefdoms took on towering significance, and where a border incursion by a small party of wandering Cossacks could provoke a full-scale diplomatic incident. It was a 'tournament of shadows' played out, for the most part, by individuals, spies, mercenaries and men who would be king.

For much of the nineteenth century the portion of the great Eurasian landmass to the north-west of India was one of the least known parts of the planet. There were other white spaces on the map of the world of course, but those were empty deserts or dense jungles. What made the lack of knowledge about Central Asia so startling was that this was no uninhabited wasteland: there were great cities out there, place names known since antiquity. Even beyond the middle decades of the century European geographers still had no idea where on the map to place significant caravan towns like Yarkand, and few of the major rivers of India had been traced to their source. They had hardly even begun to untangle the monstrous mountain knot centred on Gilgit, where the world's highest ranges lock together like the fingers of a clasped pair of hands, and when it came to the Pamirs, no one was even sure if they were a plateau or a mountain range.

It was an area crying out to be explored, and there were plenty of adventurers willing to try. But never has the boundary between scientific exploration and politics been so blurred. Many of the men who explored the region – and they were all men – were private individuals; few of them went on overt official duty, but none of them were impartial, and the news, maps and observations that they brought back to India were of the greatest significance. Was there evidence of Russia meddling in the affairs of remote Muslim kingdoms? Were goods made in Moscow flooding the bazaars of the old Silk Road? And perhaps most importantly of all, was there somewhere a chink in India's Himalayan armour, some gap in the mountains through which an invading northern army could flow?

To anyone who has seen the wildly rugged and inhospitable mountain terrain of the subcontinent's north-west corner, the idea that a full-scale military invasion could sweep down upon an unsuspecting India by way of one of those windswept passes may seem ridiculous. This does highlight something that needs to be said about the Great Game. For years most writers and historians have approached the subject from a starting point of accepting that the Russian Threat was very real and that Central Asian geopolitics was a deadly serious affair. In recent years, with the 'post 9/11' war in Afghanistan and the jostling for oil and gas rights in the former Soviet states around the Caspian Sea, there has been a good deal of chatter from commentators about 'the new Great Game'. Indeed, there are some who argue that the old Great Game never really went away. They point triumphantly to the Soviet invasion of Afghanistan in 1979 as irrefutable evidence that while the British Raj may have long since faded from the scene, expansionist Russian designs on the subcontinent have never faltered.

All that aside, few would argue that the Great Game was not taken very seriously during the nineteenth century. However, some modern historians, particularly those from India and Pakistan, convincingly argue that the whole Great Game was just that – an act, a sham – and that the Russian Threat was a deliberately constructed myth. No Cossacks, they say, were ever going to sweep down the Khyber Pass to seize India. But in a piece of textbook neo-conservative thinking – long before George W. Bush rolled into Iraq in search of weapons of mass destruction – the idea that they might do just that was deliberately encouraged, inflamed and instilled in the minds of the British public purely to justify expansionist colonial policies. As Britain's Indian armies clawed their way deeper and deeper into the mountain territory beyond the subcontinent's natural boundary at the Indus River, usurping and subjugating more and more little independent states, it could all be justified with a single phrase: the Russian Threat. That the threat was a myth was beside the point. And away to the north, these historians say, the Russians were up to the very same tricks, encouraging alarm at imaginary British influence spreading through the khanates and kingdoms of Central Asia to justify their own forward push. It is a convincing argument.

Even if it was just a game, however, even if the Russian Threat was imaginary, those who played did so in earnest. And what a motley crew they were! There were the inevitable imperial archetypes, all bristling moustaches and stiff upper lips, but they found themselves in very mixed company. Amongst those whose travels could loosely be classed under the terms of the Great Game was

Joseph Wolff, a rampaging German convert to Anglicanism who marched about Central Asia on mercy missions, searching for Jews to Christianise, refusing to tell a lie and referring to himself in the third person. There was the pompous philanderer Sir Alexander Burnes, whose penchant for Afghan women was notorious and who met his end at the hands of a Kabul mob (his womanising was the least of their complaints). The first foreigner to record a visit to Gilgit was the almost inconceivably self-important Dr Gottlieb Leitner: 'M.A., Ph.D., LL.D., D.O.L, etc' (what *do* all those letters stand for and how could anyone be so pompous as to write etcetera after their name?). Another German, he spoke thirty-odd languages, collected a spectacular human zoo of mountain folk at his Lahore headquarters, built one of the first mosques in England and turned up in Gilgit with nothing but three jars of Bovril in his pockets. And then, of course, there was the mighty Sir Francis Younghusband, a man with a magnificent moustache and an expression of permanent bemusement. He started out as a doyen of imperialism but ended his days as some kind of bizarre proto-hippie, raving from his armchair about eastern mysticism and extraterrestrials. And there were countless others, some brave and professional, some cheating charlatans, some downright crazy.

As I learnt more and more about these glorious characters, one always caught my imagination. He seemed to loiter a little way beyond the fringes of the crowd, a little out of place, a little out of time. Perhaps it is no coincidence that he was one of the most shadowy of all the Great Game figures: his origins were, until recently, a mystery; the real reason for his death is likely to remain so. While the likes of Leitner and Younghusband churned out books of travels faster than most people can read, this man left scant traces: a letter here, a report there. But for all this elusiveness there was something that shone through, something that always caught my attention. His brutal unsolved murder alone was intriguing enough, but there was more: he seemed to exude a strange intensity, setting him apart, latching him deep into my imagination. His name was George Hayward.

There is only one known photograph of George J. W. Hayward, and it is striking. Other Great Gamers appear in their 'native garb' in contrived studio portraits – robes worn self-consciously, turban cocked at a jaunty angle above pouting lips and a trembling moustache. The adventurer is perhaps flanked by a pair of fragrant Asiatic youths, and it all has an air of fancy dress and high camp. Looking like that it is hard to imagine that they ever managed to pass themselves off as Afghan horse-traders or Bokhariot pilgrims; they seem more like bit players in a Christmas pantomime. But the picture of Hayward is very different. It is a staged shot, and Hayward is in native dress, but there is nothing arch or silly about it.

The photograph is undated, the photographer unknown and the location unidentified, but given the setting and the circumstances it seems almost certain than it was taken in Kashmir in early summer 1870, during the final turbulent months of Hayward's life. The explorer stands centre stage in the garden of some rather neglected building of columns and arches with his back to the pitted, gnarled trunk of a huge tree. Clear upland sunlight streams in from the right.

The costume he is wearing is thought to be that of the Yasin Valley, the very place in which he died. His robe is of dark, coarse cloth, stiff with the grime of travel; you can almost feel it itching against your own skin. A long, curved sword is tucked into his belt, and he holds a heavy, studded shield in his left hand while his right clasps tightly at the shaft of a spear. A turban of off-white cloth is loosely bound around his head. At his feet, arranged in a great semicircle, are the huge, claw-like horns, some still attached to flyblown heads, of half a dozen enormous wild goats – the ibex and markhor he had bagged on an earlier journey – while at the very right of the frame sits an Asian man in a sloppily tied turban, looking more villainous than fragrant. And armed to the teeth, standing proud between classical columns and decapitated cloven-hoofed beasts, Hayward himself looks more like some Greek god of carnage than a foppish Victorian dandy.

It could, of course, be a moment of indulgent dressing-up, but it doesn't look like it: Hayward isn't grinning or mugging for the camera. In fact, it is his expression that is most arresting. His face is gaunt, fringed by a thick, blondish beard. His nose is long and slightly crooked, and buried under a heavy moustache you can just detect a firmly set mouth. But it is the eyes that have it. Beneath a broad, high brow, pinched into a frown of utter serious-ness, they glare away to the right of the camera from dark, intense hollows. There is nothing jaunty or jolly about him and setting out into the hills with such a man would be an alarming prospect. As one writer put it, 'He looks a most unsettling companion.'

Hayward was in some ways the epitome of the Great Game's shadowy nature, of exploration mixed with politics, but in other ways he was completely at odds with the gentleman's rules by which the game was played, choosing to make himself a perma-nent outsider, gathering no real friends and alienating people. His lonely death that bright July morning proved that. Some have chosen to see him as a suicidal fool, driven by a death wish; for others he was a man possessed, so consumed by his urge to reach his destination – the High Pamirs – that he became obliv-ious to the dangers. Still others regard him merely as a remarkably dedicated professional explorer who died in the line of duty, always seeking to further geographical knowledge no matter how challenging the circumstances. Perhaps he was all those things, and more.

He was certainly unusual. He appeared on the exploration scene from nowhere and launched himself on a mercurial career. He was one of the first two Englishmen to reach the fabled bazaar towns of Yarkand and Kashgar on the southern edge of the Taklamakan Desert; he crossed, measured and mapped numerous new passes along the Himalayan watershed and traced the source of a major Asian river. He pushed further west from Kashmir than any European had done before, and he performed staggering feats of endurance, making some of the nineteenth century's most audacious winter journeys in the Western Himalayas. He blazed brightly through the mountains for two years, and then, abruptly, was gone.

His death in that bleak valley provoked outrage in polite Victorian society. Of course it did: the death of any Englishman in such a place, at the hands of such people would. Various allegedly first-hand accounts of the murder eventually emerged into the public arena. One of these was later bowdlerised and bastardised by the poet Sir Henry Newbolt, school chum of Francis Younghusband and quivering champion in rhyming doggerel of public school values, imperialism and honourable deaths ('Play up! play up! and play the game!'). His version of Hayward's murder, *He fell among Thieves*, is excruciating:

'Ye have robb'd,' said he, 'ye have slaughter'd and made an end,
Take your ill-got plunder and bury the dead:
What will ye more of your guest and sometime friend?'
'Blood for our blood,' they said.

He laugh'd: 'If one may settle the score for five,
I am ready; but let the reckoning stand till day:
I have loved the sunlight dearly as any alive.'
'You shall die at dawn,' said they.

He flung his empty revolver down the slope,
He climb'd alone to the Eastward edge of the trees;
All night long in a dream untroubled of hope
He brooded, clasping his knees.

He did not hear the monotonous roar that fills
The ravine where the Yassin river sullenly flows;
He did not see the starlight on the Laspur hills,
Or the far Afghan snows.

He saw the April noon on his books aglow,
The wisteria trailing in at the window wide;
He heard his father's voice from the terrace below
Calling him down to ride.

He saw the grey little church across the park,
The mounds that hid the loved and honour'd dead;
The Norman arch, the chancel softly dark,
The brasses black and red.

He saw the School Close, sunny and green,
The runner beside him, the stand by the parapet wall,
The distant tape, and the crowd roaring between,
His own name over all.

He saw the dark wainscot and timber'd roof,
The long tables, and the faces merry and keen;
The College Eight and their trainer dining aloof,
The Dons on their dais serene.

He watch'd the liner's stem ploughing the foam,
He felt her trembling speed and the thrash of her screw;
He heard the passenger's voices talking of home,
He saw the flag she flew.

And now it was dawn. He rose strong on his feet,
And strode to his ruin'd camp beneath the wood;
He drank the breath of the morning cool and sweet:
His murderers round him stood.

Light on the Laspur hills was broadening fast,
The blood-red snow-peaks chill'd to a dazzling white;
He turn'd, and saw the golden circle at last,
Cut by the Eastern height.

'O glorious Life, Who dwellest in earth and sun,
I have lived, I praise and adore Thee.'
A sword swept.
Over the pass the voices one by one
Faded, and the hill slept.

Clearly Newbolt had never been to the Yasin Valley. And clearly he knew nothing about death by beheading.

I once had the misfortune to see grainy video footage of one of the wretched hostages being beheaded in Iraq. Some person of limited intelligence and deficient compassion had downloaded it on to their mobile phone and, grinning inanely, thrust it under my nose. The horrible scene had played out before I realised what I was watching, but the gurgling, the spasms, the twitching and flinching, stayed with me for days afterwards. This is exactly how Hayward would have died. One of the contemporary accounts speaks of how the assassins 'hacked off his head after the half-hacking, half-sawing way they have of killing sheep in the Himalaya'. There was no poetically smooth single stroke of a shimmering blade; Hayward's death would have been brutal, messy and unimaginably horrific.

But if wishful thinking and an urge to romanticise a thoroughly unpleasant murder is perhaps excusable, the attempt to co-opt Hayward into a rosy image of Little England, with cricket, warm beer and nuns on bicycles, is outrageous. This kind of nonsense was Newbolt's stock in trade – all foreign fields and Union Jacks – but he did Hayward a massive disservice by turning him into the perfect, straight-backed Englishman. He was nothing of the kind. He left school at 15 and knew nothing of college eights and serene dons. If he was dreaming of anywhere in his last, violent moments it would have been the bleak heights of the Pamirs, not some quaint Home Counties village.

For this is at the very heart of what attracted me to Hayward: there was something about him, something in that raw intensity, that was palpably un-Victorian, un-British. Other Great Game

explorers headed into the wilds of High Asia with armies of servants, literally tons of supplies wobbling along after them over the
passes on the backs of yaks and mules. They took vast stocks of
books and surveying gear, and complained when their bottles of
claret cracked in the sub-zero temperatures. Hayward travelled
hard and light, alone or with just a couple of servants. He often
dispensed with even the most basic of equipment, carrying no
tent, and sleeping through blizzards in the lee of overhanging
boulders. Where other travellers excelled in the flowery arts of
diplomacy in the exotic courts that they visited, Hayward proved
wantonly, wilfully inept, failing to follow correct etiquette and
offending all and sundry. But this does not seem like straightforward arrogance; it has more to do with that same unstable
intensity. And if the most English of traits is to keep quiet, not
to rock the boat or make a fuss, then Hayward was anything
but English. I'm inclined to suspect that he would have found
Newbolt's poem deeply offensive.[1]

By the time I left Pakistan that second time, Hayward, his brief,
shadowy life, and his brutal, mysterious death, were firmly
implanted in my imagination. Without realising I was doing it I
sought him out elsewhere, held up others to see if they matched
his standards – and found them wanting. Over the years I read of
other travellers and other explorers – both of nineteenth-century
Asia and beyond. Many were more dramatic, more distinct and
more endearing than George Hayward, but somehow none of
them matched that sizzling intensity.

Many of the Victorians were almost clown-like despite their
unmistakeable bravery. Burton and the other pioneers of Africa
certainly came from that eminently risible mould – but not
Hayward. In the traces he left I saw none of the self-indulgent
Orientalist romanticism of T.E. Lawrence or Wilfred Thesiger
(and none of their aristocratic sexual confusion either). Classical

Arab travellers like Mas'udi and Ibn Battutah displayed a fey
dreaminess at odds with Hayward's hard-headed practicality, and
he demonstrated none of the slick – and occasionally irksome
– self-deprecation of the best twentieth-century travel writers.
Nowhere else did I see that indefinable but unmistakably intense
aura replicated, but I did once catch a faint echo of it. It came in
the most unexpected of places: the Alaskan backwoods of the late
twentieth century.

On 6 September 1992 the emaciated body of a young American
backpacker named Chris McCandless was found in the forest
north of Anchorage. He came from a middle-class background
in the tame suburbs of Washington DC, but for the two years
before his death he had been hitchhiking back and forth across
the empty spaces of the American West, leaving a patchy, elusive
trail. His story was made famous by the writer Jon Krakauer in his
book *Into the Wild*, later made into a Hollywood movie.

Krakauer chose to romanticise McCandless, painting him as
the embodiment of some raw American frontier spirit. Others –
myself included – saw things rather differently: he was a naïve and
self-indulgent city boy, ill-equipped for the Alaskan wilderness. He
starved to death in an abandoned bus only a day's walk from the
nearest surfaced road. In this respect he is but a flea on the hem
of George Hayward's travel-stained Afghan robe, but still, there
was something about McCandless that instantly reminded me of
Hayward. Perhaps it was that determined rejection of the mainstream, that self-induced sense of otherness, that intensity. He too,
I imagine, would have been an unsettling travelling companion.

Of all the written scraps and fragments that George Hayward
left, the most famous, and that given the most significance by
those who have tried to understand him, was a bleakly sarcastic
passage of prescience. He scribbled it during a period of miserable
imprisonment in the Silk Route city of Kashgar, sketching out
future careers for himself and another travelling Englishman held
in the same town. His counterpart, he predicted, would go on to
lionised greatness, a hero of travel and exploration, feted, wined

and dined by polite British society. Meanwhile, 'In contradistinction to all this,' Hayward wrote, 'I shall wander about the wilds of Central Asia, still possessed with an insane desire to try the effects of cold steel across my throat.'

From anyone else this could be dismissed as empty Victorian bravado, but not from Hayward. Given the circumstances in which the note was written, the 'cold steel' part – prophetic as it turned out to be – could be viewed as silly hyperbole, but something about the 'insane desire' rings true. For there did seem to be some strange spark in him. Desire certainly, insanity perhaps, but whatever it was it drove him on, deeper and deeper into the mountains, further and further from home. In that, and in that alone, I sensed that he had a kindred spirit in the unfortunate hitchhiker Chris McCandless.

From my starting point in the high mountains of northern Pakistan, I travelled onwards, propelled by conventional wanderlust rather than some 'insane desire'. To the south I explored the rest of the subcontinent, from the cape of Kanyakumari to the backwaters of Bangladesh. Northwards I made my way across China from west to east. I turned through the cities of the Middle East and along north African shores, and I drifted off between the islands of Southeast Asia.

My reading and historical interests followed these extended, low-budget holidays. From the Great Game I journeyed into the wider story of the British Raj and its demise, and of European colonialism in general. India and Hinduism led me south-east to Indonesia and old Indochina; in the other direction Islam took me away towards Middle Eastern history and politics. But always the threads, the lines of communication, led back to that chaos of high mountains where the frayed borders of modern-day India, China and Pakistan break down and come apart amongst glaciers and ridges.

Looking at the map of Asia it is easy to see why: that crowded space, centred on Gilgit, really is the hub of the entire continent. Great mountain ranges sweep away in all directions from the tangled core. To the east the main Himalayan chain dips, swells and bursts into the great purple bruise of the Tibetan Plateau, with the Kun Lun bearing in from the north and the jagged splinter of the Karakoram buried between. From the north-east the Tien Shan, the Heavenly Mountain Range, rises ice-white and glittering over cold deserts and empty steppes, and arcs in to the meeting point. At its base squats the Pamirs, barren and desolate. And from the south-west, bearing inwards from the Desert of Hell and the bones of Afghanistan – like the infinite branches of some vast tree – comes the Hindu Kush, the Killer of Hindus. [2]

I might be elsewhere; I might be in steamy jungles or on coral shores, or indeed in dreary English suburbia, but somewhere in the back of my imagination that mountain knot remained. And if I looked carefully, moving through it, flickering, elusive, enigmatic and intense, disappearing, coming back into view, pushing ever onwards, possessed with an insane desire, was the figure of George Hayward.

Between long bouts of travelling and hot summers plying my sweaty chef's trade in Cornish restaurant kitchens, I stumbled in fits, starts and deferments through a journalism degree, lived for a year in Indonesia and spent every penny I ever earned on cheap flights and third-class train tickets. Before I knew it a decade had passed: ten years since 12 October 1999. I felt that I needed to do something to mark the passing of that decade. It was time, I decided, to hunt down George Hayward, to gather together whatever there was to be known about him, and to follow him on his journeys – even all the way to the location of that lonely death.

Notes

1   It is hard not to suspect that Hayward would also have been
    offended – but perhaps for other reasons – by the 2007 stage
    play, *The Great Game*. Written by an American playwright, in
    it he is glibly recast as a British aristocrat who marries a one-
    eyed Indian proto-feminist to the horror of his upper-crust
    parents (he wasn't; he didn't; he was an orphan).

2   The whole, monstrous mass of jumbled rock and ice at the
    north-west corner of the Indian subcontinent is sometimes
    known – in an attempt to simplify and make sense of it – as
    the Western Himalayas. I will use the term here when talk-
    ing in general about the vast mountain body. When talking
    about a more specific range or area I will use the individual
    names, such as the Hindu Kush, the Karakoram or the Great
    Himalaya.

3

FROM FOREST TO THE FRONTIER

It's a long way from Headingley Hall to the Hindu Kush. The former stands on the outskirts of the Yorkshire city of Leeds. Rather less grand than the name suggests, it is a modest, two-storey building. There has been a manor house on the site since medieval times, but the current building dates from the seventeenth century, with a few mismatched extensions tacked on in the Victorian era. It is fronted by a damp, slightly overgrown garden with heavyset trees crowding it in summer, standing back as skeletal sentinels in winter. The hall is an old folks' home now, where little moves beyond the flicker of the television screen and the almost imperceptible nodding of a dozen grey heads.

On the outside wall of the building the civic authorities have fixed a blue plaque. It mentions the hall's history as part of the estate of the Earl of Cardigan and lists the meagre role of notable residents, which included 'John Killingbeck, Mayor of Leeds 1677, George Hayward, Land Agent of the Earl of Cardigan, and his son George J.W. Hayward, born here in 1839, intrepid explorer in Central Asia.'

George Jonas Whitaker Hayward was born on 9 June 1839, the second of three children. That summer, thousands of miles away in Asia, the Punjab was at the centre of a hugely powerful Sikh empire under the one-eyed despot Ranjit Singh, who held sway over all of Kashmir and the modern North-West Frontier. Yarkand and Kashgar, a mystery to western geographers, were troublesome outposts on the very fringes of the crumbling Manchu Empire. Yasin was completely unknown, and Sir Alexander Burnes – moustache quivering at the prospect of the fair maidens of Kabul – had just ridden into Afghanistan at the head of the ill-omened Army of the Indus. All of which was a world away from Leeds.

As south Yorkshire land agent for the same Earl of Cardigan who would later gallop to dubious renown at the head of the Charge of the Light Brigade, George Hayward Senior would have earned a respectable income and enjoyed a lifestyle that could be described – such as these things existed in the 1840s – as middle class. The family would have had a few servants, and George Senior would have probably had some minor investments and business interests of his own. Little George would have toddled around that overgrown garden in reasonable comfort, and when his mother died in 1845 there would have been a nanny to take care of him. But they were not wealthy people; George Junior started his education in local schools and would have had little sense of privilege.

When he was 14 he was shipped south to London to enrol at the Forest School. This establishment, which still stands on the edge of Epping Forest, had opened its gates just two decades earlier. It was a decent enough place, but hardly the breeding ground of the great and the good. It catered principally for the sons of the petite bourgeoisie, not for those of lords and earls. The modern school (now admitting girls as well as boys, and priding itself on its tolerance, diversity and 'Hogwarts look-alike' dining room) marks Hayward in the rather underwhelming list of noteworthy alumni: 'immortalised by Sir Henry Newbolt in his poem *He Fell Among Thieves*,' it says. Once again, the idea that this would have earned a disgusted sneer from the man himself is hard to avoid.[1] It is unlikely that Hayward had very many memories of his time at Forest, and certainly none of endless Newboltian summer days of manly vigour 'playing the game' on the field and the running track; he only spent a year at the school. In June 1854 George Hayward Senior died, the day after his son's birthday.

For a child of the aristocracy the death of a father usually meant instant assumption of wealth and title; for a middle-class boy from Leeds it could mean a sudden descent into poverty. It certainly meant an abrupt end to a moderately expensive private education, and young George, an orphan at 15, vanishes from the school records with a single line: 'Entered business on account of his father's decease.'

For the next few years he disappears altogether. Probably he went back to Yorkshire; perhaps he lived with members of his mother's family. He may have worked in the booming textile industry of the north, or found some minor employ on the estate of the Earl of Cardigan.

It is tempting, of course, to whip out the poetic licence and engage in all sorts of Newbolt-style reconstructions of Hayward's youth: the stubborn toddler forging alone beyond the wild fringe of the garden and prompting panic among the nursemaids; the moody adolescent storming off into the woods and fields beyond the city; or the troublesome public schoolboy, intense, unsettling and with few friends, resentful of London and the petty concerns of his peers, always in trouble, speaking out of turn, and bluntly refusing to 'play the game'. But there are no notes, no records and, irresistible as such images are, they can only ever be wild fancy.

A couple of points from this unremarkable childhood are worthy of note. A middle-class upbringing with some experience of the aristocratic environment would have had a powerful impact on a nineteenth-century youth. It would, to some extent, have lifted George Hayward out of the Victorian class system altogether. He may well have encountered the sons and daughters of the earl, and must have recognised instantly that they belonged to an entirely other species. But the experience of being raised in a pleasant house with a big garden would have engendered a certain air of possibility. The young George Hayward would have

had none of the luxuries of great privilege, but equally none of
the pressures of great inheritance. It is exactly the kind of background from which upstarts and troublemakers spring. In the
smoky atmosphere of Leeds, with its textile barons and self-made
men, he could easily have rattled up the industrial ladder into the
ranks of the vulgar nouveau riche. But other factors were in play:
a year at public school is not long; connections and friendships
would barely have been made before they were broken, and then,
with the death of his father nine years after that of his mother,
Hayward was instantly cut loose. As an orphan he had no more
ties, no more connections, no one left to judge him, and from that
point it would have been far easier to drift off, into the wild. To
say more than this would be simply conjecture.

For four and a half years George Hayward is invisible, coming of
age out of sight, out of print. He reappears abruptly on 12 January
1859 when entering the army in the ranks of the 89th Regiment
of Foot, later known as the Royal Irish Fusiliers. Hayward's commission as an officer had been paid for, not by himself out of some
meagre inheritance or business earnings, but by his father's old
employer the Earl of Cardigan, an unstable and impetuous man,
not to mention a notorious philanderer. Something, some debt,
some sense of responsibility towards the child of his one-time
land agent, remained, but once again even to suggest what its
nature might have been would be the wildest of conjecture.

Her Majesty's 89th were based at Fermoy in Ireland, and it was
there that the 20-year-old Hayward went for his training. For
this reason historians long assumed that Hayward was Irish. There
was certainly plenty of Irish blood spilt on the frontiers of British
India, and some of the notably disreputable figures who haunted
its fringes were Celts. Hayward's headstrong fieriness also fitted
with the clichéd caricature of the Irish, but on reflection it could
just as easily apply to a Yorkshireman.

Training at Fermoy took two years, and it wasn't until 1862 that the young officer arrived in India to join his regiment in Multan. Multan stands near the Chenab River in modern-day Pakistan, where the fertile floodplains of the southern Punjab begin to give way to the raw deserts of Sind and the raggedly violent hills of Baluchistan. The town dates back to the days of Alexander the Great, and was seized by all the conquering armies that flowed back and forth along India's troubled western frontier: Huns, Arabs, Ghaznavids, Mughals, Sikhs and British.

After the death of Ranjit Singh in 1839 the Sikh Empire had collapsed into a chaos of internecine warfare, treachery and – quite literally – back-stabbing. The British had soon intervened and seized control, and though some of the Sikhs' vassals – most notably and crucially the Hindu Raja of Jammu – had maintained or extended their power and independence under treaties with Britain, the Punjab itself was British territory. And Multan was the Indian base of the 89th.

Hayward would almost certainly have come ashore from the steamer at Karachi. The Sindi capital was, then as now, an unlovely port sweltering on the yellow littoral of the Arabian Sea in a mess of mud and mangrove swamps. It had none of the romantic associations of Bombay, but it would have been George Hayward's first taste of Asia. He would already have seen a glimpse of the Muslim world as the steamer anchored off Aden on the southern tip of the Arabian Peninsula. He would have seen the cluster of white buildings, shimmering at the foot of the great brown-scarred buttress of the Hadramaut, and felt the hot wind coming off the desert. And he would have seen men in sweat-stained robes and white turbans swarming the dockside: Arabs, Africans, Indians and Afghans.

At Karachi it would have been more of the same, but here Aden's sizzling dryness would have been blunted by the oozing humidity of the subcontinent. A slow sea journey would have mitigated the jet lag and instant impact of new climate of today's airborne travel, but stepping ashore, beyond the reach of sea breezes into the livid, wriggling heat of South Asia would still have left the newcomer's head spinning. And the culture shock must have been every bit as intense.

A horse-drawn cart, driven by some sun-blackened man with bare feet and a scrap of cloth wound about his head, would have carried Hayward to a holding station, somewhere where papers were processed and clearances arranged. Along the way he would have been in the thick of the chaos of the Karachi street, all noise and weird smells; putrid and pungent. The pavements would have been a maelstrom of pedestrians in loose whites or shimmering reds and greens; here a huge Baluch with flying moustaches, a massive turban and a bandolier (and perhaps a knife or gun – against all government regulations); there a woman entirely cloaked in chalk-blue or mustard-yellow, or else loosely swathed in scarlet with a bare midriff and a loop of gold in her nose. This would all have had a powerful impact on anyone, even if they were not dripping with sweat and reeling at being on solid ground after long weeks at sea.

Far from the fair play and decency of young officers and raw recruits amidst Irish mists, Hayward would have had his first real exposure to the cynical, foul-mouthed and violent world of time-served British-Indian soldiery. Whether this rough, hot, noisy new environment appealed or appalled is impossible to say, but with both his parents long dead he probably didn't feel homesick.

From Karachi he would have rattled north over deserts and scrappy, stubbly fields on the newly opened Sind Railway, and rolled into Multan hot, thirsty, exhausted and disorientated. Some sniggering older soldier in Karachi might already have quoted the famous couplet to him on hearing of his destination:

> With four rare things Multan abounds,
> Heat, beggars, dust and burial grounds.

Then as now, the city, sprawling beyond its old core into the searing yellow countryside, is studded with the inlayed tombs of Sufi saints and is still watched over by a crumbling mud-walled fort. It was here that George Hayward, aged 22, joined his regiment.

Military affairs in British India in the 1860s were something of an anomaly. The colony was under the direct rule of the British crown. However, the Bombay, Bengal and Madras armies, which had begun life as the private militias of the Honourable British East India Company – essentially a trading concern that somehow became an empire – were still in existence. The 'Indian' regiments that made up this army were still commanded by British officers, and many of their foot soldiers were European too. However, since the 1857 rebellion by local soldiers (known at the time as 'the Mutiny') and the abolition of the Honourable British East India Company, there were also 'British' regiments, part of the main 'British' army, based in India. The 89th was one of these.

A posting in India's far-west ought to have brought ready chances for skirmishing and bloodshed, but the 1860s were an unusually quiet period. The dust from the Mutiny and the fall of the Sikh Empire had long since settled; the British had yet to take possession of Baluchistan; and the state of near-constant guerrilla warfare that developed later on the North-West Frontier had yet to emerge. Hayward's regiment would have rattled back and forward across north-west India to a variety of dreary peacetime postings – and all in that blistering, inescapable heat. In summer the 89th hauled itself north along the tributaries of the Indus to its hot-weather base at Murree.

Murree, not far north of the soulless grid that is the modern Pakistani capital Islamabad, is one of those lingering relics of the Raj that dot odd corners of the subcontinent; a strange flotsam and jetsam of empire left above the tide-line of history on the outer spurs of the Himalayas. They are known as 'hill stations': little visions of an imagined England built atop near-vertical conifer-studded ridges, where ladies could promenade along malls unsullied by dogs and Indians, and gentlemen could enjoy stout morning rides through the pine trees. A few of the better known examples in India still have a certain buzz amid the hordes of middle-class honeymooners up from the plains: Shimla, Darjeeling, Mussoorie. But most of the others, particularly those that were considered second-string even in the British days, have a melancholy air of decrepitude with dormer windows collaps-ing, red roofs rusting and the Gaiety Theatre and gothic church boarded up or given over to vagrants. Murree, and the chain of smaller outposts running north along the ridges, were decidedly second-string. But it was here that Hayward would have got his first glimpse of the mountains.

During the summer yellow haze runs up from the plains early in the day, making ghosts of the hills. The slopes below Murree are clouded with dense, green foliage, noisy with the hissing and creaking of insects and the hooting and trilling of birds. The town is alone and adrift in a warm yellow world where slow-creeping updrafts of hot wind carry sounds from far below and the sky is an invisible white blank. But sometimes, in the early morning, or in a sudden chill of evening after a rainstorm has muddied the streets and left the pariah dogs shivering in the ditches, the sky clears and a huge vista opens. There is rank upon rank upon rank of the lower tiers of the Margalla hills stretching away in fading purple facades, marked here and there with a smudge of wood-smoke or a spark of sunlight showing a new tin roof in some hidden vil-lage. Beyond, higher and harder, rise the Black Mountains, hiding valleys that grasp at the roaring gorge of the Indus and where, even now, the Government of Pakistan carries no authority. And further still, floating above the curve of the horizon are the high peaks; a great saw-toothed ridgeback of geological violence; black rock and white ice catching the summer sun in yellow stars or bleeding in the last of the daylight. And then, as quickly as they appeared, a yellow haze or a shivering night mist runs in and the vision is gone.

When Hayward asked —and he surely did — he would have been told quite categorically that no white man had ever been into those mountains. Somewhere up there were wild and violent places beyond the frontiers of Britain and Kashmir; places known only by name and evil reputation: Gilgit, Chilas, Hunza. Yet you could look on those places, see the very peaks that surrounded them from the high windows of the club or from the veranda of some mock-Tudor bungalow as you reclined in a cane chair and a neatly liveried bearer slid forward with a tray of whisky sodas. If Hayward, looking out towards those mountains from this environment of incongruous suburbia, had muttered something about the potential for fine trophy-shooting up in those ranges he would have been met with a dismissive scoff:

> Go to Baltistan, go to Ladakh old chap; plenty of wild goats up there, and you're always under the maharaja's protection. As for *those* hills, forget it – you can't go there. They're fanatical Mohammedans and they'd kill you as soon as look at you. And besides, the Government wouldn't let you get anywhere near the place. A civilian, maybe – though he'd end up dead just as quick – but not a soldier, no chance whatsoever. Forget it old man.

And with that the clouds would have rolled in again, the distant snows would have disappeared and the clang of a gong somewhere closer at hand would have announced that dinner was ready.

Murree might have provided a pleasant interlude, but that the dreary slog of army life in a time of peace did not appeal to George Hayward is evident. In 1863, apparently desperate for some kind of action, he purchased a lieutenancy in another regiment. The buying and selling of commissions was an odd business, clearly demonstrating that money, not merit, was all that mattered, but it was very common. In Hayward's case the cash for the upgrade was probably borrowed; chronic debt was almost a duty for young British officers in India. He purchased the position in hope of a change of pace, for his new regiment, the Scottish 79th – later to become the Cameron Highlanders – was heading for the Frontier.

Peshawar's name means 'frontier city', and that is what it has always been. Standing at the mouth of the Khyber Pass, it has been seized, ceded and sold by a long litany of invaders. It had not long been under British control after decades of being scrapped over by Sikhs and Afghans. But for all that – and for all its modern position within Pakistan – it has always been an Afghan city with more of a connection to Kabul than to Delhi, Lahore or Islamabad.

On the way there, heading west along the Grand Trunk Road, you pass through a low gap in the long yellow-brown ridge of the Margalla Hills. This unremarkable little pass is of huge significance: quite perceptibly it marks the point where you pass from the soft, bountiful, slow-moving world of the Indian subcontinent and into Central Asia. From here on in things are wilder and more dangerous; history moves with devastating rapidity and empires become transient.

Hayward must have felt some of this as his new regiment headed north-west to put down an expected uprising in the Khyber Pass. The Pashtuns of the Frontier had already been romanticised as a 'martial race' and an 'honourable adversary' – a coded acknowledgement of the fact that they had wiped the floor with the British on more than a few occasions. The chance to face them, despite the obvious risk of death, was idealised by young British soldiers. But in 1863 and 1864 no more uprisings came to pass. The regiment lingered in Peshawar; Hayward picked up a smattering of Pushtu, the language of the Pashtuns, and perhaps travelled a little way north towards Swat and Chitral, as far as the lawless conditions would allow.

By now, it seems, having gleaned what little it had to offer by way of local language skills, marksmanship and surveying techniques, George Hayward was thoroughly sick and tired of army life. In June 1865 he willingly sold his commission and walked away from the military without a backward glance. And at this point, just as when he left school exactly eleven years earlier, he disappears from the records. He was 26 years old.

When we picture the British in India it is hard not to conjure up an image of flustered memsahibs in frilly white fainting from the heat on gentle Sunday outings; of blustering colonels with gout and moustaches spluttering over a *chota peg* of whisky beneath a wafting *punkah*; of dashing young captains, all scarlet and brass on hot-blooded stallions; and above all an atmosphere of distasteful racial privilege. The only locals on the scene are inscrutable bearers in high-collared jackets and neat turbans, scuttling from the shadows with a tray of cucumber sandwiches. Or perhaps a decadent and corrupt maharaja, jewels dripping from bloated fingers, patronised and pandered to by the sahibs as he hosts them on a tiger shoot.

It is a world endlessly described as 'Kiplingesque' by people who have never read Kipling. Any mediocre travel journalist who arrives in India and discovers a hotel with a few mouldy hunting trophies on the wall and a waiter who maintains a facade of crawling subservience will instantly invoke the ghost of the Nobel Laureate. 'The India of Kipling survives in this lovingly preserved colonial hotel,' they write; 'this is a place that Rudyard Kipling would recognise.' If you actually read the *Plain Tales from the Hills* you will indeed find those overwrought ladies and puffed-up colonels, but you will also find a vivid portrait of a grimier, less salubrious world of failed entrepreneurs, fraudsters and opium addicts.

In the second half of the nineteenth century the British elite had thoroughly disengaged from the Indians they ruled, but they were not the only Europeans on the scene. By that stage there were whole generations of British adults who had been born in India. The better-off of them were sent to a little-known place called 'Home' for an almost invariably miserable schooling (this was exactly the experience of Kipling himself). But steamship tickets and English educations were expensive luxuries, and not all of the British in India were wealthy; there were plenty of Englishmen who had never seen England.

As well as military men and colonial administrators there were landholders and businessmen, tea planters and entrepreneurs. There were various oddball mercenaries in the service of rajas and maharajas, and down the social scale there were journalists, petty shopkeepers and railway engineers. Still further down the ladder there were the failures, the bankrupts and the loafers. Plenty of young British soldiers ran up enormous debts in India, and left the army too poor to go home. They scraped a miserable existence on the very fringes of European society, caused trouble and were deported by the authorities, or else smoked opium and lived in sin with native women and 'died as poor whites die in India'.

George Hayward remained in India after leaving the army, but exactly which of these worlds he occupied between 1865 and 1868 is impossible to say. In the shrunken, dislocated society of the Raj, British class consciousness intensified to levels matched only by the paranoia of the most orthodox caste-Hindus. The rules for seating precedence at dinner parties ran to pages; your station in society was fixed in stone. The 'country-born' British were looked down on by those whose birthplace was in England itself, and the 'country-educated' were almost beyond the pale.

George Hayward was at least British born, and had at least belonged to a British, rather than a native, regiment. But he was a middle-class orphan and he probably had debts; it is unlikely that he had much access to memsahibs and tiger shoots. But he did have access to the mountains.

In the 1860s Kashmir was under the control of the canny Raja of Jammu, now upgraded from plain raja, or king, to maharaja, great king. Gulab Singh, a Hindu Dogra from the petty state of Jammu on the northern edge of the Punjab, had been a vassal under the Sikh Empire of the mighty Ranjit Singh. But he was a sharp operator. Though he had some claim to royal Dogra blood, he had not inherited his title to Jammu. He had been a mere soldier in Ranjit Singh's army and had managed to get himself appointed as a client raja in reward for service to the Sikhs. But this was not enough for Gulab Singh: he had also managed to gain a good deal of autonomy – in his expansionist policies in the mountains if not in the Lahore capital itself – and before Ranjit Singh's death he had already got his claws into Baltistan and Ladakh, remote principalities in the high mountains encircling Kashmir. He had even unsuccessfully invaded Tibet.[2]

Kashmir itself was an ancient fiefdom populated almost entirely by Muslims. It had been held as a sort of gloriously romantic holiday retreat by the Mughal emperors, tussled over by Afghans, then grabbed by the Sikhs during their rapid ascendancy. Gulab Singh had every intention of making it his own.

The Sikhs were defeated in a war with the British in 1846 during the turmoil that followed Ranjit Singh's death and a huge indemnity was demanded. The Lahore court had bankrupted itself in its bout of dynastic feuding and was in no position to pay such a sum. But Gulab Singh was, and what was more, he had carefully distanced himself from the mayhem of the post-Ranjit empire and sidled as close to the British as conditions would allow.

In lieu of the demanded cash the British took certain chunks of the Sikh realm, including Kashmir, and on receipt of payment the Himalayan state was ceded to the Jammu Dogra, who became a maharaja at the very pinnacle of Indian royalty, having started out as a common soldier. In 1856, a year before his death, he bestowed the kingdom to his son Ranbir Singh who then passed the rule and the invented title of Maharaja of Kashmir down through his descendants until 1947. Essentially, the British had sold Kashmir to an outsider for £750,000. The move caused a good deal of retrospective criticism a few years later as the focus of the Great Game shifted into the high mountains. It has also left the modern subcontinent with its livid, unhealed wound and tangle of disputed borders.

But with the Himalayan state under the rule of a treaty-bound British ally, some of it at least was open to visitors. In the 1860s there was a seasonal British Resident (without full Residential powers) stationed in Kashmir to advise – and to keep an eye on – the maharaja. A steady trickle of British tourists made their way up through the Pir Panjal ranges to Srinagar, the Kashmiri capital, during the summer months, and why not? It may not quite have been the earthly paradise of the dreamy Mughal princes, but with its embroidered hem of snowy mountains, its chenar trees, cool climate and lakes, the Vale of Kashmir was certainly very pleasant. Its women were famed throughout India for their beauty,[3] and if you liked killing things – as any red-blooded Victorian ought to – there was all sorts of fun to be had up amongst the valleys and glaciers. Hayward certainly enjoyed shooting, and for the more adventurous British officers and civilians, a rough and ready stalking trip into the high wilderness of Ladakh or Baltistan in pursuit of ibex and markhor was the very best thing that India had to offer.

Exactly when and where Hayward went, and exactly how far into the Western Himalayas he travelled during this period is unknown, but it was certainly at this time that he cut his teeth in the high mountains. And it was also almost certainly at this time that he met the man who was to provide a dangerous inspiration for the young adventurer.

In the second half of the nineteenth century there can have been no more gloriously disreputable figure in all of north India than Colonel Alexander Gardner. A decrepit octogenarian, and the oldest and longest standing European resident of Srinagar, he claimed to be an American citizen (almost everything Alexander Gardner says must be prefixed with the words 'he claimed').[4]

He belonged to another age. A century earlier the pioneers of British India had positively revelled in their exotic lifestyle, sucking at *hookahs*, dressing in the finest silk turbans, taking local wives and even converting to Islam. But by the time the Punjab was subjugated and the Mutiny suppressed, such behaviour had become anathema. The trembling memsahibs of polite British-Indian society would no doubt have had a fit of the vapours at the very sight of Alexander Gardner, for the old colonel had quite unmistakably gone native. But for adventurous young men with a penchant for hunting and hiking – and for anyone with an eye to the high peaks beyond the Kashmir Valley – he was still an unmissable, if unreliable, port of call. By the 1860s and 1870s he had become a veritable tourist attraction, and 'visitors to Kashmir lost no opportunity of calling on the old adventurer'.

If you were holidaying in Srinagar during the brief summer season you might come across him unexpectedly in the malodorous alleys of the old city. Perhaps you have strayed from your path, and now, a little flustered, are trying to find your way back out to less cramped, less claustrophobic quarters. All around you are jostling mobs of Kashmiris, Baltis, Ladakhis and Afghans, men with all manner of faces and all manner of costumes. But the figure now lurching towards you would stand out anywhere. He is 6ft tall, as thin as a poplar tree, and quite clearly very ancient indeed. He lives, one imagines, somewhere back along the rat-run of alleys and overhangs, deep in the heart of the native quarter, in some squalid lodging of damp papers and dirty bedding, shared – you cannot help but assume – with a local female some years the colonel's junior.

If it is a normal day he will be wearing his regular and no doubt thoroughly shabby attire, but perhaps he has been invited to dinner by some amused Englishman in anticipation of a ripping yarn or two. If this is the case then he will be dressed in all his particularly unique finery. And what a sight he is! The stick-thin legs bow out slightly in narrow trousers as he bears his weight on the tip of long sword; a jacket that splays out Indian-style from the waist is bound about with a bright sash, and on his head a bulky turban is crowned with a plume of peacock feathers. On the superannuated 6ft giant this costume would be striking enough even if it was not all cut from a cloth of bright tartan. But the astonishing nature of the garb is nothing to the face of the man that wears it. A black beard shot through with streaks of badger grey flies out in all directions beneath an enormous crag of a nose – and the eyes! They swivel wildly, glaring furiously in all directions. He also appears to have difficulty swallowing. A strong gust from the mountains could probably knock him down but he looks utterly terrifying nonetheless.

You wonder for a moment if this is some bastard progeny of Rob Roy Macgregor and a concubine of Ranjit Singh, and start to back away. But you have caught the old man's blazing eye. He limps towards you glowering furiously, collars you, and in English, 'quaint, graphic and wonderfully good considering his fifty years among the asiatics', he begins to tell you his story.

Alexander Haughton Campbell Gardner was born in 1785 to a Scottish father and an Anglo-Spanish mother in the little town of St Xavier at the mouth of the Colorado River …

You cough and politely interrupt. You don't wish to be rude (you are still rather frightened, and he *is* carrying a very sharp sword), but if the colonel was born at the mouth of the Colorado River, then why on earth is he speaking with a distinctly Irish accent? He glares at you furiously with those swivelling eyes and mumbles something about a brief interlude in Ireland during his twenties, then goes on with the tale.

The story with which Colonel Alexander Gardner (it's unclear whether his military title was ever conferred on him by anyone other than himself) regaled his wide-eyed visitors was one of the greatest ever told. It abounds with the most spectacular adventures, with narrow escapes, bloody battles, daring victories, crushing defeats, service in any number of exotic armies and tragic heartbreak. He had seen almost every corner of Central Asia and the Western Himalayas, and had been to all of the places that would obsess explorers, geographers and politicians for years to come – he claimed.

From that unlikely starting point at the mouth of the Colorado (or the source of the Mississippi or the shores of Lake Superior – it depended on his mood) he embarked on the most improbable career. After a brief and unexplained spell in Ireland (why he went there at a time when Irishmen were already beginning to leave the Old Country in droves for a life in the New World is anyone's guess – perhaps he just wanted to pick up the accent), an equally brief return to the United States, and an even briefer stopover in Spain, he was off to Central Asia.

Gardner claimed – he *claimed* – that his brother was working for the Russians on the chilly northern coast of the Caspian Sea and that he had gone there to join him in his employment as a mining engineer. But when the brother fell off his horse and died in late 1817, the Russians became distinctly unfriendly. For some reason, instead of doing what anyone else would have done and returning to Europe or America, Gardner smuggled himself across the Caspian to its wild eastern shore, leapt into the saddle, took the *nom-de-guerre* 'Arb Shah' and galloped off into the sunrise. There followed a fourteen-year period of the most jaw-dropping adventure. He wandered right, left and centre through the territory of Afghans, Turkomen, Uzbeks and Hazaras; he gathered around him a posse of local reprobates and lived by his wits – begging, borrowing and stealing to survive.

Sometime in the early 1820s, after already visiting all of the towns of Central Asia, he and his little band crossed into Afghanistan for the second time and headed for Kabul with the intention of enlisting in the army of the then king, Dost Mohammad. However, before they reached the capital they ran into Habibullah Khan, the thoroughly unpleasant estranged nephew of Dost Mohammad, who was then fighting his own guerrilla insurgency from the mountains (such things have been going on in Afghanistan for a very long time). Never one to be inspired by principle, Gardner was quick to sign up for Habibullah's campaign.

For the next two and a half years the colonel thundered around the outer ramparts of the Hindu Kush, harrying government patrols and launching attacks on camel trains and caravans. In the process he managed to kidnap a beautiful young wife for himself.

How the lady in question reacted to finding herself wed to a 6ft giant, already gashed about with a variety of horrible war wounds (he had some fourteen by the end of his career) and speaking Dari with an Irish accent, is not known. But she did bear him a son.

If things had gone differently Gardner might have retired to grow opium poppies in some remote mountain valley; his bloodline would have dissolved into the genetic melting pot of Afghanistan, and we would never have heard of him. However, in a twist almost unprecedented in Afghan history, the central government actually managed to defeat the insurgents.

Habibullah's rebels were definitively routed and their leader severely wounded. When Gardner, himself bleeding from various new sabre cuts, returned from the battlefield to his fortified home he knew at once that something terrible had happened:

> The silence was oppressive when I rode through the gateway of the fort, and my men instinctively fell back, when an old *mullah* (who had remained faithful to our party) came out to meet me ... the aged *mullah*, at first stood gazing at me in a sort of wild abstraction, and then recounted the tale of the massacre of all I loved.

Gardner's beautiful wife and his 'noble boy' had been brutally murdered by Dost Mohammad's soldiers. The old Mullah had tried to protect the baby, but the men had snatched it from him and stabbed it to death. Gardner listened in horror as the tale was told:

> I sank on my knees and involuntarily offered up a prayer for vengeance to the most high God. Seeing my attitude the *mullah*, in a low solemn tone, breathed the Mohammedan prayers proper to the presence of the dead, in which my *sowars* [orderlies], who had silently followed with bent heads, fervently joined. Tear after tear trickled down the pallid and withered cheeks of the priest as he concluded. Rising, I forced myself and him away from the room, gave him all the money I had for the interment of the dead,

and with fevered brain rode away for ever from my once happy mountain home.

With this gut-wrenching tragedy, a story that has so far gone from interesting to astonishing by way of improbable now becomes downright flabbergasting. Pursued and penniless – not to mention still bleeding profusely – Gardner and his ragged band of outlaws took to the hills. They subsisted on herbs, wild mushrooms and carrion – including the carcass of 'some hyena-like animal' which was 'disgustingly rotten' – and had a number of close scrapes with units of hostile horsemen, before passing, sometime in late 1826, into the high mountains.

This is the section of the tale that most interested later travellers and geographers, for even during Gardner's retirement in the 1860s and 1870s few of the places he claimed now to have visited had been seen by foreigners. It was also the part that raised the most eyebrows, for in his late eighties, Gardner's recollections were nothing if not a little hazy.

Over a patchy three-year period he claimed to have crossed the Pamirs, surviving an attack from a pack of ravenous wolves en route, to reach the deserts of Eastern Turkestan. He made a casual stopover in Yarkand before crossing the high passes of the Karakoram – disguised as a Haji – and descending on Kashmir via Ladakh.

These would have been some of the most audacious mountain journeys ever undertaken. In the high Pamirs wolves are the least of your troubles; it is one of the most inhospitable places on earth – one experienced polar explorer declared that it was colder than the Arctic. Yarkand and the other cities of the Taklamakan Desert were troublesome, treacherous places, as later travellers – George Hayward included – would find out. And the passes over the Karakoram watershed and down to Ladakh were absolute deathtraps, combining brutal weather and severe physical conditions with extreme altitude. But Colonel Gardner took it all in his stride – he claimed.

In Srinagar he heard a whisper that his old commander Habibullah was once again launching attacks from the hard brown hills of Afghanistan. On a whim he decided to join him, but rather than taking the obvious and easy southern route he ploughed due west through the mountains, seeing Gilgit, Chitral and Kafiristan decades before any other westerner.

He eventually emerged at Kandahar, where he was summarily tossed into a dungeon, Habibullah's insurgents having been defeated once more. Gardner's jailors kept him festering for a full nine months, but as soon as he was released, again demonstrating that singular absence of principle, he applied to Dost Mohammad to join the very army that had murdered his own wife and child. Dost Mohammad refused – quite sensibly, it must be said – but he eventually found work in the militia of the Afghan governor of Peshawar. Then, in late 1831, he continued east to the Punjab and, having now apparently swapped the moniker Arb Shah for that of 'Gordana Khan', signed up for a post in the army of Ranjit Singh.

At this point, with a certain degree of relief, we can drop the 'he claimed' for there are verified records of Gardner during his time fighting for the Sikhs. He was there for more than a decade, and in a lapse into thoroughly uncharacteristic loyalty he actually remained in Lahore throughout the bloody power struggle that followed Ranjit Singh's death. But he was back on form as soon as things were quiet in the Punjab: he returned to Kashmir to take up a post as commandant of the artillery of the new Maharaja Gulab Singh, a man whose character he had previously described as 'one of the most repulsive it is possible to imagine'. Evidently the delights of Kashmir tempered any qualms he might have had about his new employer, for he remained there for the rest of his days, dying peacefully in his bed in 1877 at the age of – he claimed – 91.

If the self-related biography of Alexander Gardner raises a certain healthy scepticism today, there were also plenty of doubtful cynics at the time. Debate as to the veracity of his tale raged both before and after his death. And there do seem to be an awful lot of gaps and inconsistencies in the story. For a start, no town by the name of St Xavier has ever stood at the mouth, source, banks or shore of any American body of water, and that thick Irish brogue, rumbling from between toothless gums, was undeniable.

Gardner left accounts of his travels in a jumble of scarcely legible handwritten notes and incomplete journals. Various people borrowed and studied these both before and after the colonel's death (and an alarming number of these would-be biographers died while in possession of them – prompting rumours of a curse). Gardner's papers only serve to muddy the waters still further. Some sections – such as that dealing with the guerrilla campaign in Afghanistan and the murder of his young family – are rich with vivid detail; others amount to nothing more than a list of place names.

Many of the old colonel's itineraries through the cities and caravan towns of Afghanistan and Central Asia could have been cobbled together from any nineteenth-century atlas. But the section of his journey that pressed into what was terra incognita at the time – namely the crossing of the Pamirs to Yarkand, onwards over the Karakoram and then west again to Kafiristan – is precisely the section where Gardner is at his most vague. Geographical descriptions are hazy, timescales imprecise and places visited along the way unidentifiable.

But even so, many who heard his stories were convinced. Andrew Wilson, a successful Indian-born journalist who wandered the Himalayas with a sharp eye and a sharper pen, met Gardner in 1873 and saw no reason to doubt what he heard. He also pointed out the need to take into account the colonel's immense age. 'If (as I have no reason to believe) he occasionally confused hearsay with his own experience, it could scarcely be wondered at considering his years, and there is no doubt as to the general facts of his career,' wrote Wilson. The enigmatic explorer Ney Elias, who actually did visit many of the key staging posts on Gardner's improbable itineraries in later decades, was also a believer: 'There appears to me to be good internal evidence that, as regards the main routes he professes to have travelled, Gardner's story is truthful.'

Others, however, were less charitable. Sir Henry Yule – the eminent geographer, co-author of *Hobson-Jobson*, the mighty dictionary-encyclopaedia of Anglo-India, and greatest translator of Marco Polo's *Travels* – poured as much scorn on Gardner's story as Victorian decorum would allow. He compared him, appropriately enough, to the Abominable Snowman:

> Geography, like Divinity has its Apocrypha … I am sorry to include under this head the diary of Colonel Gardiner [sic] … [A]mid the phantasmagoria of antres vast and deserts idle, of scenery weird and uncouth nomenclature … we alight upon … familiar names as if from the clouds; they link to nothing before or behind; and the traveller's tracks remind us of that uncanny creature which is said to haunt the eternal snows of the Sikkim Himalaya and whose footsteps are found only at intervals of forty or fifty yards.

Perhaps most damning of all is the very part of the story that we know to be true – the service in Ranjit Singh's military. Gardner was by no means the only foreigner in charge of Punjabi troops. In the first half of the nineteenth century the Sikh army was a veritable French Foreign Legion – only with fewer questions asked.

The Sikhs have long prided themselves as a martial race, but Ranjit Singh was ever the pragmatist and recognised the superior techniques and technology of his main subcontinental rivals – the British. Eager to inject modern European practices into his soldiery he recruited any wandering foreigner with a passable military CV who arrived in the Punjab. Some of his most senior generals were former Napoleonic officers; the most famous was the Italian, Paolo di Avitabile, a brutal sadist who subjugated

Peshawar for the Sikhs. There were plenty of others, and few of them were particularly savoury characters. A surprising number declared themselves to be American. If the presence of American citizens in the Punjab in the 1820s is puzzling, then the accents of these supposed Yankees were even more bizarre: many of them sounded distinctly Cockney, Scottish or, like Gardner, Irish. They were of course British deserters. Sick of heat, drill and drudgery in the East India Company Army, more than a few soldiers went AWOL and slipped across the western frontier in search of an easier – and more lucrative – life.

Colonel Gardner's Irish accent had long raised a few suspicions in this direction, and half a century after his death a British historian, ploughing through the old Punjab records, stumbled upon what appeared to be a confirmation. An entry from December 1831 mentioned the arrival in Lahore of a pair of British renegades. They had done a runner from a warship in Bombay 'not being satisfied with their position', and made their way to Peshawar for service with the Afghan governor. Still not satisfied after six months, they headed to Lahore 'having heard of the liberality' of Ranjit Singh. Neither had been further into Central Asia than the Khyber Pass. One was named Khora; the other was Alexander Gardner.

This appears to be the convicting evidence. Gardner was just another deserter; his fabulous biography was nothing more than a hearty Irish stew of odds and ends gleaned from the stories he heard from other unsavoury foreigners in Sikh employ – some of whom really had been to Afghanistan. He was a fraud and a liar, and ought to be utterly discredited. With this, you might assume the prosecution presents a watertight case. But still, but still …

Perhaps it is just the same romanticism that keeps people searching for that Abominable Snowman; surely the octogenarian colonel, spinning his yarns in Srinagar, could still be telling the truth? If he had lied to so many other people, then why not also to Ranjit Singh? The Sikhs wanted experienced European soldiers, not half-wild Afghan mercenaries, and service with the defeated Habibullah Khan would be one job to judiciously leave off the résumé. In 1832 Gardner met Josiah Harlan – a mighty oddball and perhaps the only verifiably authentic American in the Sikh army; he ended his days trying to introduce camels and Kabul grapes to the Wild West. Gardner's story was already in place at that time and Harlan seemed to regard him as a fellow American. Could he not simply have met Khora, a real British runaway, in Peshawar and agreed to share a back-story? Because, for all the gaps and improbabilities, so much of the story *is* convincing.

With his tale finished on that crowded Srinagar alleyway, Colonel Gardner turns and hobbles away, leaving you slightly dazed. It couldn't be true; it *can't* be true. The omissions, the inconsistencies, the Irish accent and that irrefutable note in the Punjab archives. But then, he told it so well. Every one of the fourteen wounds, including the gash on his throat that made swallowing difficult, had a plausible tale of Afghan violence attached to it. When he told of the battle with the wolves of the Pamir you could almost hear their growls and the sound of their paws pattering the snow, almost smell their hot, rank breath. And when the old man spoke of the brutal murder of his Afghan wife and child, even after so many years, his eyes had unmistakably filled with tears.

You want to press him on all these points, to seek some flash of clarity that will either confirm it all as the incredible truth, or damn him forever as a liar and charlatan. You call out to the disappearing back – 'Colonel Gardner!' – but he only raises a long, withered hand without turning or stopping. You start forward into the crowd of hill folk, stumbling over a Balti tugging a bundle of onions. You catch yourself before you fall and look up just in time to see a flash of tartan disappearing between a tall Pashtun with a huge turban and a Dogra woman with a gold nose stud and a basket of vegetables on her head.

'Colonel Gardner!' You dash through the throng, weaving between lines of Ladakhi coolies, to the point where the old man disappeared. There is no sign of him, and here the bazaar splits three ways down darker, dirtier alleys. You start down one, falter, go back to the junction and take another turn. But it is hopeless, and you come to stand, sweating, heartbeat pounding in your ears, and the sound of a throaty Irish chuckle echoing from somewhere in the distance.

The truth is that we will never really know.

In a way it doesn't really matter whether Alexander Gardner had actually been to all the places he claimed to have visited, or whether the various scars were simply the result of a drunken brawl in some Bombay tavern. Plenty of real-life adventurers have been inspired by the fiction of John Buchan and Joseph Conrad, and for two later generations of travellers the old man exerted a powerful influence. Alexander Burnes had visited him in Srinagar even before George Hayward was born, and had borrowed a wad of notes and journals from him. These were lost forever when the Afghan mob killed Burnes and torched his Kabul residence in 1841, prompting an uprising that led to the most catastrophic retreat in British military history: 16,000 British and Indian soldiers and hangers-on were massacred along the road back to India. Later Himalayan wanderers also called in to see the colonel. Dr Leitner did, and was impressed – and Leitner was usually impressed by no one but himself. Douglas Forsyth, the Punjab commissioner who took part in the first official mission to Yarkand and Kashgar, met him and had his stories in mind when he made his own crossing of the Karakoram watershed. And there were others.

It must be remembered that the kind of travels Gardner spoke of were simply no longer possible by the 1860s. There might remain some large unexplored chunks of mountainous country, but the borders of British India were increasingly well-defined, and the authorities were increasingly averse to British subjects crossing them on anything but official business. In Gardner's heyday Britain was still a newcomer in the subcontinent, matched if not overshadowed by the Sikhs. Few people in Central Asia had even heard of it. But by the latter part of the century most of the independent rulers west and north of the Punjab knew all about Britain and resented its increasing dominance. Gone were the days when anyone could dress as a Pashtun and slip over the border for a life of romantic roguery. Fifty years earlier a blue-eyed stranger passing through the kingdom would have been an intriguing oddity; now he would be suspected – rightly or wrongly – as a British agent and dealt a suitable fate. Gardner's past was as foreign a country to the young men who heard his tale as the days of the Magic Bus and the Hippie Trail through Afghanistan are to today's *Lonely Planet*-clutching backpackers.

The journalist Andrew Wilson summed this up perfectly in 1873:

> There was something almost appalling to hear this ancient warrior discourse of what have now become almost prehistoric times ... Listening to his graphic narrations, Central Asia vividly appeared as it was more than half a century ago, when Englishmen could traverse it not only in tolerable safety, but usually as honoured guests.

George Hayward probably sought out Gardner in Srinagar while he was stocking up for a hunting trip to Baltistan. He must have listened to the colonel's tales with a strong sense of the mediocrity of his own petty little shooting treks into the nearby ranges, and he probably felt again the tug of the restlessness that had ruined his army career.

The stories certainly had a powerful effect. Hayward's later tent-less dashes across high passes dressed native-style were an anachronism in the age of the well-stocked, multi-staffed professional expedition, but they were eerily reminiscent of a penniless escape to the mountains after the rout of a rebel army some forty years earlier. During his brief exploring career Hayward even made enquiries about the possibility of publishing

Gardner's journals. For him they must have read exactly as Wilfred Thesiger's tales of the Arabian Empty Quarter and the Iraqi Marshes do for the romantic traveller today – potent liquor indeed.

The first twenty-nine years of George Hayward's life had been relatively unremarkable, and all the more indistinct for it. A middle-class childhood, a truncated education and the early death of his parents are all worth a passing note, but they were hardly unique and did nothing to mark him out amongst the hundreds of other young British officers who arrived in India in the 1860s. The obvious dissatisfaction with army life is interesting, but in itself it made him no more than an average drop-out, destined for a life of loafing around north-west India before an obscure and impoverished end in some backwater station.

But something else caused a spark in George Hayward during the years after he returned to civvie street. The wild yarns of Alexander Gardner unquestionably played a part, but whether there was more to it than that we can only guess: a moment of revelation – of the kind described by other explorers and mountaineers – at some lonely campsite on the edge of a Baltistan glacier during a shooting trip? A lingering fascination left by that first glimpse from Murree of the lawless mountains of the Western Himalayas? Or just the need to escape a chronic debt, a failed enterprise or a broken heart? We will never know.

But something propelled George Hayward, pushed him forward to emerge once again from historical obscurity. And that the brief, blazing career that followed was no accident, that it was exactly the path that he had chosen, is plainly evident; for he reappears in the records abruptly and unexpectedly in the most unlikely of places. Not in some second-string hill station; not in the service of a corrupt maharaja; nor in the report of a scandal in Shimla or a financial impropriety in Bombay. In fact, when he next turns up he is not even in India.

In the late 1860s the India Office – home base of the administration of the Jewel in the Crown, the biggest and most important of Britain's colonial possessions – occupied part of what is now the Foreign and Commonwealth Office in Westminster. The building is a great hulk of pale grey stone amid the other grim edifices of government across from St James' Park, and just in view of Buckingham Palace. Statues of buxom Venuses and barrel-chested military men stare out from high wall niches, but Doric columns and arched windows do nothing to allay the imposing militarism. Union Jacks flutter damply at the head of tall flagpoles.

It is a place that even before the days of strict anti-terrorist security would have seen most chancers and timewasters shrivel and retreat even before reaching the threshold, so the young man who waited nervously in some antechamber in the bowels of the building one morning in early 1868 must have been drawing on all his supplies of intensity and courage. Perhaps he came straight up to London from Southampton, peering from the carriage windows as the train rattled north. It was six years since he had seen England, and now the strangely blunted landscape of the Home Counties, the heavy green fields and the orderly towns and villages must have looked as alien and incomprehensible as the chaos of Karachi and the scorched earth of Sind had when he first arrived in India. Uncomfortable in an ill-fitting suit and still dazed from the confinement of the long sea voyage from Bombay, he would have shivered in the London fog as he got down at Victoria Station; it was more cloying, more depressing than the mists of Murree.

He was taking a wild chance by asking for this interview, and in fact had no business to be in the India Office at all – he was not even applying for any official government work. But the man he was waiting to see was Sir Henry Rawlinson. Rawlinson was serving for the second time on the government's India Council, but he was no mere pen-pusher. He was a time-served soldier and

a veteran of the catastrophic First Afghan War. He had been a dip-
lomat in Baghdad and Tehran – places as outlandish and politically
troublesome then as they are today – and was an esteemed scholar
of Persian language, history and culture. He was also intensely
hawkish when it came to the subject of the Russian Threat and
the Great Game.

But the young man waiting to meet this imposing person was
– officially at least – appealing to Rawlinson not in his political
capacity. For Sir Henry, while table-thumping and demanding
action against Russian advances in Central Asia in the India
Office by day, was by night the vice-president of the strictly apolitical Royal Geographical Society.

The modern headquarters of the Royal Geographical Society
(RGS), a rather more gentle building of red brick and white windows, lies some 2 miles away across London to the north-west of
the old India Office. It is beyond the Natural History Museum
and across the road from Hyde Park and Kensington Gardens, the
muddy curve of the Serpentine, and what passes for wilderness
in central London. Today there is a plate-glass facade and helpful
ladies with name tags at the reception desk. The Reading Room,
down a short flight of stairs and with coin-operated lockers outside the door (bags are not permitted, though you may use a
laptop computer), is bright and air-conditioned, with strip lights
and internet plug-in points. There is an online catalogue of the
archives. But a hint of old grandeur remains, and an echo of the
strange meeting of scholarly science and wildly romantic adventure that the society has long represented; as well as academic
journals the library stocks all the latest *Lonely Planet* guidebooks.

Founded in 1830 from the ashes of a number of other organi-
sations, the Victorian era was the RGS' heyday. In its mission to
further the interests of science and geography it was the sponsor
and inspiration for virtually all of the celebrated journeys of the
day. Burton, Speke, Livingstone, Darwin all sallied forth with a
RGS bursary in their pocket and a crate of RGS surveying equipment in their luggage. The discoveries they made were announced

in the journal of the society, and the papers revealing the location of the source of an African river or the marriage customs of some wild Borneo tribe were read out in the hallowed London chambers to a bearded and bespectacled audience of Fellows.

There is simply nothing comparable in existence today. In the 1860s the RGS combined the authority of the House of Lords, the stature of an Oxbridge university, the excitement of a Boy Scout troop for grown ups and the function of a top-end travel agent. And it was clearly a thoroughly exclusive club. The moustached gentlemen who marched into the hearts of darkness in the name of science, civilisation and the RGS were no fly-by-night vagabonds. A few of them might end up going spectacularly gaga out in the jungle, but they set out with the highest of qualifications. They were professional scholars and scientists, and men with long and distinguished careers.

So the young man must have known that his own qualifications for approaching such an organisation were minimal. He was an unconnected unknown with nothing more to his name than an undistinguished and brief military career; a command of a few Asian languages no better than that of any other India-served soldier; some rudimentary sketching and surveying skills; and an ample stock of bravery. If he had gone straight to the RGS headquarters he would have been lucky if they didn't throw him out on to the street. Even here, in the India Office, waiting on some upright, leather-backed chair in a draughty hallway, the absurdity of what he was doing must have struck him. But the young man was possessed with an insane desire, and this was perhaps the most insane thing he had ever done. He would carry off the coming interview on self-confidence alone.

And he had clearly done his homework. He must have known that the RGS president, the staid and serious – and insistently dovish – Scottish geologist Sir Roderick Murchison would never have given him the time of day. He had chosen instead to go straight to Rawlinson. The political pronouncements and the enthusiasm for Central Asia of the society's vice-president were well known; by approaching him on his political turf, the young man might just be in with a chance.

For Rawlinson, the wilds of Central Asia and the high mountains of the Western Himalayas were not only scientifically intriguing, they were also of the deepest geopolitical significance. So when the thin young man in the ill-fitting suit, unaccustomed to his surroundings and unmistakably fresh off the boat, was shown into his office, he listened with scepticism, but also with interest.

The young man – who said his name was George Hayward, that he was a Yorkshireman but that his parents were dead and that his principal experience in the field of exploration had been a few shooting trips in Kashmir – had a certain intensity about him that was both disquieting and intriguing. And he definitely had courage, for he now announced to the vice-president of the Royal Geographical Society that he was 'desirous of active employment'. He wanted to explore. He had no money to speak of, but he wanted the society to sponsor him, and he would go absolutely anywhere Rawlinson cared to suggest, the more remote and dangerous the better.

Notes

1   One other notable former student that Forest judiciously omit from their list of noteworthy alumni is Ahmed Omar Saeed Sheikh, the Islamist extremist who, in 2002, kidnapped and murdered – by beheading – the American journalist Daniel Pearl in Pakistan. Somewhere in that nugget of gruesome information there is a kernel of unhappy irony.

2   The attack on Tibet by Gulab Singh's Dogra troops in 1841 was as audacious as it was outrageous, and was the last attempt to invade the country before the notorious British 'Mission to Lhasa' under the mighty Francis Younghusband more than half a century later. Gulab's leading general Zorawar had had his

confidence buoyed by the feeble defence offered to his attacks by the Tibetans' ethnic and linguistic brethren in Ladakh and Baltistan and had expected more of the same – inept amateur soldiers with antiquated weapons – in Tibet itself. What he actually encountered was a far more aggressive adversary, both in the Buddhist army and the hideous weather. The invaders were routed and only a few straggling survivors ever made it back across the passes to tell the tale. The only cold comfort that Gulab Singh could have taken when he heard the news was in knowing that a remarkably similar fate had befallen the British at exactly the same time – further west in Afghanistan. Their Army of the Indus had been totally annihilated on the ignominious retreat from Kabul.

3   Despite the long-standing legends of delightful maidens, it was said that 'if you want beautiful Kashmiris do not go to Kashmir to look for them'. As well as saffron and high-quality shawls, Kashmir had long been famous for exporting the more fragrant of its womenfolk. Fair-skinned, dark-eyed Kashmiri beauties abounded in Bombay brothels and Hyderabad harems, but centuries of such flesh trade had, according to one theorising Englishman who considered the question in the 1870s, caused a sort of natural selection in reverse in the Valley itself: 'A continuous process of eliminating the pretty girls and leaving the ugly ones to continue the race, must lower the standard of beauty.' The gallivanting French botanist Victor Jaquemont was moved to a particularly vicious outburst by his disappointment on arrival in the Himalayas: 'Know that I have never seen anywhere such hideous witches as in Kashmir.'

4   Even the spelling of Alexander Gardner's name is a matter of confusion. Some sources, both contemporary and more recent, refer to him as 'Gardiner'. However, Major Hugh Pearse, who edited the old colonel's papers in the 1890s, had him down as Gardner, so that is how he appears here.

4

A MOST UNSETTLING COMPANION

He saw them as he was heading back down the valley towards his camp: six bulky creamy-brown shapes moving slowly across the distant mountainside. The man dropped instantly behind a stony bank, checked that his rifle was loaded, then peered tentatively over the cusp. The creatures had moved along the slope towards him now, and he could make out what they were – half a dozen enormous male argali. His breaths shortened with a sharp shot of adrenalin: one of these huge wild sheep would provide a decent meal of fresh meat, but that was less important than the thrill of the chase. Argali were the most highly prized trophy for sportsmen in these mountains.

He watched them from his stony hiding spot. They were almost 4ft high at the shoulder, with thick, downy hair the colour of clotted cream on their underbellies and forelegs, and coarser, darker wool on their backs. Their horns were enormous: great twists of rough grey-brown that seemed almost too heavy for the animals to lift. They picked their way slowly over the barren ground, pausing from time to time to graze some invisible scrap of vegetation that had managed to survive in this desolate wilderness. Occasionally a shard of stone dislodged by their hooves skittered away down the mountainside. The man hardly dared to breathe. It was stunningly cold, and now that he had stopped moving he felt the chill quickly seeping through his layers of heavy winter clothing.

It was 9 October 1868. He had been camped out in this spectacularly inhospitable valley in the uninhabitable wastes between Ladakh, Tibet and the Karakoram watershed for the last nine days, and it was growing colder every day. Keeping a journal was proving difficult for the ink froze in the pens, and small mountain birds overcame their natural fear of man to seek warmth and shelter in the tents of the camp. The bone-numbing temperature was matched by a searing dryness, for this valley – the Chang Chenmo – lay within the high-altitude desert of the trans-Himalayan rain shadow; breathing was an agony and snow was limited to a dappling of icy patches. Past meanderings of a grey stream had cut the valley floor into a series of level, stony terraces. Beyond these the mountain slopes swept upwards, stark and brown, without any fleck of green or even a stunted juniper bush or patch of yellow grass; they rose to heights marked with thin skeins of ice. There was no grazing for the great mob of horses and yaks that the man had brought to carry his baggage, and it seemed incredible that the valley could support even the tiny wagtails that shared his tent, let alone the magnificent argali rams that he was now stalking.

Eventually, before they came within range, the beasts turned uphill and disappeared into a narrow ravine, bearing away at a right-angle to the main valley. The man waited patiently behind the blind of cold stone, but they did not reappear. It was very still, and though the slightest sound would echo to the far mountain-side and beyond, there was no wind to carry his scent towards the quarry. Slowly, cautiously and with infinite patience, he began to creep towards the mouth of the ravine, suppressing the urge to shiver in the extreme temperature.

The man's name was Robert Shaw, and he had every intention of being the first Englishman to reach Yarkand and Kashgar.

Shaw was a native of Somerset, a gently pastoral English county about as far removed from the chilly wilderness of Chang Chenmo as could be imagined. His family were wealthy, and though his father had died when he was a small child they remained comfortable. When he was just 3 years old he had been dragged through a tour of Europe by a sternly Anglican mother with a horror of Catholics and an angry obsession with the Sins of Man that bordered on a fetish. Sickly little Robert, instilled with Christian virtues and plagued by chest infections from an early age, was educated at the grand Marlborough College. Despite his weak constitution, he somehow managed to pass the Sandhurst entrance examination. However, his chronic tendency to 'rheumatic fever' meant that the army was not for him. He went to Cambridge instead, and after graduating came out to India in search of a more benign climate.

In partnership with his brother-in-law, a certain John Younghusband – whose own son would go on to be one of the greatest of all Himalayan explorers and Great Gamers – Shaw bought a tea plantation in the tranquil Kangra Valley. This gentle country on the outer flanks of the Himalayas due north of Delhi is just the environment for a man with fragile lungs. The air is fresh, the brooks sing and the pine forests are peaceful. The distant snows look like a postcard of the Swiss Alps, tea grows well and life is good. When John Younghusband was offered a military promotion he gave up his share of the business and Shaw became the sole owner of the estate. He might have been expected to remain there. However, Robert Shaw was a man of ambition, and he took himself far too seriously for a life of obscurity in the foothills.

The mysterious country of Eastern Turkestan[1] had long fascinated the British. Lying somewhere beyond the great bastion of the Himalayas, it was a place of rumour and conjecture. The area was bounded by vast mountain ranges and immense deserts.

It was populated by Turkic Muslims with green eyes and thick beards, and over the centuries the region had been tentatively held, then lost, then recaptured by the Chinese. That was as far as western knowledge of Eastern Turkestan went. Its cities – Kashgar, Yarkand, Hotan – were known by name and renown, but not by location, and even in the mid-nineteenth century the *Travels* of Marco Polo was still just about the most authoritative information available on the region.

The area was all the more intriguing – and all the more politically significant – at the end of the 1860s, for the rule of the ailing Chinese Manchu Empire there had been shaken off, and Eastern Turkestan now formed an independent Muslim kingdom. At the same time the Russians were rumoured to have advanced through Kazakh and Kirghiz country to establish frontier posts high in the Tien Shan and were now poised, if not to invade, then at least to monopolise trade in the region.

It was to this unknown country, some 500 miles north of his tranquil Kangra home, beyond some of the most extreme terrain on earth, that Robert Shaw turned. To get there would be a mighty triumph. A Russian-Kazakh was rumoured to have visited the region a few years earlier. In 1865 a rebellious British surveyor named Johnson, working on the highly ambitious mapping project of British India, had disobeyed orders and slipped across the Karakoram – in as much as you can slip across an 8,000m mountain range – and got as far as Hotan. A German with the delightful name of Schlagintweit had got himself murdered in Kashgar a decade before that, and of course, Alexander Gardner *claimed* to have been there years ago.

But as he carefully stalked the herd of argali, Robert Shaw felt secure in the knowledge that he would be the first bone fide, verifiable Englishman to visit these parts, and that he would certainly be the first foreigner to do so in such well-planned style.

For several decades explorers, surveyors and spies had tentatively felt out potential 'India-Turkestan trade routes' through the mountain barrier north of Kashmir. Local caravans had been plying the passes for centuries, but the traffic was exclusive and low-key – and it had never been exploited by the rulers of India. Now Shaw, as a plantation owner, was convinced that the Muslim cities across the Karakoram and Kun Lun ranges would provide a lucrative market for Indian-grown tea.

But although the forging of trade links was the stated *raison d'être* for his expedition, he admitted himself that going in the guise of a trader was, for the most part, mere expedience: 'it seemed that the only chance was to go in the character of a merchant. Asiatics who travel do so from one of three motives, and they can understand no other. Their journeys are either religious, commercial, or political,' he wrote. Shaw had no official political status, and national and religious pride made him 'determined to go as an Englishman' and avoid the indignity of disguising himself as a native pilgrim. He went as a trader, and in this character, he claimed, he would be able openly to get a full impression of the state of Eastern Turkestan, both politically and economically. To be fair, he did have genuine commercial interests. His large caravan was loaded with luxurious gifts for the despotic rulers of the country, and samplers of tea, cloth and other British goods. But there was more to it than that. Shaw was clearly motivated by something that it would be vulgar, and perhaps a little unchristian, to declare: the lust for glory.

He had been planning the trip for a long time, and had made a month-long reconnaissance of Ladakh, the northernmost possession of the Maharaja of Kashmir, the previous year. In the Ladakhi capital Leh he had quizzed the local traders who regularly crossed the high passes to Yarkand about their journeys, and spoke at length to the recently appointed British Resident in Ladakh, who had also been spying out possible routes north across the mountains. It was on this visit to Leh that Shaw had his first encounter with the Muslim people of Central Asia:

> I was preparing to study the Tibetan manners[2] and customs more attentively, but the first walk through the town at once dispelled

all the rather contemptuous interest which I had begun to take in the people of the place, by introducing a greater interest in lieu thereof. For stalking about the streets, or seated in silent rows along the bazaar, were to be seen men of a different type from those around. Their large white turbans, their beards, their long and ample outer robes, reaching nearly to the ground, and open in front showing a shorter under-coat girt at the waist, their heavy riding boots of black leather, all gave them an imposing air; while their dignified manners, so respectful to others, and yet so free from Indian cringing or Tibetan buffoonery, made them seem like men among monkeys compared with the people around them.

Shaw was every inch the Victorian bigot, with a distinct streak of religious chauvinism inherited from his mother. But these 'Toorkees', he felt, were 'good fellows'; some, he pointed out approvingly, were almost as white as Englishmen! He returned from Leh all the more determined to visit their homeland. And so it was that on 6 May the following year he set out from his planter's bungalow in Kangra on his self-appointed mission to be the 'first Englishman into Yarkand'.

Shaw himself admits that his 'progress at first was not very rapid'. He had a vast amount of baggage and supplies, the scenery was lovely, the weather fine and there was always the distraction of a sporting detour into a side valley in pursuit of mountain goats. Besides, there was no need to rush: it was not a race and Shaw had no rivals in his journey to Turkestan. He made a stately progress through the Himalayas and arrived in Leh at the beginning of August. En route he had enjoyed lakeside picnics, rescued a Yarkandi orphan whose parents had died in the Kullu Valley on their return from the Haj pilgrimage to Mecca, and shot vast numbers of wild animals. In Leh he still felt in no particular rush to proceed, and enjoyed the company of the British Resident, a medical doctor named Cayley, and of the 'fine fellows' from Turkestan.

At the end of August Douglas Forsyth, a government commissioner in the Punjab, arrived. Forsyth was India's principal expert on Eastern Turkestan – despite never having been there. He had been obsessed with the region for years, and was a keen advocate of trans-Himalayan trade. Shaw readily admitted that his initial inspiration to travel to Yarkand and Kashgar had 'been lit at the flame of Forsyth's enthusiasm', but seemed entirely unconcerned by thoughts that he might now be trespassing on the commissioner's territory.

Forsyth, as a state employee, was banned from travelling into the terra incognita beyond the Indian and Kashmiri frontiers. Now, doubtless immensely jealous of the civilian tea planter's freedom to explore, he did his best to discourage him. But Shaw was not to be swayed; in fact, Forsyth's obvious annoyance rather tickled him. Forsyth, Shaw wrote somewhat smugly, was:

> trying to dissuade me from my expedition on account of its possible dangers. But men very often fear perils for others which they would not in their own case, and I believe Mr. Forsyth would be more than ready to go to Yarkand himself, did the Government allow him.

But the government did not allow him; the glory would all be Shaw's.

Shaw was a rather pompous and self-important man who prided himself on his organisational skills and his talent for oriental diplomacy – though others would come to criticise the sluggish pace of his journey and a tendency to inaction in difficult circumstances. In photographs he appears with his mouth turned arrogantly downwards and his chest thrust out with a faint air of aggression. The ill-health, the weakness of the lungs and the aborted army career had clearly left him with a chip on his shoulder, but it was a chip that he whittled on the lathe of bitterness into a headstrong arrogance. 'Look at me now!' he seems to crow as he glowers down the length of his nose from the sepia images; 'Little Robert! The one they said would never cut it on the battlefield, the one they laughed at for his coughing and wheezing

– crossing the Karakoram and the Kun Lun! The first Englishman into Yarkand and Kashgar! Pioneer of trans-Himalayan trade!'

And one thing was certain: he did not want to share the glory with anyone else. In Leh a young traveller by the name of Thorpe had eagerly asked to join the expedition, but Shaw, with lordly condescension, had turned him down, offering the somewhat contrived explanation that he had already sent word of his approach across the mountains and that the Yarkandis would be expecting one Englishman, not two. Thorpe got the message: 'with great good-nature, he gave in to these reasons, and consented to abandon his intention of accompanying me – preferring to do that rather than risk the failure of my expedition.'[3] The monumental self-importance in this statement from Shaw is obvious. But it was also written after his return from Eastern Turkestan. In his published account of the journey it is the first of many oh-so-subtle but thoroughly catty attempts to cast in the worst possible light a certain other English traveller – one less inclined to capitulation and good-natured retreat.

Finally, on 20 September, Shaw set out from Leh, heading for Turkestan. He had frittered away the best part of two months in the Ladakhi capital, apparently showing no concern for the fact that the most hospitable season for high-altitude journeys was rapidly passing him by. By the time his cumbersome caravan hit the road the approaching winter was rapidly pushing night-time temperatures far below zero, and bringing the first dustings of snow to the higher slopes. But even with enormous mountain passes ahead of him, Shaw still showed no inclination to rush. He dawdled along over the Chang La, the first pass out of Leh, and down the other side towards the Pangong Lake, struggling to accrue more supplies and pack animals in the hamlets along the way, and bullying the local villagers horribly.

Shaw's enormous luggage, with tents, tinned food and wine and the bulky samples of Indian tea and cloth, required a large number of baggage animals. In Leh the caravan trade and the market in horseflesh was largely controlled by mixed-race families with bloodlines extending on both side of the Himalayan water-shed. These Turki-Ladakhis were known as Arghons, and were, by all accounts, well versed in the art of swindling travellers.

'Like most half-castes, they possess all of the evil qualities of both races without any of their virtues,' wrote Shaw, haughtily. Given these attitudes, it would be hard not to feel a certain wicked pleasure on seeing the Arghons, with smirking protestations of honour, presenting the exasperated tea-planting racist with a skin-and-bones clutch of ruined old nags of neither the quantity nor the quality that he had paid for. He was eventually obliged to leave most of his baggage in Leh in the care of a servant with instructions to obtain more horses and send them on after him.

He managed, by way of threatening the headman with a stick, to obtain a dozen more horses in the village of Tangtse, just after the Chang La Pass, though he complained that they were 'hardly bigger than rats' and were given to collapsing under their loads. In Chagra, near the head of the Pangong Lake, he took on another ten ponies, as well as five yaks – the huge, hairy beasts of the high mountains which would prove much more useful for load-carry-ing on the steep passes. As Shaw turned north-east from the lake towards Chang Chenmo, he already had an enormous cavalcade of loaded animals and a flock of sheep to supply fresh meat – not to mention a large staff of local porters and caravaneers, as well as those who had been with him since Kangra. This included the Muslim table-servant Kabeer, who Shaw picked on and mocked endlessly, and Rozee, the Yarkandi orphan rescued in Kullu.

The route Shaw was following was not the usual one. Traditionally trade from Ladakh to the oases of Eastern Turkestan had been carried due north from Leh across the forbidding Karakoram Pass. Crossing this grim 18,000ft cleft in the moun-tains was no stroll in the park. The route to its summit was strewn with the bleached bones and dried-out hides of the hundreds of pack animals – and not a few men – that had died along the way. In winter it was an absolute deathtrap. Shaw had chosen instead to head further east, via Chang Chenmo and across the Lingzi

Thung Plateau, before descending on Yarkand. This alternative route had been known to – and largely ignored by – local traders for many years. But Shaw, and Forsyth, and the Leh Resident Dr Cayley who had reconnoitred the first part of the road the previous year, all suspected that it would prove an easier, if longer, way into Turkestan. They had dreams of it becoming a sort of trans-Himalayan motorway, with tea, cloth and all the other riches of India rattling along an easy, paved road through the mountains.

The severe cold and the sound of cracking claret bottles from his baggage did nothing to temper Shaw's dreams of such a bountiful commercial future as he moved on from Chagra, the last Ladakhi settlement before the extreme altitude obliterated all possibility of permanent human habitation, and entered the frozen desert of Chang Chenmo.

The extra horses and the baggage from Leh had still not been sent on, and Shaw was beginning to have grave doubts about the appropriateness of the name of the man in whose charge he had left his possessions: he was called Momin, which means 'Faithful'. He decided therefore to slow the pace even further, and to wait a while in Chang Chenmo in the hope that the baggage would materialise (quite what made him choose this spectacularly desolate spot to camp out, rather than the slightly more temperate locales back down near Pangong Lake, is unclear). Also, before leaving Leh Shaw had sent his munshi (secretary-cum-translator), Diwan Bakhsh, and a caravan man named Jooma on ahead across the mountains to deliver a letter to the Yarkandi authorities, warning them of his approach. He decided that it would be expedient to give them a little more time to complete their mission before proceeding himself.

And so it was that on 9 October, having been wandering around the same valley in fruitless search of things to shoot for the previous week, Shaw found himself stalking that herd of six proud argali rams, some of the finest specimens he had ever seen.

He picked his way delicately over the stony hillside, struggling to suppress the momentary spasms of hypothermic shivering that overcame him from time to time. In the windless silence, sharpened by the bitter cold, the sound of every movement – a dislodged shard of frozen stone, the accidental click of gunmetal against brass coat buttons, even the chattering of teeth – seemed amplified to the point where it would roar around the whole Chang Chenmo Valley. Shaw stalked on, hoping desperately that the argali would not suddenly emerge again from the ravine with him in full view, creeping across the open ground.

As he drew nearer to the mouth of the gorge he became ever more cautious, moving more delicately, gently folding and unfolding his gloved hands over the stock of his rifle. And then, just as he was approaching the point where his quarry – hopefully unaware and moving slowly uphill with their backs to him – would come into view, Shaw glanced down into the main valley. Another spasm passed over him, but of rage this time rather than cold, for standing in the middle of the valley, casual and careless and in full view of the ravine, was the figure of a man, starkly outlined against the patches of icy snow.

Fury knotted in Shaw's belly as he glanced between the figure of the man and the ravine from which he assumed the argali would now be fleeing. Somehow restraining the powerful urge to scream in frustration and what must have been a similarly powerful urge to turn his gun on the intruder, he stalked on with little hope. When he reached the opening of the ravine he saw the argali, six distant, dwindling creamy brown dots in full flight up the high slopes and far out of range. In a filthy temper Shaw turned, shouldered his rifle, and descended on the disturber, plotting a suitable punishment and muttering whatever cuss-words were permissible for a man of such upright Christian morality.

To Shaw's surprise the man was not a member of his own party. He was a Ladakhi, but what would even a Ladakhi be doing here in Chang Chenmo at this late and miserable season? Shaw had assumed that from now until reaching the frontiers of Turkestan he would meet no one. His puzzlement deepened as the man reached into a greasy pocket and handed over a scrap of paper.

On it was a note, in English, in a thin, spidery scrawl. As Shaw read it, standing in a snowdrift in the middle of the Chang Chenmo Valley, his anger at the lost argali was instantly forgotten, replaced by a much deeper fury.

The note was from another Englishman, now hammering up the valley from Leh in the same direction, but at a much faster pace. He was barely two days behind Shaw, and, presumably unaware that the tea planter had come to a temporary halt, had written to suggest that he wait and that they meet.

Shaw was outraged. This was supposed to be his journey, and his alone! It had been many months in the preparation; *he*, little coughing, wheezing Robert, would be the first Englishman into Yarkand; he would not share the glory with anyone! How dare this newcomer even consider following the same route!

Just before leaving Leh three weeks earlier a rumour had reached Shaw via Cayley that another English traveller was making his way up from the plains with the intention of reaching Yarkand. Having already deflected the good-natured Thorpe, Shaw had hastily penned a note to the same self-important effect, warning off this unknown newcomer. He fired the missive off along the road to the south and headed out of Leh having forgotten all about it. But it seemed that the message had had no effect, for here was this new English traveller, sending his own notes, ploughing north at a formidable pace, and in serious danger of overtaking Shaw.

He read the note again, trembling with frustrated outrage. 'Going to Yarkand,' it said, 'propose a meeting.' Who could this infuriating person be? Shaw scanned to the bottom of the scrap of paper and there read the name of the man he would soon be describing as 'the thorn in my side': George Hayward. Evidently that meeting with Henry Rawlinson in London had gone very well indeed.

The outlandish region that Rawlinson had suggested for George Hayward's exploring urge was the High Pamirs. Of all the monumental mountain ranges that lock together in Central Asia, the Pamirs are perhaps the strangest and wildest. They are also – on the map at least – the ugliest. All of the others form distinct linear chains. The Kun Lun and the Karakoram sweep in as long, jagged lines from the east; as does the Great Himalaya and its southern attendant, the Pir Panjal, swimming beneath its belly like a sucker-fish. From the opposite direction the Hindu Kush, though broken and fanning out in its south-west extreme, still maintains a distinct course inwards to the core of the knot. And some 200 miles away to the north the Tien Shan is a long, glittering line, walling off the Kazakh Steppe from the deserts of Eastern Turkestan. But between the Hindu Kush and the Tien Shan lies the odd man out, the ugly kid, without direction or destination. This is the Pamirs; a bulky outcrop of rock and ice, filling the gap between the other ranges. It is still a vast range in its own right, the highest peaks rising to some 25,000ft, but it lacks the long razor-backs of connected mountains. More a great up-welling wart of land, the gaps between the summits are shallower and broader. There are no deep valleys to shelter rhododendron forests, wheat fields and little kingdoms ruled from poplar-wood palaces. Instead, there is only bitter wind and driving sleet, and occasional sheets of frozen, muddy water. No one lives in the High Pamirs. They were known to the classical Arab and Persian geographers as the *Bam-i-Dunya*, the Roof of the World.

Today they are still one of the most remote and inaccessible places on earth, and they remain a great geopolitical tangle too. Their bulk occupies the entire eastern half of Tajikistan, poorest and most broken of all the ex-Soviet states of Central Asia. But the Pamirs also spill over, northwards into the fringes of Kyrgyzstan, north-east into Xinjiang and south, through Afghanistan's narrow Wakhan tail to rub up against the Hindu Kush in the furthest reaches of Pakistan.

In the mid-nineteenth century they were all the more mysterious and troublesome. Hardly anyone had ever been there, although Marco Polo and the medieval Arab travellers had mentioned them and various wanderers had skirted their fringes over the centuries – and, inevitably, Alexander Gardner *claimed* to have had his battle with wolves on their icy slopes.

In fact, a verifiable, trustworthy Englishman in the employ of Sir Alexander Burnes had actually made it to the Pamirs in 1838. In February, the very worst time of year for such a journey, Lieutenant John Wood had traced what he thought was the source of the Oxus, one of the great rivers of antiquity, to the Sir-i-Kol, a chilly puddle in a gutter of the Roof of the World. Perhaps it was appropriate that his goal was a body of water for everything else about his journey through a mountain range as far from the sea as anywhere on earth was anything but: Wood was a naval officer.

But despite Wood's journey thirty years earlier, in 1868 the Pamirs remained almost completely unknown, and still held all manner of geographical secrets locked in those windswept valleys. Various doubts had been raised about the authenticity of Wood's claim for Sir-i-Kol as the source of the Oxus, and there were other rivers, including the Oxus' classical counterpart the Jaxartes – the hydrology of which had not been entirely disentangled – which were suspected to rise in the Pamirs.[4] In fact, in spite of the accounts of Wood and Gardner which made it clear that while not a place of towering alpine summits, the Pamirs were anything but flat, there was still a common misconception that they constituted not a mountain range, but a plateau.

What was more, the potential political significance of these unknown uplands was enormous. Like some great muscle-bound doorman, the Pamirs separated the lawless hills of Afghanistan from the ill-defined western frontiers of Kashmir; and held the desert outposts of Eastern Turkestan at arm's length from the khanates of the Central Asian Steppe. It was towards this latter region that the British authorities had been looking most nervously in recent years.

Throughout the 1860s the Russians had been advancing at a tremendous rate through Central Asia, seizing more and more territory each season, and edging ever closer to the northern marches of Afghanistan. On the other side of the Pamirs the Chinese had been kicked out of Eastern Turkestan and the caravan cities of Yarkand and Kashgar now presided over an independent Muslim fiefdom, which itself appeared ever more vulnerable as rumours emerged of new Russian frontier garrisons high in the Tien Shan – garrisons that looked suspiciously like the forward supply posts for a forthcoming invasion. The Pamirs lay at the very heart of all this. The rivers that issued from their glaciers and muddy lakes might have huge importance in the future demarcation of international borders; a firm grip on their geography would put an imperial player at a massive tactical advantage. But first someone actually needed to go there to see how things stood.

For Hayward there could hardly have been a better destination. The Pamirs formed part of the same great mountain mass that he had been tentatively skirting for years – as a distant prospect from the foothills of Murree, in the hard ridges of the Frontier north of Peshawar, and in the Baltistan glaciers beyond the Vale of Kashmir. Now, finally, he would have the chance to plunge deep amongst them. The Pamirs were almost completely unknown, yet well placed in history and politics. To get there would surely prove an extreme physical challenge, and the journey would be wildly dangerous. And perhaps most appealingly of all, the Pamirs had even been a key destination on the wayward itineraries of Alexander Gardner.

Rawlinson had drawn up a memorandum for Hayward, sketching out the official aims of his journey. This is long lost today, and what precisely his main object was is not entirely certain. His own ideas would seem to shift over the next two years. In the early stages he seemed to consider the Pamirs to be merely the turning point on a journey that would scout out the trading routes through the mountains from India's north-west; at other times he fixated more on the vexed issue of the 'source of the Oxus' and the general hydrology of 'the lake region of the Pamir'. But gradually, as attempts to reach his goal were thwarted, as the odds of success and even survival shrank, the Pamirs seemed to swell and grow and come to occupy mythical proportions in Hayward's mind. They were some kind of madness-inducing Holy Grail, an obsession of which the geographical and political significance had become irrelevant. All that mattered was that he reach them, that he get there in spite of all those who would stop him, that he stand, howling in triumph on the ice-bound summits of that bleak mountain mass. And then? By the end he had long since stopped thinking about the future.

But for now, in 1868, he had a goal and a mission. He had ample bravery and enthusiasm; he had a memorandum from Rawlinson; a stock of lightweight surveying equipment, including a special miniature artificial horizon for taking bearings, designed by a Captain Christopher George; and a bursary of £300 from the Royal Geographical Society. Within weeks he was at sea again, heading back to India.

This was all highly irregular by the standards of the RGS. They did not usually employ travellers. Sponsorship was available, but generally for journeys that had already been planned by men with existing expertise in their chosen field – the lakes of Africa, for example. From time to time the society also mounted its own expeditions, but again, these were carefully planned operations run by established explorers, and were never in places as politically contentious as Central Asia. On the face of it, what Hayward had managed seems as improbable as some unwashed, dreadlocked backpacker with a vague interest in Asia turning up unannounced at the RGS headquarters today and within minutes being handed £20,000 and an air ticket to Kabul.

For this reason some have wondered if this really was the whole story. Hayward's sudden appearance in London, 'desirous of active employment', was improbable enough; Rawlinson's positive response all the more so. And so there has been speculation over the years about both Hayward's exact status and Rawlinson's exact role – their first meeting had, after all, taken place in the India Office. However, there is simply no evidence to suggest that Rawlinson was acting in his government rather than in his RGS capacity when he dispatched Hayward to the Pamirs, and that the British Indian Government would later prove deeply unhelpful to Hayward firmly suggests that he had no official status, secret or otherwise.

What seems more likely is that Hayward was simply lucky, and had presented himself to Rawlinson at an opportune moment. As a government advisor and an ever-hawkish proclaimer of the Russian Threat, Rawlinson was not averse to compromising the strictly apolitical status of the RGS from time to time. Equally, he was not averse to gentle manoeuvres against his superior, the society's president, Sir Roderick Murchison. Unlike Rawlinson, Murchison was an avowed Russian Threat sceptic, viewing the idea of a tsarist invasion of India as a 'chimera' and a 'phantom'. He considered the recent Russian advances in Central Asia and the developments in Eastern Turkestan to be of no political significance to the British in India. But not Rawlinson, and when an intense young man with a severe case of wanderlust and an existing interest in that part of the world turned up, he simply decided to take a chance – a chance with ulterior motives perhaps, but no conspiracy.

Indeed, despite the fact that Hayward had set out under his directions, Rawlinson was always at pains to point out that the young man was an independent traveller. Addressing a meeting of the RGS on 9 November 1868 (when Hayward himself was sleeping out under the stars in sub-zero temperatures at a campsite called Zinchin in the valley of the Karakash River), Rawlinson stated that Hayward had gone 'at his own risk and responsibility'. He had received, Rawlinson said, 'some small pecuniary assistance from the Geographical Society by way of outfit'. In truth, £300 was not so small an amount, and was by far the largest sum granted by the society to a traveller that year. But no matter; Hayward was 'not an officer of the government, and he would deserve all the more credit if he came back with any great geographical results'.

If the final tragic outcome eventually made Rawlinson regret his decision to point Hayward in the direction of the Pamirs, the young man's indisputable demonstration of determination and skill as an explorer in the preceding two years would strongly suggest that it had been justified.

From the moment George Hayward stepped ashore on his return to India he hardly stopped moving, wasting as little time as possible and rushing straight upcountry to his old summertime billet at Murree. It was the height of summer and his former regiment, the 89th, would have been in town.

Any old comrades who ran into Hayward on the Murree Mall that August would have seen a man already so far gone from the routines of military life and petty leave-time pleasures that they would scarcely have recognised him. The conversation would have been halting, embarrassed almost. Regimental gossip and talk of the chance for a dust-up with Johnny Pathan on the Frontier would have been of little interest to Hayward now, and the soldier would have sensed his attention drifting, his intense, deep-set eyes shifting beyond the dormer windows and chimney pots of Murree, searching for something on the lost northern horizon. After a few moments they would have parted ways with a half-hearted suggestion of another meeting later – 'See you at the Club perhaps? I'm sure the chaps would love to hear your news ...' But Hayward would probably have been hardly listening, and the soldier would have gone on his way along the Mall with a somewhat puzzled backwards glance and a mumble of consternation: 'Always was an odd cove.'

Hayward spent a couple of brief weeks in Murree preparing for his journey. He had already decided to travel as light as possible, and, doubtless inspired by Alexander Gardner, he was determined to go in native disguise. He had kitted himself out in the garb of a Pashtun, and, brimming with naïve confidence, was convinced that his smattering of pidgin Pushtu was all he would need to pull it off.

His first thought was to head for the Pamirs by way of the North-West Frontier, turning north from Peshawar towards Chitral – then still a locked mountain kingdom notorious for slave-trading and banditry. He had the views of Gardner to go on about the practicality of this route, and in Murree he had also studied the report of a wandering Yarkandi merchant named Mahamed Amin about trade routes through the mountains. The Turki's statements confirmed that the journey from Peshawar to Eastern Turkestan – and onwards to the Pamirs – via Chitral posed few geographical challenges. Hayward considered Amin trustworthy and declared that the Chitral road 'must then be considered as not only the most direct route from Peshawar to Yarkand (and Badakhshan) but also the easier for trading purposes'. Hayward was entirely correct about this: the route north from Peshawar would indeed have been the quickest way into Eastern Turkestan. But he was also aware that even the Yarkandi merchants usually avoided this road – not because of landslips or high passes, but because of its lawless nature, the slave raids of Chitral and the depredations of marauding bands of the Siah-Posh, the wild pagans of Kafiristan.

None of this would have stopped Hayward from trying the route, but in the summer of 1868 the entire Frontier was in exactly the kind of ferment that had been uncharacteristically absent during his unhappy army service. With everywhere between Peshawar and Kabul in a state of uprising, the British Punjab Government did not respond kindly to the idea of a disguised Englishman wandering off into the hills with a compass and artificial horizon to get himself killed. The Lieutenant-Governor of the Punjab effectively banned him from making the journey.

It was only in the face of this initial disappointment that Hayward turned eastward to the most obvious alternative route to the Pamirs – a circuitous and far more physically demanding but infinitely more politically safe option that involved crossing

breadth of the entire South Asian n. untain system at just about its
highest point. He would go via Leh, L. dakh, Yarkand and Kashgar.

In Murree, Hayward penned his firs letter back to the Royal
Geographical Society, addressing it to the president, Sir Roderick
Murchison. Over the next two years he wou. send many of these
letters out of the Himalayas, sometimes to M. chison, but more
often to the man he considered his direct empk er at the RGS
– Sir Henry Rawlinson. He also sent a great ma. letters to a
Colonel Showers, an officer serving in India. Hayw. rd's exact
relationship with Showers is unclear, but the tone of t ese letters – which Showers forwarded to the RGS – suggests t at he
was more an acquaintance with a particular interest in Hayw. rd's
explorations than a close personal friend. They contained no. e
of the confessional, none of the off-the-record indiscretions and
informalities of, for example, Robert Shaw's missives from the
mountains to his friends and family. They stuck firmly to the
practicalities of Hayward's journeys, and, with a few of the more
heated political passages excised, were quite fit for publication in
the society's journals.

Over the next two years the tone of these letters would
harden, their focus becoming narrower and more insular, the
ever larger, ever more abstract presence of the Pamirs looming
darker and darker over the page. But this first note to Murchison
that Hayward wrote on 15 August was full of boyish energy
and enthusiasm:

Sir,

I have much pleasure in informing you of my arrival here
on my way to Central Asia. It has been my endeavour to be as
expeditious as possible and by travelling up country via Central
India instead of the usual route up the River Indus, have saved
much time.

According to the wishes expressed in Sir H Rawlinson's
memorandum for my guidance, it was my intention to have
endeavoured to penetrate into Badakhshan from Peshawar, but

having been seriously warned by the Lieutenant Governor of the Punjab 'that you will not only endanger your own life but be likely to compromise the British Government' I have abandoned the idea of going from Peshawar and am now about starting for Cashmere [Kashmir] and thence to Yarkand without delay, this being the safer route under the present circumstances. By proceeding by it I hope eventually to be able to accomplish successfully the objects in view. I am convinced that there is little danger in Yarkand itself to anyone acting with ordinary precaution, even in the event of being discovered to be an Englishman. The greater difficulty will be in returning from Yarkand by the Pamir Steppe, exploring the steppe and Badakhshan and leaving through the difficult country lying between the Hindu Kush and the North West Frontier. But as by the time I arrive at Yarkand I ought to be quite 'au fait' at keeping up the disguise I shall assume, I feel very confident of success.

Should it be in my power during my travels to forward reports, plans or information I will not fail to do so. But I fear that the great distance such communications will have to be sent before they can reach the frontier will effectually hinder my being able to do so – if even it would be advisable to send any from the fact of the necessity of being in disguise. Hoping I may be able to succeed in returning with much valuable information, scientific and geographical.

I have the honour to be, Sir, Your obedient servant,

Geo. J. W. Hayward

The excitement is palpable; the native disguise and the possibility of being beyond the reach of communication are obviously relished. In his intense urgency he even struggles to stay within the confines of a sheet of blue A4 writing paper: the words bunch up at the edge of the page, bending down the right-hand margin as if there is no time even to start a fresh line. Hayward is on his way. This is precisely the kind of adventure he had been looking for – and had never found – in the army.

With only the barest minimum of equipment (he had no tent, for example, despite the fact that he would be crossing the highest mountain ranges on earth with the winter already advancing), he set out from Murree on 26 August. By this time Shaw had already been idling away the summer in Leh for almost a month.

Murree itself was almost 300 miles further from the Ladakhi capital than Kangra, but unlike Shaw, Hayward was very much concerned about the advancing season. He headed for the hills at a spectacular pace, making double marches every day. He made it from Murree to Leh via Kashmir in a month, riding into the dusty town, with its squat houses and towering mud-walled palace ringed by barren brown mountains, on 21 September, just one day after Shaw had finally departed for Turkestan.

Shaw's dawdling along the road up from the plains, and his leisurely summer holiday in Leh, is quite frankly bizarre. Leaving Kangra at the beginning of May he had every opportunity to make it over the Karakoram passes before the first snowfall, and even taking into account his large luggage and attempts at letter-writing advance diplomacy he could quite feasibly have been in Eastern Turkestan before Hayward even arrived back in India. In contrast Hayward was, quite literally, a man on a mission.

He was in Leh for only a week, organising horses and supplies. With so little to carry he seemed to be far less vexed by the swindling Arghons than Shaw. He was relaxed and philosophical about the overcharging: 'Directly too an Englishman goes to purchase, they ask about three times the animal's value, deeming us, I suppose, fair game for being cheated.' Still, he managed to get hold of some of the finer Yarkandi ponies, superior beasts to the local Ladakhi nags, which were 'small, and hardly fit for the severe work attending so long a journey'. He also took on two local horsemen, one of whom had been to Yarkand before and was confident of the route. Still tent-less, and still dressed in his Afghan robes and turban, Hayward scoured the bazaar for thick, sheepskin-lined clothes for himself and the servants, and also bought a pair of local snowshoes and hired some yaks to carry the supplies.

He was so eager to be on his way that he could not bear to spend one more night than was necessary in Leh. Though most of the day had been taken up with last-minute wrangles over horses and equipment, on the evening of 29 September his little party made their way out of town, heading south-east along the north bank of the Indus. Leh's upland oasis of auburn poplars and willows slipped away behind them and they passed into a stark grey gravel world. South, across the river, the snow on the ridge of the bony Stok Kangri range would have flamed in the last light as the sun fell away to the west, towards the Pamirs. For the previous month Hayward had already been deep amongst the mountains, and had already crossed the Great Himalaya itself. But the road up to Leh was well-trodden; it was only now that he was moving into the true wild. He must have been elated. It was already dark when they reached the little hamlet of Thikse with its huge Buddhist monastery and camped for the night.

The next day Hayward branched away from the Indus, pulling steeply uphill to cross the Chang La Pass then dropping down towards Pangong Lake. In Tangtse, the first real village after the pass, Hayward was forced to halt for two days to make final arrangements with supplies and animals. From here on in anything he had forgotten he would have to do without. In Tangtse he took on four local yak drivers who knew the road to the first Turki outpost at Shahidulla, some 350 miles away across some of the most inhospitable territory on earth. These Ladakhi villagers were known, appropriately enough given their wrinkled, leathery complexion, as Bhoots. So with his little train in good order, and accompanied by two pairs of old Bhoots, Hayward headed north to Chang Chenmo.

He was well aware that he was following closely in the footsteps of another traveller. If Shaw's haughty note telling him to retreat had reached him on the way to Leh he must have been rather baffled by its tone. For Hayward the presence of another Englishman on the road was not an annoyance; it was simply an odd coincidence. Hayward never saw Shaw as a rival or a challenger and he was not jealous of the chance to be 'first Englishman into Yarkand'; for him the Turki trading towns were merely staging posts en route for a greater, more tantalising goal – the Pamirs. He simply didn't understand why Shaw might resent his presence.

From Tangtse he had sent one of the Bhoots ahead with a note for Shaw, suggesting that he wait and let him catch up. To Hayward it must have seemed silly not to travel together at least as far as the Turkestan frontier. By the time the messenger returned Hayward was already approaching Chang Chenmo. The Bhoot's strange story of a foul-tempered Englishman yelling at him in the middle of a snowdrift must have puzzled Hayward still further, as must have Shaw's return message, again telling him in no uncertain terms that he ought at once to turn around and retreat. Hayward penned a reply from his cold campsite (he had already recorded a temperature of -15°C one morning). He had been sent by the Royal Geographical Society, he explained; great men in hallowed London halls were relying on him to complete his journey in the name of science, and he most certainly would not be turning back towards Leh. However, he had no wish to compromise any plans Shaw had laid, and his own interest in Yarkand and Kashgar was merely as way stations to be hurried through. That such a casual, dismissive attitude towards the very places that Shaw considered 'a kind of Eldorado' might have enraged the tea planter still further probably never occurred to him.

And so it was that on 14 October a rather prickly Robert Shaw, reining in his anger with all the Victorian decorum he could muster, rode over to Hayward's threadbare camp in the Chang Chenmo for what must have been a rather chilly meeting in more ways than one.

Previous writers have felt the urge to describe Hayward as 'young' in comparison to Shaw's apparent maturity. And indeed it is an obvious way to read the glaring contrast between the two men:

one on a highly organised, carefully diplomatic expedition cost-
ing vast sums of money; the other tent-less and dressed as an
Afghan, huddling over a guttering campfire with a few local companions. These are surely the travelling styles of an older and a
younger man respectively. But anyone who cares to check birth
dates and to do a little backwards counting on their fingers will
find that it was actually Shaw who was younger – albeit by only a
year. Hayward was not long past his thirtieth birthday; Shaw was
still in his late twenties.

But they were radically different, and given the difference
it is perhaps easy to understand Shaw's hostility. Dismounting
at Hayward's little camp and glancing over its meagre outfit,
Shaw must have felt rather like a top-end tourist on some eye-
wateringly expensive organised Himalayan trek. One with a
silky-tongued guide in reflective eyeshades and an army of porters and cooks, who, on the second day of walking, runs into a
lone backpacker, carrying his own rucksack along the same trail,
moving at twice the speed and with only the sketch map in the
Lonely Planet for guidance.

The wealthy tourist booked this once-in-a-lifetime Himalayan
experience eighteen months ago; the backpacker came up on
a whim from dope-smoking in Pokhara just a week back after
finding that all the flights to Goa were fully booked. For the tourist the backpacker is indeed likely to be 'a thorn in the side'. His
dreadlocked, unprepared presence instantly shatters any illusion
of intrepidness and reveals the truth – that this is just another
generic, cookie-cutter holiday that thousands of others have
done before. The fact that the backpacker is happily lugging his
own pack, wearing a pair of regular trainers and doing 'double
marches' daily makes the tourist feel suddenly a little soft, despite
the blisters already throbbing inside his £200 trekking boots. It
also raises a certain squeamishness about all those rubber-sandaled
porters. And the backpacker's thrifty, ten-dollar-a-day budget
brings home to the tourist the slightly uncomfortable fact that
somebody, somewhere, is making a great deal of money out of

him (though perhaps not in this case an Arghon horse-trader). In short, he starts to feel a bit silly.

And if, as he makes his carefully guided way around the Annapurna Circuit, or along the Everest Base-camp route, the tourist finds himself repeatedly running into the same backpacker, airing his socks in the sunshine or cheerfully chewing down the cheapest *dhal bhat* in the most basic teahouse, it's not surprising that he comes to resent his presence to such an extent that he begins to fantasise about shoving him off some narrow footbridge into a mountain ravine. For the backpacker's part, if he's the unbearably snobbish kind (and Hayward wasn't), then he'll have contempt for the tourist, and will indeed use that very word – 'tourist' – as a sneering insult. But if he's not, then he'll likely just consider the tourist as merely a slightly odd fellow traveller.

The analogy is unfair of course: Shaw was no tourist on a well-trodden trail. He was stepping into a blank on the map; he would be the first Englishman into Yarkand, and his initial crossing of the Karakoram would be undertaken in atrocious winter conditions (that he only had himself to blame for this is beside the point). But sketching the two men as tourist and backpacker is probably the best way to understand how they felt about each other, particularly in the case of Shaw. Hayward had, he felt, rudely intruded on an adventure that was supposed to be exclusively his. That Hayward's journey to Yarkand was just a casual second choice after the best option proved impossible must have stung him deeply. The lightness of Hayward's baggage and the speed at which he was travelling might also have made Shaw feel a little ridiculous for all his flapping around over horses and supplies in Leh: clearly a crossing of the Karakoram wasn't quite so big an undertaking as he had made it out to be.

Shaw almost certainly also resented Hayward's presence for another, more embarrassing reason. The tea planter's journey had absolutely no scientific purpose whatsoever. He later claimed to have considered surveying during his initial preparations. 'But I asked myself, is this not attempting too much?' he wrote in somewhat pompous fashion. He decided against it, with the cryptic, Zen-like utterance: 'After all, we do not desire to know a country in order to map it, but we map it in order to know it.' The Turkis, he argued, would be suspicious of mapmaking. This was all somewhat disingenuous; the truth was that Shaw simply had no scientific skills; he had no idea how to survey properly, and even his grasp of basic Himalayan geography was shaky. None of this would matter if he made his journey alone: he would still be lauded for its political value, and indeed its romance. But now that a professional explorer – a capable draughtsman and a trained surveyor commissioned directly by the most august body in all geographical science no less – had turned up, Shaw's thunder was in serious danger of being stolen. No one would pay much attention to his account if some upstart emerged at the same time with the first accurate map of Eastern Turkestan. Small wonder then that he did so little to help smooth Hayward's journey over the coming months, and unsurprising that he made some uncharitable remarks in private letters back over the mountains. But the discrediting comments about Hayward that Shaw eventually scattered through his unashamedly populist published account of the journey do leave a rather nasty taste in the mouth: Hayward never even got to see his own report in print; he was long-dead by the time *Visits to High Tartary, Kashgar and Yarkand* appeared.

But that all still lay ahead. As George Hayward invited him to share a meagre meal at his little Chang Chenmo campsite (no frozen claret bottles here), Shaw would have felt utterly miserable. Of all the passes, in all the mountains, he must have wondered, why did you have to pick mine?

Any hopes Shaw harboured of convincing Hayward to turn back were soon abandoned over dinner. Hayward, probably aware that the RGS had taken an unusual chance in sponsoring an unknown, took his responsibility to the society very seriously indeed, and for the next two years was always at pains to point out – in case there were any doubters – just how hard he was

trying to reach the Pamirs. There was no way that he was going
back to Leh. Shaw instead brought to bear the same 'reason' with
which he had deflected his earlier would-be companion, Thorpe.
He had sent notice ahead that he was travelling alone, therefore
for two Englishmen to arrive at Shahidulla, the Turki frontier post,
would be disastrous for their chances of success, he claimed.

Whether Hayward was convinced by this or whether he was
just humouring Shaw is not clear (though the former seems more
likely: Hayward never had a bad word to say about Shaw in his letters or reports, and if he was aware of Shaw's occasional attempts
to undermine him, he never let on), but he agreed to let him go
on ahead. For his part, Shaw said, once he arrived in Shahidulla
he would attempt to obtain permission for Hayward to enter the
country too – though only if he 'saw an opportunity' to do so.

Shaw also had one more demand to make of Hayward, and to
be fair, this one was quite reasonable: he wanted him to drop his
Afghan disguise. Shaw himself was making no attempt to hide
his nationality, and he had some justification for thinking that
to do otherwise was a bad idea: 'it would require a most perfect
acquaintance both with the Afghan language (Pooshtoo) and also
with the Mahammadan religious ceremonial, (an acquaintance
only to be obtained by years of expatriation) to pass muster as
an Afghan in a bigoted Mussulman country which swarms with
Afghan merchants and soldiers,' he wrote. Hayward saw reason
and, perhaps a little sadly, he changed out of his rather indulgent
Gardneresque robes.

And so it was that two days later Robert Shaw headed on
towards Shahidulla by the most direct route, leaving Hayward
behind, and, one suspects, secretly hoping that some fortuitous
avalanche might intervene and that that would be the last he
saw of him. It wasn't, of course, though it would be almost eight
months before they next met face to face.

Having watched Shaw's unwieldy caravan shambling out of camp at an excruciatingly slow pace, Hayward realised that he would need to be given a serious head start if he was not simply to be overtaken again within days. He was left in the freezing Chang Chenmo with time to kill, but unlike Shaw, there was no way that he was simply going to fritter it away wandering aimlessly around in search of argali. His first move was to branch north-west from the main Chang Chenmo into the Kugrang Valley. The landscape was spectacularly barren and without any visible vegetation, but even this wasteland somehow managed to support a sizable population of large animals. Hayward shot a pair of wild yak from a herd of about forty that he came across near the head of the valley.

Three years earlier the rebel surveyor, Johnson, had disobeyed orders and headed to Hotan via the Chang Chenmo, the first Englishman to take such a route. In doing so he produced the first map of this trans-Himalayan region that was not based entirely on conjecture and second-hand rumours. Hayward was carrying a copy, but as he scrambled to the top of the short, steep pass at the head of the Kugrang and looked out over the wild chaos of mountains beyond, he began to have his first doubts about the accuracy of Johnson's work.

According to the map, just beyond the pass should have lain the headwaters of the Yarkand, the river that led down through the mountains to the town of the same name before disappearing into the vast shifting-sand wastes of the Taklamakan Desert. Hayward had planned to follow this river on down to the plains, but peering down into the barren valleys below there was no sign of it whatsoever, and no obvious route northwards. The suspicion that Johnson had got his rivers in a mighty muddle began to form, and the further Hayward pushed into the mountains over the coming weeks the more obvious it became that this was the case. By the end he was declaring that 'Mr Johnson's map is pure imagination, not even hearsay'. It was disentangling this knot and putting the headwaters of the rivers of Eastern Turkestan where they actually should be that eventually proved to be Hayward's own greatest geographical triumph.

With no obvious route north from Kugrang itself, Hayward and his party headed back down the valley into Chang Chenmo. He spotted the herd of yak he had stalked three days earlier and went in for another shot. He managed to kill another of these great shaggy wild cattle. It was, Hayward decided, 'a very game beast', having charged furiously at him several times before finally going down in the snow. However, he had doubts about the future potential of the valley as a destination for bloodthirsty sportsmen with high-power rifles. Yaks may well be game beasts and may be rather bad tempered, but lumbering around the valley floor and so big you could hardly miss them, they were not much of a challenge. 'I must say that it is hardly worth one's while coming up so far to kill a yak or two when in my humble opinion so much better sport is to be had in Kashmir, for no sport in the world can be fairer than ibex and markhor shooting,' wrote Hayward.

The days were bright and sunny, but the temperature was extreme, never coming even close to the melting point of water. On the way down from Kugrang the first of the horses died – the best of them, unhappily – its feet ruined by the frozen ground and its lungs destroyed by the cold, dry air. The nights that Hayward and his men spent in the open air, huddled between snoring yaks and smouldering camp fires, must have been horrendously uncomfortable.

Back in the Chang Chenmo Hayward sent some of his men back towards Pangong Lake for more fuel and food, and penned a last few hurried letters: 'all communication between civilisation and the wilds of Central Asia was about to be severed.' And then, having given Shaw eight days' grace, he headed east, crossing the 18,839ft Chang Lang Pass (where his enamel paint box cracked in the intense cold and his paintbrushes froze together as he attempted to capture the scene in watercolours) and dropping towards the freezing, wind-scoured wasteland of the Lingzi Thung Plateau.

The Lingzi Thung, some 17,000ft above sea level, is a bleak expanse of roughly level ground, 50 miles long and 25 miles wide, bounded on all sides by jagged mountains. It took three days to cross. Snow had yet to fall here at the end of October but the journey across the flatlands was still a horrible experience. Each morning after the stinging stillness of first light a wind began to rise. By midday bitter gusts laden with sharp grey dust were shrieking across the plain. Hayward and his men slogged across this wilderness, squinting and shivering. The servants complained bitterly. Another pony collapsed and was left behind. The Ladakhi guides had forgotten to mention the complete absence of water or firewood on the Lingzi Thung, and they had carried none with them.

Halfway across the plain they stumbled upon the frozen, dried out carcasses of a yak and a horse, and then, a little further on they spotted a long blanket-wrapped bundle lying on the stony ground, the howling wind tugging at the cloth. It was the body of a man, a Yarkandi traveller 'wrapt up as if asleep', who had succumbed to the cold. The little party paused in gloomy silence over this macabre scene. Hayward wanted to bury the body, but the shivering, miserable servants huddling together for shelter refused to go near the desiccated corpse, and, considering for a moment the practicalities of digging a grave in the frozen ground without the aid of a shovel, Hayward thought better of it. With an uneasy backward glance, they went on, leaving the wrapped bundle alone in the middle of the plain.

But despite the conditions, Hayward never stopped working. He took bearings whenever there were peaks and ridges that could be marked on a future map, noting them down with stinging fingers in his pocketbook. He measured altitude at every opportunity by taking the temperature of boiling water,[5] and recorded the air temperature three times every day – it was -24°C at breakfast on their first day on the Lingzi Thung. Throughout all his journeys, no matter how desperate the conditions, he kept this up, ever eager to prove to his masters in London that he was the man for the job.

On 30 October Hayward's party gladly passed beyond the northern edge of the plateau and returned to narrowing mountain valleys, where at least there was occasional shelter from the wind. The normal route that the Ladakhi yak drivers knew ran due north from the Lingzi Thung, meeting the Karakash River, where it bent north-west towards Shahidulla. But the obvious inaccuracy of Johnson's map that Hayward had recognised had played on his mind as he shivered across the plateau, and he now decided to break west from the established path into uncharted territory in search of the true hydrology of the Karakoram. The servants and yak drivers, doubtless still dwelling on the frozen corpse they had seen a few days earlier, were 'anything but pleased' when Hayward ordered them to break camp on 1 November, and led them and the footsore, hungry yaks and horses into the unknown.

It was indeed risky to leave the main route: the temperatures were severe, the horses and yaks were in a sorry state and they had no idea when they would find fuel, grass and water. But Hayward, to the consternation of the Ladakhis, was thoroughly enjoying himself as they picked their way along treeless gorges, over an unmapped pass which he christened Kizil (or Red, on account of the colour of its frozen ground), and down into the upper valley of the Karakash. He realised with some delight that he was now over the final grand watershed of the entire mountain system of Asia: beyond the vast ridge of the Karakoram. Just to the south, all the icy streams drained into the Shyok, which in turn led down to the Indus, the great river of western India. But the chilly grey stream in the belly of this narrow valley must lead on down to the deserts of Turkestan – another world entirely. And what made it all the better was that this landscape was unknown and unmapped: 'Notwithstanding the great cold I enjoyed my exploration thoroughly for all this country was totally unexplored. I doubt if any human being had ever been down this valley – probably not – and it was interesting in the extreme,' wrote Hayward.

Moving down the valley, he scaled every ridge that he could in search of new views and new bearings, though his fingers were frostbitten from holding the brass surveying equipment in the sub-zero temperatures: 'It was certainly the coldest work I ever experienced and when on some high ridge of mountain after taking the bearings of the peaks all round, it was often difficult enough to write them down legibly.'

Disaster almost struck on one of these solo ridge climbs. Early on the morning of 8 November Hayward scrambled up some 4,000ft of near vertical mountainside for a view across the Karakoram to the south and the Kun Lun to the north, and the 'interminable mass of mountains' between. Having jotted down bearings in his notebook with frostbitten fingers, he prepared to scramble back down towards camp. As he was buckling on the leather belt in which he carried his lightweight surveying equipment, the strap of the sextant case snapped, and the little brass measuring device went bouncing away down the rocky slope. Hayward must have uttered some colourful language on that high hillside, and he began his descent in a state of utter despair. Without a sextant he would be unable to take bearings of latitude, and he would be completely crippled as a surveyor. There was, he knew, no such thing as a sextant in Turkestan, and it would be impossible now to send back across the mountains to India for a replacement.

The seriousness of the loss would be enormous, for he was planning to have seen the Pamirs and the unknown valleys of the North-West Frontier before he next had chance to visit a reputable supplier of map-making equipment. Thoughts of angry and disappointed scientific grandees in the RGS headquarters must have played on his mind as he scrambled down the mountain. He had doubted that he would ever find the dropped sextant, but even when he caught sight of it, glinting in the sunlight amongst the rocks 300ft below the point where he had dropped it, he was still despairing. 'I felt sure it was smashed to pieces for I had unpleasant reminiscences of once dropping a pair of binoculars out shooting on a hillside in Cashmere [Kashmir] and I remembered the state I picked them up in.' But to his delighted astonishment, when he reached the spot the sextant was completely unharmed. Hayward, in high spirits, returned to the valley floor as the servants were breaking camp. He named the spot Khush Maidan – Happy Valley – in honour of his good luck.

Heading on from Happy Valley the terrain became more and more rocky and the loaded yaks and horses, already thin and exhausted, struggled to make headway. Hayward, with spectacular understatement, described the condition of the route here as 'indifferent'. The going was so hard that where the valley suddenly turned sharply to the north-east they took to the surface of the frozen river, the slippery ice proving an easier road than the rocky shoreline.

Until this point Hayward had not even been entirely sure what river he was following. According to Johnson's 'deplorably inaccurate' map it should have been the Yarkand, but with this change of course – away from Yarkand itself – Hayward was certain that it was in fact the Karakash, the river that led to Shahidulla and onwards to Hotan. In all the surveying that he did Hayward was admirably assiduous in refusing ever to fill white spaces with conjecture; if he hadn't been there himself, if he hadn't taken the bearings and scribbled the notes in his own pocketbook, then the map would have to remain blank. He was scathing of his mapmaking predecessor's glib liberties with accuracy.

Hayward was sure that the true Yarkand River must be somewhere close at hand, perhaps just one or two valleys to the west, and he was greatly tempted to head off in search of it. But he had already made a long detour; supplies were almost exhausted and the horses were close to collapse. Only two yaks remained alive, and the servants were probably on the brink of mutiny after all he had put them through. Grudgingly he decided to leave the mystery of the Yarkand for another day, and pressed on along the Karakash towards Shahidulla.

They picked their way along the gradually descending valley, and four days later came to a point where the river turned to the west. Here they rejoined the established trail to Shahidulla, that from which they had split eleven days earlier. Hayward was delighted: he had now proved beyond doubt that the river he had been following was the real Karakash, and that Johnson had been wildly misguided when he marked its source 170 miles to the east in the Kun Lun. Quibbles over maps were doubtless of little interest to his exhausted Ladakhi companions, but they were equally happy to be back on a known road where the going for the exhausted beasts was easier.

Disaster for Hayward almost struck again just after their return to the main route. Towards the end of the day he realised with horror that he had lost his notebook. The loss would have been as devastating as that of a sextant, for it contained all the bearings and measurements of his journey so far: 'there was a nice to do, for if I did not find it my labours had been in vain.' Hayward ordered the men to set up camp, and then turned back up the valley alone, retracing his own footprints through the slushy snow, furious with himself for such carelessness. To his enormous relief he eventually found the little book lying by the side of the river at the point where, he confided to his journal, he had stopped to shoot fish.

Hayward judiciously avoided mentioning this incident in his official report, and with good reason. The fellows of the RGS would doubtless have been unimpressed by the image of a traveller in whom they had invested so seriously, gleefully unloading his revolver into the icy waters of the Karakash River in a moment of ridiculous self-indulgent abandon – there is some hint of insanity in the idea of shooting fish. For his part, Hayward was simply delighted to have avoided disaster twice. He trudged back down the valley towards camp in high spirits:

> Truly my luck was great to find so small a book in such a place; and this was an eventful week in accidents – first my sextant, bounding down a hillside and [sic] was not smashed to atoms, and this day I lost my valuable field book and found it again.

And what was more, it was growing warmer by the day as they descended the valley, almost scraping above freezing point at midday. He would, he expected, soon run into the first camps of Kirghiz nomads. Shahidulla was not far ahead; beyond it lay the cities of Eastern Turkestan, and beyond them, the Pamirs.

Robert Shaw, meanwhile, was already established in Shahidulla. From Chang Chenmo he had lumbered north across the Lingzi Thung – his unfortunate table servant Kabeer, a man from the steaming plains of India, suffering terribly from the cold and receiving scant sympathy from Shaw. Kabeer moaned as he staggered over the icy plateau that neither he, his father nor his grandfather had ever been to such a cold place as this, and that 'he did not know what stones have fallen into his life!' Shaw was contemptuous – though he did send back a rescue party after Kabeer was left behind and collapsed at the side of the road.

Picking his way along the usual route north from the Lingzi Thung (with the exhausted yaks and ponies beginning to fail and the suffering Kabeer trailing in his wake) Shaw came to the Karakash, downstream of the uncharted section that Hayward would soon explore, and turned towards Shahidulla. On 7 November, while Hayward was camped out some 50 miles to the south in Khush Maidan, Shaw scrambled ahead of his caravan to the top of a hill that surveyed the lower valley and saw his first human habitation since leaving the villages at the head of the Pangong Lake. It was a yurt, the portable, felt-walled tent of some travelling Kirghiz herders. There were horses and yaks tethered outside, and a man in a long tunic and high riding boots minding a herd of cows nearby. Wood-smoke was escaping from a hole in the roof of the yurt, rising into the cold air of the upland valley. It was the perfect Central Asian cliché, and Shaw was delighted.

'I can't describe to you my sensations at beholding this novel scene,' he wrote. 'I felt I had now indeed begun my travels. Now, at length, my dreams of Toorks and Kirghiz were realised, and I was coming into contact with tribes and nations hitherto entirely

cut off from intercourse with Europeans.'This last part was rather
overdoing it: Johnson had visited the country just three years
earlier, as Gardner claimed to have done, as had the murdered
German Schlagintweit. A Russian who had been held as a slave in
Uzbek country at the end of the eighteenth century had escaped
through Yarkand and had even written a book about the journey.
At least one of his countrymen had been into the region much
more recently, and doubtless a few other wandering foreigners
had drifted along this stretch of the Silk Route in the centuries
between Marco Polo and Robert Shaw. And meanwhile, travelling Yarkandis and Kashgaris, while certainly exotic, were by no
means unknown at local horse fairs and cheap caravanserais in
India. But still, Shaw's enthusiasm is forgivable.

Three days later he arrived in Shahidulla. The first view of the
Turki frontier post was not quite as inspiring as the earlier Kirghiz
pastoral. There was little there except a squat, mud-walled fort with
a stubby tower at each corner. It had been built several years earlier
by the ever opportunistic Maharaja of Kashmir, looking to expand
his realm far beyond its natural extreme on the Himalayan watershed during the chaos that followed the ejection of the Chinese
from Eastern Turkestan. But it had now been abandoned by the
maharaja, who, Shaw pointed out quite reasonably, 'has no more
right to Shahidoolla than I have', and the Turkis had moved in.

They welcomed Shaw heartily and he was quickly established
in the fort's best rooms – though he was at pains to point out
to his British correspondents that 'you must remember the fort
much resembles an English pig-stye, and not picture to yourself
apartments of Oriental luxury'.

The munshi Shaw had sent on ahead from Leh was already in
Yarkand, and the Turki soldiers at Shahidulla had known of his
approach for a month. However, they explained, by way of sign
language and a tiny common vocabulary (Shaw knew no Turki,
and his hosts had no knowledge of Persian or Hindi), the usurper
king of Eastern Turkestan, Yaqub Beg, was away on the country's
western frontier, and they were still awaiting official permission

for Shaw to proceed towards Yarkand. Until it arrived he would have to remain in Shahidulla.

Shaw was, for the time being, quite happy with the situation and set about organising yak-shooting day trips and learning as many Turki words as he could. After a couple of days an official emissary, a nobleman in silk robes, arrived from Yarkand as Mihmandar, or 'welcomer of guests'. With him was an elderly Tibetan-speaker, and, by way of this old man on the Mihmandar's side and a Ladakhi called Tashee who knew both Tibetan and Hindi on Shaw's side, they were able to converse. They were soon getting on famously, with lots of indulgent laughter and hearty backslapping. The Turkis, Shaw decided, were 'just like public schoolboys, of boisterous spirits, but perfectly well bred'.

While some people might consider being cooped up in a pigsty in a desolate mountain valley with a raucous bunch of Old Etonions to be hell on earth, it suited Shaw very well, and he was happy to ignore the fact that he was, de facto, a prisoner. He also, in a piece of spectacular hypocrisy after his stern admonishments over Hayward's Afghan get-up, decided to 'assume the full Moghul dress'. He kitted himself out with black riding boots and a silk tunic, twisted a scarf around his waist and threw a long brown robe over his shoulders. A red Kashmir shawl was conjured up from his baggage which he decided made a splendid turban. 'I flatter myself that I look like a dignified Toork,' he wrote – and his new best friend, the Mihmandar, apparently agreed.

But for all these larks and high jinks, something was troubling Shaw, 'my chief source of anxiety, the incubus that constantly weighs upon me': somewhere up there in the mountains, moving closer day by day, was George Hayward. Shaw explained this anxiety in the same terms that he had used to justify his obsession with travelling alone from the very start: he had written in advance to tell the Turki authorities that there was only one Englishman approaching. The concern was to some extent reasonable: the rulers of Eastern Turkestan were certainly suspicious of outsiders. But the very fact that Hayward, despite Shaw's confident predictions to the contrary, was eventually allowed to proceed to Yarkand and Kashgar makes it clear that he was worrying about nothing. And indeed, it is hard not to conclude that the horror of Hayward's approach was, in truth, based largely on the same emotions that would afflict our high-paying tourist on finding his experience of an 'untouched' mountain village marred by the arrival of his dreaded, dreadlocked nemesis – the backpacker.

Shaw had a moment of false hope when a Ladakhi caravan came shambling down into Shahidulla with a rumour that Hayward had returned to Leh. But it soon faded a few days later when the other Englishman's imminent approach was confirmed. Shaw had already told his 'public schoolboy' friends about Hayward, and they had, he claimed, been not best pleased. Still, on 20 November, Hayward, his footsore Ladakhis and little herd of exhausted yaks and ponies, arrived at the frontier post. Shaw did not rush out to welcome them and was doubtless rather pleased when they were housed, not in the best rooms in the fort, but in the ruins of some older building, 600 yards away across the reedy valley floor.

Shaw claimed in his letters and book that, to his fury, Hayward announced on arrival that he was in the tea planter's employ. Shaw said that he was able to hide this compromising lie from the Turkis because the conveyance of Hayward's Hindi message had to go through his own Ladakhi translator. Hayward, unsurprisingly, makes no mention of this in his own account, but it seems rather unlikely that he would have said such a thing. Perhaps he had indeed mentioned that he knew Shaw, and that Shaw was expecting him – which was all true – and then Shaw, jealous and resentful as always, was a little creative with the truth in his letters home.

In *Visits to High Tartary, Yarkand and Kashgar*, this is the first of a number of incidents of bad behaviour from Hayward that Shaw mentions. Many of them seem decidedly unlikely. He claimed later to have seen the letter that Hayward sent on to Yaqub Beg from Shahidulla, asking for admittance to Turkestan. In it, Shaw

claims, Hayward described himself as a trader. Hayward himself
(unaware of the derogatory claims that Shaw would later make)
said that the letter simply stated 'that I had travelled a distance of
8,000 miles, occupying six months; and now, having arrived on
the borders of Turkestan, sent forward asking permission to enter
his country and have the honour of an interview'. Hayward was
not stupid; he must have known that his depleted, tent-less little
caravan would never pass for a trading operation, and it seems
unlikely that he might have claimed that this was what it was.

Likewise, Shaw also claimed that after he arrived in Yarkand,
Hayward marred his first meeting with the governor – Eastern
Turkestan's second-in-command – by sitting with the soles of
his feet pointing rudely at the dignitary. Again, this seems highly
unlikely. Hayward was not as steeped in the ways and mores of
Central Asia as many earlier travellers had been (and neither was
Shaw, for all his pompous pride in his diplomatic skill). But again,
he had been in India, where the same rule applies, long enough,
and had already been in Central Asia for some weeks when this
event is claimed to have occurred. Like Shaw's other slurs it has
the distinct ring of untruth – and it should be remembered that
by the time these claims were published in 1871, Hayward was
never going to be able to challenge them.

In Shahidulla that November, book deals and RGS reports
were all still a world away but Shaw had no intention of being
friendly. Once established in the ruined fort, Hayward, naturally,
asked to see him. Shaw, who now felt that he was on excellent
terms with the Turkis, was able to engineer matters to avoid
this, sending one of his own men as a translator having told the
Mihmandar that there was no need for the two English travellers
to meet.

George Hayward, 600 yards away, was apparently unaware that
Shaw was refusing to see him, and seems never to have found
out the truth. He always assumed that they were being deliberately kept apart by the Turki soldiers. Over the next couple of
days, however, the two men's perplexed servants carried a series

of slightly tetchy letters back and forth over the muddy ground between the modern fort and the ruin. Shaw had opened the correspondence on the first night after Hayward's arrival with a stern letter, yet again advising him to turn around and go back to Leh, and telling him that he had no chance of being allowed into Eastern Turkestan. Shaw still seemed not entirely to have grasped the fact that Hayward's goal had never been Yarkand and Kashgar, but the mountains that lay beyond them.

Hayward sent back a note, patiently explaining yet again, his responsibilities to the RGS, and that he was duty bound at very least to try to reach the Pamirs via Kashgar. He was not going to give up. He also wrote that he would very much like to see Shaw to discuss their respective plans.

The Mihmandar, who by now had managed to dupe Shaw into thinking he was calling the shots, was quite happy for the two men to meet. But he was equally happy to 'obey' Shaw's 'orders', and declare permission for such a meeting refused.

Shaw was delighted at having been able so firmly to establish in the minds of the Turkis that he wanted nothing whatsoever to do with Hayward, and he rather enjoyed the fact that his rival was isolated across the valley in the ruins, apparently with no hope of proceeding. But still, he had now been in Shahidulla for more than a fortnight, and the close proximity of 'the incubus', even though gratifyingly quarantined, must have made matters worse. On the morning of 24 November he declared that he was 'frightfully weary of this life', and that he 'could not stand it any longer'. Some of his nay-saying servants, ever given to prophesies of doom, had been predicting that they might be stuck in Shahidulla for months, if not forever, and their endless pessimism was obviously beginning to get to Shaw.

But on the very same day the depression abruptly lifted as a messenger arrived from Yarkand with news that permission had finally been granted for him to proceed, and that an even more senior emissary was waiting for him a few days along the road. Shaw was ecstatic, and the next morning, accompanied by the Mihmandar, he set out for Yarkand. He must have glanced back at the miserable ruin where the unseen, unmet Hayward was camped out – perhaps a thin coil of cooking smoke rising above the crumbling walls – with smirking satisfaction. Shaw was genuinely convinced of the powers of his own 'understanding of Orientals' and his capacity for silky-tongued diplomacy. As he had judged that Hayward possessed neither of these dubious skills, he was quite certain that he would never be allowed to continue. As he headed downhill from Shahidulla towards the Sanju Pass, he must finally have felt that he had rid himself of 'the thorn in my flesh'. Hayward, he assumed, would either have to return to Leh or face the deeply unattractive prospect of an eternity in Shahidulla. That Hayward might have the imagination to come up with a third option never even occurred to him.

The journey down to Yarkand was a delight. Shaw got his first hazy, indistinct glimpse of 'what looked like a distant sea' beyond the mass of declining ridges: the plains of Eastern Turkestan. The official who had come to meet him on the road – a Yoozbashi: an officer of a hundred men – was charming, and soon trumped the Mihmandar in the best-buddy stakes. The hospitality was lavish, with Shaw fed handsomely on great banquets of rice and mutton at every stop. The road had been repaired in preparation of his advance, and a game of the famous Central Asian sport of horseback rugby over the carcass of a goat – known as *buzkashi* in Afghanistan, and, according to Shaw, as 'ooghlak' here – was even staged for him. It was little wonder that Shaw, never the most modest of men, allowed his self-importance to spiral to dizzying heights: he was going to be the first Englishman into Yarkand, and he was, it seemed, going to be hailed as a king on arrival there.

He penned a few letters and sent them back to Shahidulla in the hope that some local caravan might carry them back over the mountains to Leh. He wrote one to his sister in England, telling her that 'I am being received in the most handsome manner', and confiding gleefully that 'I now dress entirely as a Turkee, turban, robe and everything'. He had been delayed in Shahidulla for eighteen days, he wrote, a delay 'chiefly caused by the arrival (most inopportunely) of a second Englishman'. This was palpably untrue: Shaw had already been delayed for two weeks before Hayward ever reached the frontier, and his presence appeared to have had no bearing on Shaw's departure.

'I am afraid,' he continued:

> that the other Englishman, Hayward, who is sent by the RGS but has not prepared his way as I have, will not be allowed to come on. He is kept under guard at Shahdulla Khoja [sic] and we were not allowed to communicate, or rather I was obliged to say don't let him meet me.

Shaw was clearly anything but 'afraid' about the prospect of Hayward's failure; he was positively delighted by it.

The letter did make it back across the mountains, and it was forwarded to England by the Punjab commissioner Douglas Forsyth. Forsyth had apparently forgotten his earlier jealousy. It seems that Shaw had been sending him whinging letters ever since first running into Hayward in Chang Chenmo. Forsyth, the man with by far the most qualifications for a visit to Eastern Turkestan, must have been deeply dismayed to see yet another Englishman taking advantage of civilian status to infringe on the playground of his imagination. He decided to throw his lot in with Shaw.

As early as February 1869, when Shaw and Hayward were both still deep in Turkestan, Forsyth was already writing to the Royal Geographical Society, doing his very best to undermine their own man in Central Asia:

> The way for Mr Shaw's entry was carefully prepared ... Mr Hayward's approach was <u>not</u> made smooth beforehand, it appeared, and as the people of that country are naturally suspicious they have hindered his advance.
>
> I may add that Mr Shaw is one of our most enterprising settlers in the Kangra Valley. After receiving a University education

he came out to India to set up as a tea planter ... To him, therefore, rather than to anyone else, will be due all the credit should we hereafter find our mercantile relations with Yarkand established on a sound basis.

Even if Mr Hayward should fail to penetrate into those regions, I feel that your Society will ere long receive most valuable and reliable information regarding those unknown regions from one whom I am glad to be able to call my friend.

The emphatic underscoring of the 'not'; the mention of Shaw's university degree (in contrast to Hayward's background as a drop-out of dubious origins); the insistence that Hayward would deserve no credit whatsoever for any positive developments in Eastern Turkestan – all seem deeply unfair. And it also makes clear something that Hayward must have already known: that no one was looking out for him, that he would always be on his own.

On 8 December Shaw finally came in view of Yarkand. The prospect was not the most beautiful: a flaking mud wall rising above the dusty plain (the mountains now lay away to the south), topped at the corners by unwieldy, pagoda-roofed watchtowers added during the Chinese occupation. The only structure within the walls that rose into view was an enormous set of gallows. This was hardly a vision of Eldorado, but nothing could dampen Shaw's spirits. He rode through the main gateway with the Mihmandar on one side and the Yoozbashi on the other, and was soon established in fine comfort in a specially prepared townhouse in the fortified quarter of the town.

The king, Yaqub Beg, was away campaigning on the flanks of the Tien Shan, and had in any case shifted his court to Kashgar. But Shaw was quickly given an audience with Eastern Turkestan's second-in-command, the Shagawal. Inevitably, he felt that he had struck up an instant rapport with this even more senior Turki.

There was no question of him continuing to Kashgar until expressed permission had been received from Yaqub Beg, but, once again, Shaw put any suspicion that he was a prisoner from his mind – how could he be when the Turkis were daily feasting him on the tenderest lamb and the juiciest melons and grapes, and were draping a new silk robe over his shoulders at each meeting? They had even had their own confused interpretation of European furniture made especially for him – with a table only two feet off the ground and chairs that towered over it. Never one to be concerned with time schedules or hurrying, Shaw settled down in his new quarters; he could do little else – he was not allowed to leave them.

But by the time a week had passed and there had been no further developments beyond more silk robes and more overflowing dinner plates, Shaw was beginning to have the nagging suspicion that the Turkis were toying with him. His servants, who unlike Shaw were allowed to wander the town, were also bringing him reports that the scaffold he had seen poking up above the walls was being put into almost daily usage, and that a crude interpretation of Sharia law was strictly enforced with violent lashings. Though the Turkis might well be 'fine fellows', the government in Yarkand was anything but soft. With his 'diplomatic skills' there was little Shaw could do but passively to continue waiting. Then he began to hear strange rumours from the direction of Shahidulla.

On 15 December Shaw's munshi, Diwan Bakhsh, with whom he had been reunited, was asked by a Turki official if he knew where Hayward was. The puzzled munshi replied that he had no idea, and later told an equally puzzled Shaw of the cryptic question. As far as he knew Hayward could only be still stuck in Shahidulla, or sensibly on the road back to Leh. The following day the munshi brought Shaw another titbit of gossip: the Turkis were declaring Hayward 'lost', whatever that meant, and saying that he had 'gone off to look for some water'. Shaw was still none-the-wiser until the next morning, when his old friend the Yoozbashi came to visit.

Hayward, the Yoozbashi explained, had done something that Shaw – who was eventually to receive some criticism back in India for the way he let the Turkis walk all over him – would never have dreamed of doing. Two weeks earlier, just one day after Shaw had ridden out of Shahidulla, assuming that his rival was in for a lengthy spell of detention, Hayward had broken out of captivity and headed west into the mountains. He had escaped, and he hadn't been heard of since.

Notes

1   The region known as Eastern Turkestan in the 1860s is now the restive Muslim-majority Chinese state of Xinjiang, but it has a confusing number of aliases. As well as Eastern Turkestan, the old spelling of the Chinese name, Sinkiang, still crops up, as do the monikers Kashgaria and Uighuristan, naming the place for its most famous city and its principal ethnic group respectively. And this wilderness of deserts, mountains and cold oases is also sometimes known, perhaps most effectively, as Chinese Tartary or Chinese Central Asia.

2   By 'Tibetan' Shaw means Ladakhi – the culture and ethnicity of Ladakh is essentially Tibetan, and in the nineteenth century the two areas were nowhere near as firmly separated as they are today.

3   A sad footnote to the story of the good-natured Thorpe: deflected, he returned south to Kashmir, and two months later, after taking a brisk walk up the Takht-i-Suliman, a hill that stands above the lakeside in Srinagar, he collapsed and died. Exactly the same kind of rumours of Kashmiri foul play that would eventually swirl around Hayward's demise soon attached themselves to the death of Thorpe, for he had recently published a pamphlet entitled 'Cashmere

Misgovernment'. However, Dr Cayley, descending from Leh to see out the worst of the winter at a lower altitude, was on hand to examine the body. As far as he was concerned, Thorpe had died of a 'rupture of the heart'.

4   Today we know that the Jaxartes, now known as the Syr Darya, rises just north of the Pamirs in the Tien Shan.

5   Water boils at decreasing temperatures as you ascend from sea level. Although it is not an entirely accurate method of ascertaining altitude, with a control taken at a place of known height it was the only practical option available for nineteenth-century explorers. Yet kindling any kind of fire in such conditions must have proved a challenge for Hayward.

5

FUGITIVE ON THE UPPER YARKAND

On the morning of 26 November 1868, George Hayward was awake well before dawn. In the inky blackness that falls over the mountains in the hours between the fading of the stars and the rising of the sun, the ruined fort at Shahidulla was a little hive of stealthy activity and muffled voices. A cold breakfast was hurriedly scoffed; a yak, its snorts of protest stifled by its driver, was loaded with a week's starvation rations for four men; and shadowy figures shivered and hugged themselves in the bitter cold.

Though they had been unmistakably under arrest since arriving in Shahidulla six days earlier, Hayward and his men had not been kept under a particularly strict guard. The Turki soldiers sent to watch over them found the frontier post as wretched and desolate a spot as they did, and as far as they were concerned their charges had no way of escaping. There were only two obvious routes out of Shahidulla: if Hayward continued along the road to Yarkand without permission he would be stopped within a few miles; if he went back the way he had come towards Ladakh, then all the better. They saw no need to post a sentry outside the

Englishman's miserable quarters overnight; much better to enjoy the comfort of the best rooms of the modern fort, newly vacated by Robert Shaw.

Glancing anxiously over the crumbling walls across the shingle-and-reeds bed of the valley, Hayward saw no flicker of light. The Turkis were still sleeping. In urgent whispers he told the men who would stay behind to take care of the camp and to keep quiet when the guards asked after him. By this time the outline of the walls, the dark hollows of faces and the jagged ridges of the surrounding mountains had begun to form from the gloom and a faint red stain was seeping from the eastern edge of the night. Quickly, with a last few whispered instructions, Hayward and three of the Ladakhis from Tangtse shouldered small packs and one hunting rifle, hurried out of the ruins and scurried across the valley floor, driving the loaded yak before them. Within minutes they were striking uphill away from Shahidulla along a steep side valley to the west. Short, urgent steps changed to long strides, and the yak grunted its way sure-footedly along the trail. Behind them, the still-sleeping fort fell out of view and the sun cleared the ridges, casting shallow warmth on to the backs of their necks. Hayward must have been elated. Like Shaw, he had doubted that he would ever be allowed to proceed from the frontier post, but unlike Shaw, he was completely unprepared to patiently wait.

If one thing is obvious from George Hayward's chronically peripatetic years in Asia, it is his horror of staying in one place. It was not captivity as such that was anathema to Hayward; it was stasis. From the moment he arrived in India in possession of an RGS mission until the morning of his death two years later, he scarcely stopped. It was as if the idea of spending one more night than was strictly necessary at the same spot terrified him. He had, after all, rushed out of Leh the very moment his caravan was ready, even though the shadows were already lengthening. Any other man would have waited until the next morning – after all, what was a loss of twelve hours? But to Hayward a week, a day, even twelve hours was everything. Every moment had to be capitalised on, every opportunity taken. In some ways he seems like a fugitive, always glancing over his shoulder, never sleeping in the same bed twice. Perhaps he really did have the sense that something – real or imagined; debt or depression – was pursuing him, but perhaps it was simply that a grim prescience weighed on his soul: he knew that his time was short.

Feet itching and frustration mounting as he paced the ruins back in Shahidulla, his mind had turned again and again to Johnson's hopeless map, to the work he himself had already done along the Upper Karakash, and the knowledge that the true source of the Yarkand must lie somewhere close at hand to the west. If he was not allowed to continue into Turkestan, as seemed likely, he would have to head back to Ladakh and seek some other route to the Pamirs. But by late November the passes down into Kashmir would already be blocked with snow and he would have to fritter away some six cold, uneventful months in a dusty guesthouse in Leh. Such a prospect might not have troubled Robert Shaw, but for Hayward 'the idea of passing a winter in Ladak [sic] doing nothing was not to be entertained'. It would probably have driven him crazy. Instead, preferring not to think about what would happen later, he was determined to push into the mountains west of Shahidulla, and to put right all that Johnson had got so horribly wrong.

But that had left him with the problem of the Turki guards. They would probably have allowed him to make some tame day-time excursion on to the slopes in search of yak or goats to shoot, but they would have insisted on coming with him. And they would have been wildly suspicious if they had seen him whipping out compass, sextant and notebook on every ridge, for in the independent fiefdoms of Central Asia surveying was seen – with good reason – as tantamount to spying, and spies were not treated kindly. In any case, the Turkis certainly would not have allowed Hayward to stray off further afield. There was nothing else for it: he would have to escape.

Watching jealously from a distance as Shaw's party had trotted out of the new fort to begin their royal progress to Yarkand the previous day had probably pushed him to act. So now here he was, striding up a steep valley that rose due west from Shahidulla towards the 17,093ft Kirghiz Pass. The sun was rising; every step took him further from the frontier post, and every backward glance revealed no angry search party hurrying in pursuit – the Turki guards were still snoring under their blankets in the fort.

Hayward was a very happy fugitive. Ahead lay unknown country and over the next twenty days he would travel harder and faster than he had ever done before, covering huge distances in terrible conditions, breaking new ground the whole way, and making discoveries that would eventually earn him the Founder's Gold Medal of the Royal Geographical Society.

Hayward spent that first night out of Shahidulla at a high campground called Kulshish Kun, and the next morning, still apparently unpursued, he pressed on to the Kirghiz Pass. This high saddle of land, scoured by a biting wind, gave a magnificent view out over the ranges. He could pick out mountains he had surveyed from the Lingzi Thung, more than 100 miles away to the east; whilst ahead to the west was truly wild country, an upland chaos of rock and ice. To the south-west the high white flanks of the Karakoram formed a long, jagged wall; while the Kun Lun bore away to the north-west as the outer bastion of the whole mountain mass. Thousands of feet down below Hayward could just about trace the westward course of what he knew must be the Yarkand River. This first view alone afforded a significant new discovery: the Karakoram and the Kun Lun, often regarded as the same range, were clearly separate mountain systems, rising in distinct lines and divided by the valley of the Yarkand.

He spent long hours on the pass, taking bearings and scribbling notes while the Ladakhis shivered patiently nearby. 'Not a tree, bush, or shrub, met the eye anywhere,' wrote Hayward. 'It was solely a magnificent panorama of snowy peaks and glaciers, as the last rays of the setting sun tinged their loftiest summits with a ray of golden light.'

Finally, the last observations made and scribbled down with numbed fingers, they started downhill in the gathering dusk, dropping some 3,000ft in darkness and only making camp at nine o' clock, huddling in the mouth of a narrow gorge over a fire of thorny brushwood. Still there was no sign of the guards from Shahidulla.

The next morning they scrambled on downhill and soon came into the narrow gorge of the Yarkand River – the true Yarkand River, which flowed away to the west then turned north to the deserts of Turkestan. Pausing briefly beside the icy waters, Hayward decided first to push on downstream. Though he was eager to trace the river to its source, none of this area had been mapped, and he wanted to cover as much of the country as possible. That night they camped beside the river.

This was not completely unknown country: the traditional Ladakh-Yarkand trade route, after crossing the mighty Karakoram Pass, had come this way, meeting the river just above the junction to the Kirghiz Pass and following it downstream for a way before turning due south to the plains. But the whole region had recently been declared off-limits by Yaqub Beg, the new ruler of Eastern Turkestan. Traders from Leh now had to follow another road, over the ridges to the east and down to Shahidulla.

Yaqub Beg had ruled this wild country forbidden not because it contained any precious secrets or because it strayed into politically sensitive territory; he had closed it because it was dangerous. Caravans passing through this way were so often attacked by Kunjuti bandits that the situation had become an embarrassment. In the name of security, and with no sense of irony, the new Turkestan Government had declared that any trader who compromised his own safety by travelling along the Upper Yarkand River would be beheaded.

Hayward was unconcerned by that law, and the idea that he might be being pursued by angry Turki soldiers probably delighted him. But the thought that there could still be a few marauding bandits haunting these cold defiles was a real concern. Every traveller in the mountains had heard horrific stories about the Kunjuti raiders, descending on caravans in a sudden avalanche of rusty sabres and long-barrelled muskets; no one relished the idea of encountering them.

The Kunjuti homeland, a spectacular upland fiefdom, lay 150 miles to the west, across some of the highest mountains on earth. But robber bands strayed far and wide from their remote villages in search of plunder. Today Kunjut – part of modern Pakistan – is better known as Hunza. It is an absurdly beautiful valley, with two rival principalities – independent even within Pakistan until the 1970s – facing each other across a narrow gorge; Hunza on the west bank, Nagar on the east. These lost worlds occupy narrow strips of tiny terraced fields and orchards. Villages with roofs of pine and walls of creamy earth stand in clusters of tall poplars, where golden apricots are spread to dry in the glass-sharp sunlight. There are precious stones in the glacier-fed streams, and above rise impossibly high mountains: vicious, unclimbed Ultar, heavy-set Shishpar and the sheer granite spire of Bubulmating looming in the west; Rakaposhi, sweeping up in one single 15,000ft wall from the valley floor, to the east. It is the kind of hyperbolic landscape that is normally found only in the cover art of fantasy novels. And if Hunza looks like a kingdom of elves and fairies, the real inhabitants are hardly disappointing. The Hunzakuts are a people of pale eyes and auburn hair, speaking a language completely unrelated to any other. They brew wine and brandy from the fruits of their valley and live to a great age. Clichés of Shangri La are irresistible, and once upon a time, in the late twentieth century, foreign tourists came here in droves, up the Karakoram Highway, to what might just have been the most beautiful place on earth. Today, Hunza still floats serenely 6,000ft above Pakistan's yawning abyss, but any traveller who makes it there now will find himself a throwback to another era, outnumbered twenty-to-one by bankrupt gift shops, empty guesthouses and one-time tour guides long since gone back to their fields.

The Hunzakuts are Ismaeli Muslims, disinclined to fast or pray, and much given to drinking and dancing. Today they are often patronisingly proclaimed by westerners as 'the right kind of Muslims'. They are famous for their hospitality and kindness. But 150 years ago the mere mention of the name of this glorious mountain paradise was enough to prompt terror in Yarkandi horse traders and Ladakhi caravan men. It had exactly the kind of reputation for violence, hostility and certain death to all strangers that blights the tribal badlands of the North-West Frontier today. And worse yet, the Kunjutis ranged far beyond their own country, plundering caravans everywhere from Baltistan to the foothills above Kashgar; from Ladakh to the lower Indus Valley. Like the Chitralis and their pagan neighbours further west (also idealised as inhabitants of an earthly paradise today), they were notorious for slave trading. Anyone seized by the Kunjutis would, if he wasn't immediately slaughtered, likely end up on sale like a bolt of cloth in the bazaars of northern Afghanistan. Anywhere the Kunjutis travelled was dangerous country, and they had ready access to the upper reaches of the Yarkand River by way of their own high-altitude back door – the Shimshal Pass.

As Hayward and the Ladakhis drove their single yak on down the banks of the Yarkand the next morning they must have glanced nervously up at the crags and slopes, wondering if someone was watching them. Their party – small and ill-equipped – was precisely the kind that the Kunjutis swooped upon most eagerly. The sense of unease only grew that evening when they came across fresh tracks of camels and horses in the snow beside the river. Hayward decided that they should stop and wait until they could continue under cover of darkness. If the tracks had been left by local hill men then news of his whereabouts would quickly reach the Turki guards; if they were the footprints of a Kunjuti raiding party then 'to be carried off by them and sold into slavery, would most effectually put a stop to further exploration'.

Huddling out of sight behind a bank of stone, they kindled a small fire and waited until the moon had risen before pressing on downstream in the cold darkness. They had already been on the move since first light, but Hayward seemed to be in the grip of one of the truly frenzied moments of exploration that sometimes overtook him. He simply could not stop moving. Darkness, exhaustion, sub-zero temperatures, terrible terrain: none of it would bring him to a halt. Had he stopped to make camp again he would never have slept, so all consuming was his urge to continue.

Pushing on through the gloom, scrambling over rocks and boulders, the roar of the river filling the narrow valley, they continued some 9 miles before the trail came to a halt before a sheer cliff, dropping into the icy waters. It was now the middle of the night, but incredibly, despite having been walking all day over harsh ground, Hayward did not give the order to camp and to tackle this new obstacle in the morning. Instead, he and the baffled, exhausted Ladakhis – who must have wondered just what kind of demon this crazy foreigner was – set about trying to build a bridge. They cut whatever lengths of brush and branches they could find in the meagre scrub on the banks and attempted to lay them across the bitterly cold torrent. But as they stumbled around in the darkness the river simply swallowed up whatever they threw at it. After an hour – an hour that Hayward bitterly described as 'wasted' in his report – they gave up.

But again, instead of finally agreeing to camp until dawn, Hayward cast about for another option. Pushing the men and the bellowing yak back upstream for a mile in the frosty moonlight, he struck straight up the loose scree slopes in the hope of bypassing the cliff face higher above. This was atrocious terrain on which to walk – even in daylight, even fresh from rest. Each footfall sent a miniature avalanche of gravel back down the hillside; breath screamed in bursting lungs, exhaustion seared up calves and thighs. It was ground that 'gives way and lets one down about as fast as one progresses upwards' was all that Hayward had to say about it.

Eventually, having passed the sheer section of riverbank far below, they dropped back down towards the valley floor, only to come to a halt a short distance further on where a huge debris flow from the high slopes ran down to meet the river. Hayward might have even tried to cut across this impossible surface, but a new thought had come to him, standing there in the freezing darkness, peering at the shadowy crags above. If a search party had set out from Shahidulla, even if they were travelling much more slowly than he was – which they almost certainly were – they would probably have crossed the Kirghiz Pass by now. If he didn't hurry back up the valley they would cut him off and he would never reach the source of the Yarkand. Ordering the exhausted Ladakhis and the increasingly ill-tempered yak to perform an abrupt about turn, Hayward marched on – back over the very same hellish scree that he had just crossed in the opposite direction.

He hammered on up the valley until they found the ashes of the little fire they had lit at dusk while hiding from the unseen, unknown caravan. Hayward allowed a brief rest here through what remained of the night. But he wasn't done yet. As soon as the first hint of daylight spilled down into the valley, with aching limbs and ruined feet, he ordered his men onwards, upstream.

Leaving the Ladakhis to slog on up the banks of the river, Hayward struck out alone up the sheer mountainside in search of a high vantage point from which to survey the surrounding peaks. He had spotted a likely crag from the valley floor, and inevitably, once he started his climb nothing would convince him to turn back. The ascent was across the same kind of hideous scree that they had scrambled over in the hours of darkness. Anyone who has ever slogged over this type of surface to some high peak in the biting cold of a mountain dawn will know just how soul-destroying it can be. Each painful upward step seems to gain no more than an inch or two of ground; weary feet bog amongst heavy grit; a misplaced footfall sends you slithering back down in seconds what took agonised minutes to ascend; and niggling stones continuously work their way into boots and under tender soles. It took Hayward five hours to reach the top.

But the view, he declared, 'was an ample reward for the toil of the ascent'. Gasping for breath in the thin air, limbs throbbing with the burn of the climb, Hayward looked out on a dizzying expanse of mountains:

> Far away to the south and south-west stretched the high peaks and glaciers of the Karakoram and Muztagh Range ... Beyond where the river sweeps out west, the snowy peaks above the Kunjoot country were in sight towards Sarikol. East and west extended the whole chain of the Kuen Luen and the Kilian Mountains, the last range to be crossed before the steppes and plains of Turkistan are reached, while immediately below lay the confined ravine up which the road ascends to the Yangi Pass, now full in sight beneath me.

It was a panorama of some 200 miles, stretching from the peaks due north of Leh, to the icy giants above Hunza.

Hayward was almost 19,000ft above sea level as he shivered on this rocky vantage point, and although the midday sun was high overhead, the temperature was -15°C. Still, the surveying opportunities were too good to miss, and wincing at the cold, he dug out his pocketbook, unbuckled his compass and sextant, and began trying to make sense of the chaos around him.

All of the mountains were enormous, and the calculations that he made declared many of them to tower above 25,000ft. But one peak, looming far away to the south, was higher than all the others. Hayward scribbled, shivered, tilted his artificial horizon, fiddled with his compass, and concluded that it was 28,278ft tall. He was sure that it must be 'one of the highest mountains in the world'. He was right: the rough dagger of rock on his far horizon was K2, the second tallest peak on earth.

K2, a strangely elusive mountain that loiters out of view behind the surrounding giants, had been spotted by surveyors in western Kashmir on a couple of fleeting occasions a decade earlier, and though its height had been calculated, so rarely had it been seen that the accuracy of the figure was not assured. In the 1860s it was still a contender for the world's highest mountain. No one had ever seen it from the north, however, and Hayward had no way of knowing that he was looking at the same mountain. In his notebook he simply recorded it as yet another 'Snowy Peak', but remarkably, given the distance of his vantage point and the severity of the conditions, he calculated its height to within 30ft of the modern estimate.

Eventually, on the brink of hypothermia, Hayward put away his notebook, buckled his equipment belt and took one last look out over the mountains:

> I had reached many higher altitudes, but never any commanding so extensive a view of such a stupendous mass of mountains; and it was with a feeling of regret that I turned to leave a spot from where the peaks and glaciers could so well be seen, stretching far away on every side in their solemn grandeur.

He scrambled back down the mountainside, his knees and back now taking the strain that had all been on his lungs and heart on the way up, and met the Ladakhis waiting far below in the chilly shade of the valley. They slogged on upstream through the afternoon, and finally made camp at the same spot they had left the morning of the previous day, the last place where they had slept or eaten properly. In the thirty-six hours since starting out from this campsite they had covered 55 miles of spectacularly harsh mountain terrain, in sub-zero temperatures, and with no more than a couple of hours rest.

This had been a stupendous bout of travelling. It certainly impressed the Fellows of the RGS when finally they heard of it, and some have chosen to see it as perhaps the finest example of Hayward's dedicated professionalism as an explorer. But, in truth, he had rarely seemed closer to insanity, rarely seemed so utterly consumed. And the whole episode was insane – the frantic attempts to build a bridge from brushwood in the freezing darkness, the furious ploughing up nightmare slopes of slithering gravel only to make an abrupt about turn in the middle of the night. Once again, it was that horror of stopping or slowing the pace taken to ridiculous extremes, taken to the point where even sleep was deemed an unconscionable waste of time. Hayward's journey that cold November had resembled the possessed, almost crazy drive of an Alexander the Great heading for India, of a Napoleon slogging through the snow towards Moscow, of a Captain Cook relentlessly banging his head against the ice of the Bering Sea in search of the North-West Passage. The difference was that Hayward had condensed all that no-surrender excess of ambition into one single day of marching; his exhausted army, driven to the brink of collapse by its frenzied commander, was merely three Ladakhis and a yak.

It was -18°C at breakfast the next morning. They had already been out of Shahidulla for six days and their meagre supplies were almost exhausted. The yak too was on its last legs. But Hayward had no thought of turning back to the frontier post, and when they reached the junction of the side valley that they had previously descended from the Kirghiz Pass and found no angry Turki sentries waiting for them, he was delighted.

Though he didn't know it at the time, the Turkis were indeed out searching for him. Hayward's servants who had remained in Shahidulla had done an admirable job at playing dumb, and the soldiers had no idea where to start looking. They had sent men out in every direction, but unequipped for the freezing temperatures they never got far before slogging miserably back into camp. They were starting to suspect that Hayward must have been seized by Kunjutis, and guessed that he was probably already bound, gagged and en route for sale in Badakhshan. Doubtless they were also nervously fingering their own throats and wondering how Yaqub Beg would react on hearing this news.

But for Hayward, the road to the source of the Yarkand was open. Their stock of food was almost exhausted, however, so he decided to send one of the men back across the pass with instructions to

sneak into camp at Shahidulla and have fresh supplies sent out to a
rendezvous point in the mountains to the south. The place selected
for the meeting was a spot called Aktagh on the road down from
the Karakoram Pass. According to Johnson's map it lay somewhere
further up the same river they were now following, and they ought
to reach it within a couple of days. Hayward should have known
by now that he ought to have long since used Johnson's dubious
cartography to kindle a campfire, but it was all he had to go on
and none of his Ladakhi companions had ever travelled this way.
The messenger headed off uphill for Shahidulla, and they pressed
on upstream, expecting to meet him again within a couple of days.
In fact, the road to the Karakoram Pass branched off along another
side valley further up the river, and Aktagh lay far to the south-east
behind a great spur of mountains; they would miss their rendezvous
and their fresh supplies by 50 miles.

For the next week they worked their way along the valley. The
temperature grew ever colder as they climbed steadily higher.
Ahead, slipping in and out of view between the sheer ridges of
brown rock that hemmed the valley, the great white wall of the
main Karakoram Range rose into an icy sky. They now had no
food left at all but were still pushing through long days marching, and Hayward was still scrambling up every ridge and spur
to survey the surrounding peaks. There was not even any grazing for the poor yak and, a few days up the valley, the wretched
creature finally collapsed. There had no longer been anything for
it to carry anyway, and the Ladakhis put it out of its misery and
butchered enough of its greasy flesh to keep themselves from
sharing its fate.

Each day the great southern wall of mountains drew closer,
each day it grew colder and each day the river shrank still further. Hayward knew that its source must be somewhere close at
hand, but he also knew that they were approaching the very limit
of their capabilities. The Ladakhis had been spectacularly tough
travelling companions, but without food they could hardly continue. Hayward himself must have been almost beyond the point

of exhaustion – though he never mentions fatigue in his report. And worse yet, great banks of angry cloud were now beginning to well up behind the high ridge of the Karakoram. In this place, in their hungry, shattered state, without a tent and with firewood increasingly hard to come by, a heavy snowfall would be as disastrous as the arrival of a band of Kunjuti robbers.

But Hayward still pushed on – he was too close to turn back now. Finally, on the afternoon of 8 December, he scrambled up one last hillside, following what was now no more than an icy trickle, and reached the source of the Yarkand. It lay in a gloomy basin of roughly level ground, 16,656ft above sea level, surrounded by towering peaks rising like frozen meringue.

This was it: the source of the Yarkand; the wellspring of the river that ran many hundreds of miles down into the lost desert wastes of western China, the object that Hayward had been striving for during the last fortnight, and that he could quite easily have killed himself and his men in trying to reach. And all it was at this miserable time of the year, under a heavy sky filled with brooding snow clouds, was a puddle of frozen mud.

It was ridiculously cold, almost -30°C at first light. But Hayward still insisted on spending a night at the frozen spring, and on taking bearings of all the surrounding country. He even dragged out his paint box and, somehow managing to stop the brushes from freezing, he made a quick watercolour impression of the scene.

Hayward was no great artist, but a basic skill with a brush was the nineteenth-century equivalent of a basic skill with a camera today – an essential for any serious explorer. And Hayward's watercolours, though occasionally a little cartoonish, are at least effective, capturing something of the barren grey-and-brown starkness of the high mountains, though without quite doing justice to their grandeur. His rendering on heavy paper of the source of the Yarkand was not one of his best works – a smear of what is obviously ice trickling off out of sight down a steep slope and that meringuey mess of mountains beyond, streaked with dirty cloud. The strokes are certainly broad, but given the conditions it is doubtful that Constable or Turner could have done any better.

Watching the mountains swimming out of view behind ominous black thunderheads as he painted, Hayward finally recognised the precariousness of his situation. It was time to return to Shahidulla. On the afternoon of 9 December he set out downhill, back along the valley. The journey now takes on the character of an ignominious retreat – the broken army stumbling back from the frontier. But unlike Alexander, Napoleon or Cook, Hayward had succeeded: he had reached his goal; the Upper Yarkand had been mapped to its source. Such an achievement may seem insignificant today – the tracing of some obscure stream to its muddy fount – but in the nineteenth-century heyday of exploration men had died for much less.

The snow that had been threatening for days finally started to fall as they made their way back down the valley, shivering and exhausted. They pushed on long into the night before huddling together to sleep in the lee of an overhanging boulder.

It took them three miserable days to reach the point where the old trade route from Aktagh and the Karakoram Pass branched in from the right to meet the Yarkand River. They had struggled at an agonisingly slow pace over the last part of the descent, for one of the Ladakhis was now ill. Hayward blamed the sickness on the fact that the men had eaten what was left of the yak meat raw when no wood could be found for a cooking fire; more likely the man was simply on the brink of exhausted collapse. Hayward too must have been suffering. The driving determination that had done in lieu of food over the previous week would have gone now, for he had already mapped and surveyed this valley. The return journey was merely a tiresome slog.

As they shambled to the mouth of the junction of the side valley that would lead them to Aktagh, and from there back to Shahidulla by the most direct route, the ravine was filled with the sound of hooves clattering over frozen rock and of harsh voices calling back and forth. Hayward and the Ladakhis were probably too exhausted even to bother hiding by this stage, but as a long train of loaded pack horses, bearing downhill on the other side of the valley, came into view, they happily realised that the newcomers were neither Turki soldiers nor Kunjuti robbers. They were simply local traders, bringing one of the last caravans of the year in from Leh by the forbidden route.

But for the traders the sight of three ragged strangers standing amongst the rocks, without baggage animals and one of them carrying a gun, was a cause for alarm in this notorious place. They screamed and shouted and waved their sticks, doing whatever they could to ward off what they assumed were villainous Kunjutis. It took a great deal of effort with sign language to convince them that they had nothing to fear, but once they had tentatively picked across the frozen stream and realised that Hayward and his men were not going to rob and kidnap them, they were all smiles. And better yet, they took pity on the exhausted explorers. Hayward and the Ladakhis spent that night with the traders, sitting around a roaring camp fire and eating the first proper meal they had enjoyed for over a week.

In the morning they went their separate ways. The traders loaded their horses and trotted on down the river towards Yarkand. They had, they said, been given special permission by the Turki authorities to take this road, and had decided that the directness of the route outweighed the risk of kidnap and robbery. Before they left they kindly gave Hayward enough food to last for three days. Immensely grateful for this lifesaving charity, Hayward made them a gift of a pair of hunting knives. They were delighted, and promised to look out for the Englishman in Yarkand.

Two days later, trudging wearily into Aktagh, Hayward finally ran into a two-man search party from Shahidulla. The Turkis were astonished to see him still alive. In fragments of some kind of

High Asian lingua franca they explained to Hayward just what a furore his escape had caused. The Panjabashi – the official in charge of the frontier post – was in a state of despair, knowing exactly how he would be punished for allowing the Englishman to get away. His return would be very warmly welcomed indeed. And better yet, from what Hayward could make out, the soldiers seemed to be saying that permission had now arrived from the plains – he was to be allowed to continue to Yarkand.

From Aktagh they trudged back to Shahidulla with the two Turkis leading the way. It was still bitterly cold, and the going was far from good. All along the route they passed the bleached bones of the pack animals that had died coming down from Leh. There was virtually no fuel or water to be found, and the pleasure of pushing into uncharted territory was all gone now. Finally, on 16 December, Shahidulla came into view, the miserable ruin where Hayward had previously camped out now looking as welcoming as a cosy cottage. The frontier post, in its gloomy valley was, Hayward wrote, 'a dreary and desolate place at any time, but it appeared almost charming just then'.

He had been out in the hills for twenty days, with food for just seven; the temperature had remained below freezing virtually the whole time; and he had covered over 300 miles of hard ground. Geographically speaking, he had not only located the source of one of the major rivers of the country; he had also firmly established the nature of the Karakoram and Kun Lun as distinct ranges and he had taken a huge number of bearings that would allow a vast white blank on the map – currently only traced with Johnson's conjectural fantasies – to be filled. With that distant view of K2 he had even managed to connect his surveying work in these unknown northern mountains with the more extensively mapped country of Kashmir – though neither he, nor anyone else for that matter, ever seemed to realise the significance of the huge peak he had spotted on the far southern skyline as he crouched on that windswept buttress on 30 November. For his own part, all Hayward could say was that 'the result of the expedition was very satisfactory'.

But now there was unknown territory of a very different kind ahead of him.

The country north of the Shahidulla frontier post was wild and strange. In the mid-nineteenth century it was known to Europeans only enough to make it all the more tantalising. Herodotus had reported gold-digging ants the size of foxes in the deserts there; more than 2,000 years later, the credulous might still have believed that such things could exist in Eastern Turkestan.

A vast area, bigger than France, it was formidably walled off from the outside world, almost completely ringed by huge mountains. To the south lay the Kun Lun, and behind them the full might of the Karakoram and Himalayan ranges. To the north was the long line of the Tien Shan, and in the west was the solid back wall of the Pamirs. Only in the far east did a gap open through the mountains, but it merely led through bleak desert to the Tibetan Plateau and the windswept Mongolian Steppe. These massive ramparts shielded no hidden Eden: the gaping space between, though largely flat and in places below sea level, was every bit as inhospitable as the highest glaciers. Almost all of Eastern Turkestan was taken up by the Taklamakan Desert– an evil expanse of shifting yellow sand almost 1,000 miles long and over 400 miles wide. Only the Sahara is bigger. Well-worn guidebook myth has it that the name, Taklamakan, means 'Go in and you won't come out'. This is untrue, but it was true that the desert could easily swallow not just men and caravans, but also whole rivers and even cities.[1]

There were strange, unsettling stories about the desert: tales of ghost armies marching out of the sandstorms that howled across the dunes and of a race savage, hair-covered men living far out amongst the sands where no normal human could survive. Marco Polo wrote of these rumours in the thirteenth century; Robert Shaw heard the same stories repeated by the locals 600 years later.

For all its vast size, human life in Eastern Turkestan was pinned into the narrowest of margins. Teetering on the brink of bleak oblivion, oasis townships were strung along the desert littoral where glacier-fed streams flowed down from the mountains. These places, with their strange, enigmatic names, carried with them the whiff of silk and spice and camel wool: Kashgar, Yarkand, Hotan, Turfan. All were adrift in a vast landscape, chokingly hot and scoured by devilish dust storms from the desert in summer and bitterly cold in the grey of winter. They lay within sight of the mountains, an icy wall floating above the horizon, as if clinging to something solid, something immovable in a land otherwise unhinged from steadying features. Over the millennia the Taklamakan has destroyed whole civilisations: far out in the sands there are buried cities and desiccated towns. It was not a place to inspire a sense of security.

Swathes of uninhabitable land separated one caravan town from the next, and the further you went along the desert's southern edge from Kashgar – the most westerly city – the bigger the gaps became. In human terms, Eastern Turkestan had more of the characteristics of a chain of islands than of a country. Indeed, although the indigenous people of the region are today known collectively as Uighurs after an ancient tribe, it is a designation of the twentieth century. In Hayward's day people were known simply by the island-city from which they hailed: Yarkandis, Kashgaris, Hotanliks.

Such a wildly hostile land might be expected to be utterly cut off from the outside world, its people isolated for centuries. The truth was rather different and a glance at the map explains why. Eastern Turkestan – a roughly egg-shaped blemish on the face of the world – lies at the very heart of the Eurasian continent. As humanity flowed back and forth over grand millennial timescales, nomads, traders and invaders simply had to pass through this country.

Today Eastern Turkestan, with its new name, Xinjiang, meaning 'New Frontier', is Chinese territory. For well over 1,000 years it has shared a fate with its more famous southern neighbour, Tibet. Like the Land of the Lamas, Eastern Turkestan has long existed on the peripheries of China, repeatedly falling in and out of its shadow as imperial power waxed and waned over the centuries. Like Tibet it has always been restive; like Tibet it has repeatedly slipped out of effective Chinese control; but like Tibet its periods of total independence have been transient and often chaotic. The Chinese have always regarded Eastern Turkestan, like Tibet, as an integral part of their country, with historical records dating back to the early first millennium AD to support the claim. But, like the Tibetans, many of the Uighur people would beg to differ (though without the glamour of Buddhism or the media figurehead of the Dalai Lama, Xinjiang is no one's cause célèbre).

For the truth is that from the earliest days the native people of Eastern Turkestan have been anything but Chinese. The most ancient corpses, dug from desert tombs, mummified by the parched air of Central Asia, show that 3,000 years ago the oases were occupied by men with fair hair and long noses. But whoever these ancient Caucasians were, wherever they came from, they have long gone, swept away by later migrations.

It was in the sixth century that the first of the Turkic tribes dropped down from the high passes of the Tien Shan into the tall stands of poplar trees around the streams and wells at the desert edge. The Turkis are the great race of Central Asia. Their own legends say that they are descended from Japhet, a son of Noah, born under the ribbed slopes of Mount Ararat in the high, clear air of Eastern Anatolia. A people of the steppes, they were only ever loosely rooted in their landscape, shifting with the seasons and the herds over huge distances. The Kirghiz, a Turkic people, originated thousands of miles north of their modern mountains, while the most famous Turkis of all only moved west into their eponymous homeland 1,000 years ago. Today their names are marked across the map – Uighurs, Kirghiz, Kazakhs, Uzbeks, Turkmen and, of course, Turks. Their languages are spoken from the marches of China to the fringes of Europe.

And it was Turkic people who settled in Yarkand, Kashgar and the other towns of the country that took their name – Eastern Turkestan. Other peoples came here too, following the trading links of the old Silk Route, bringing goods, ideas and religions – first Buddhism, then Manichaeism and Nestorian Christianity, and then, in the tenth century, as Arab armies pushed into Central Asia and met with Turkic hordes: Islam.

Even before the first mournful Arabic prayer call drifted out over the wastes of the Taklamakan, the towns were a ragbag of all the peoples who had made their way east along improbable roads through impossible mountains: Afghans and Persians, Indians and Tibetans, and Turkic cousins from all the countries further west. There were even a handful of Jews in Yarkand and Kashgar.[2] And in the wild mountains that fringed the country there were camps of Persian-speaking Tajiks and wandering tribes of Kirghiz. 'The Bedouin Arabs of Central Asia', Hayward called them, who, 'like those children of the desert possess no fixed habitation'. Marco Polo came this way too.

More often than not, even when the Chinese yoke was temporarily shrugged off, it was outsiders who took the throne. After the mighty pan-Asian Mongol empire collapsed in the thirteenth century, Eastern Turkestan had fallen to a string of transient, short-lived dynasties dominated by men from across the mountains in modern-day Uzbekistan. The country was rarely under a single firm hand and, floating island-like in the desert, the caravan towns were often lawlessly independent city states.

In the seventeenth century the Chinese, who had been tranquil since the ignominy of the Mongol rout, picked themselves up once more in the form of the expansionist Manchu Dynasty and returned to Eastern Turkestan. Their rule lasted longer than anyone's had for many centuries, but by the early decades of the nineteenth century the inevitable dynastic decline into decrepitude had begun, and, pressured by British bullying on the eastern seaboard and Russian advances on the western frontiers, the edges of the empire began to crumble.

From 1825 onwards Eastern Turkestan was in chaos. As if a string of often ferocious internal uprisings throughout their western realms weren't bad enough for the embattled Chinese, Kokandis from the Ferghana Valley in modern Uzbekistan, some of them the descendants of the men who had ruled Eastern Turkestan in the bloody pre-Manchu interim, began to attack from across the mountains. For more than twenty years Kashgar, Yarkand and the other towns of the country fell repeatedly to these chancing warlords. Like all warlords, they were better at winning than governing, and the petty dictatorships that bloomed all along the edge of the Taklamakan rarely lasted more than a few months before the Chinese, somehow still refusing to let go altogether, returned. But each rebellion was more violent than the last, each new invading mob from the west descended more rapidly, seized power more bloodily and ruled more chaotically.

Worst of all was the dope-smoking monster Wali Khan, who burnt the walls of Kashgar in 1857 and killed even any muezzin who dared raise his voice to call prayer when the self-styled king was passing. Khan's brutal rule lasted a mere seventy-seven days before the Chinese returned yet again – though with little hope of holding on for long. By the mid-nineteenth century Eastern Turkestan was, by modern standards, a failed state. But then, apparently out of nowhere, came a man who, by 1868, seemed to have changed all that.

Mohamed Yaqub Beg was a self-made man, a masterful soldier and a wily politician – the archetypal Central Asian upstart in the tradition of Tamerlane. If he was alive today he would be some warlord in Afghanistan at the head of a private army, a Kalashnikov-toting militia of brooding men with sinister smiles in charge of a fiefdom on the southern banks of the Oxus. He would be visited in his armed compound by white men with reflective sunglasses in helicopters and bearded Afghans on motorbikes, all of whom would give him suitcases full of American dollars without ever truly convincing him to back anyone but himself.

But, born near Andijan in the Ferghana Valley sometime in the early nineteenth century, he would go even further, carving out for himself a vast kingdom from thin air and carnage, and kicking the Chinese more decisively out of Eastern Turkestan than they had been kicked out for many centuries.

Ferghana – now the most troubled corner of modern Uzbekistan – was known since the Middle Ages as a place of rebels and rabble-rousers. It was also famous for its horses, the half-mythical heavenly steeds that sweated blood and could gallop the length of Asia. In the nineteenth century it was the cradle of the Kokand Khanate, one of the Central Asian fiefdoms that would fall to Russian rule long before the century was out.

Yaqub Beg came from commoner stock, though his father was said to have been a magistrate. According to legend he had been a professional dancer in his youth, but as dancing boys in that part of the world are usually little more than male prostitutes, and as Yaqub was from a family not completely without substance, the story seems like nothing but self-conscious myth-making. He apparently rose as a courtier and soldier of Kokand, and was eventually – the classic nascent warlord – given control of his own fortress and militia on the banks of the Jaxartes where he had licence to extort tolls from travellers. But it was events hundreds of miles away, across the Pamirs in Eastern Turkestan, that would allow him to rise to glory.

In 1862 there had been yet another violent uprising against Manchu rule. This time the initial outbreak had come not in Eastern Turkestan itself, but amongst the ethnic Chinese Muslims, today known as the Hui, in Gansu, a narrow bottleneck of Chinese territory between the Tibetan Plateau, the Mongol Steppe and the Turkic desert. This was one of the most violent upheavals yet, effectively cutting off Turkestan from the Chinese heartlands. By 1864 the revolt had spread to the west. In Hotan the entire Chinese population – some 7,000 people – was massacred in a single day, and all the way along the string of desert oases, Chinese soldiers and civilians found themselves besieged in the new garrisons they had built outside the old Muslim quarters. In Kashgar, it was said, they were reduced to eating cats and dogs, then their saddles and boot straps, and finally each other, while in Yarkand, when the roar of the surrounding mob made it clear that the garrison was about to be stormed, the Chinese governor calmly tapped out the smouldering contents of his tobacco pipe on to a carefully laid trail of gunpowder that led to the powder store and blew himself, his family and whatever remained of Chinese rule in Turkestan to some Confucian heaven.

This countrywide outbreak of violence was spontaneous; it answered to no authority, and men who would not be king often found themselves in possession of slippery power that they had no idea how to wield. One such man was a turncoat Kirghiz brigand named Siddiq Beg, formerly in the service of the Chinese, who overran Kashgar with his nomad militia and proclaimed independence at the end of 1864. Desperate for some kind of legitimacy, he sent over the mountains to Kokand for help in maintaining his rule. The Khan of Kokand sent a local noble, a descendant of an earlier rebel in Eastern Turkestan, to Kashgar. His name was Buzurg Khan. By all accounts Buzurg was not up to the job, but in charge of his army was a man who had until recently commanded a fort on the Jaxartes, and who, wicked rumours suggested, had been a dancing boy in his youth.

Yaqub Beg roared into Kashgar, capturing and executing the Kirghiz rabble, including, apparently, their unfortunate leader Siddiq to whose cry for help he was responding. He then set about seizing the string of southern oases, and putting an end to the siege of the last surviving Chinese in their fortress outside Old Kashgar. While Yaqub Beg tore east along the old Silk Route, Buzurg Khan simply idled away his days in the palace in Kashgar, slipping further into ineffectual torpor. In 1866 it required little more than the posting of a guard of soldiers around his chambers and the reading of a simple proclamation for Yaqub Beg to complete a coup that, considering the usual standards of the region, was remarkably bloodless. The boy from the Ferghana Valley was now the King of Eastern

Turkestan. Buzurg was kept under house arrest before eventually being hustled out of the country on a pilgrimage to Mecca, from where he returned to Kokand a broken man.

In 1867 Yaqub Beg, now enjoying the Turkic title Atalik Ghazi, or Father-Leader of the Holy Warriors, took Hotan and consolidated his rule all along the southern edge of the Taklamakan. For the first time in decades much of Eastern Turkestan was under effective central control. Justice was rough, but the Chinese had gone – maybe even for good – and there was some kind of peace. In 1868 Yaqub Beg had yet to seize the towns along the northern edge of the desert, but he would do so within two years, having made himself a king without a pedigree, ruling over the vast space between China, Russia and British India – the three great powers of Asia.

Garbled reports of all these violent shenanigans in Eastern Turkestan had long since leached down out of the Himalayas to reach the ears of the British in India, and west over the Tien Shan to catch the attention of the Russians. The world quickly began to take notice of Yaqub Beg. Before long his name would be discussed over the morning papers in the drawing rooms of England, his emissaries would be received in the great capitals of the world, and he would be invested as an Emir by the leader of all Islam, the Ottoman Sultan in Istanbul. But in 1868 no European had met him face to face, no one knew anything of the nature of his government, or even of the country he ruled. All that could be surmised was that he was ruthless – he must have been to have risen from nowhere and betrayed his own masters – and that he would very likely fall under the category of 'Oriental despot'.

As George Hayward unpacked the little he had carried during his escapade in the mountains and enjoyed his first change of clothes for three weeks, he knew that he would soon be deep within the territory of this unknown man. Over the coming months

Hayward would be entirely at Yaqub Beg's mercy; the success of his mission, and even his life, depended totally on the whims of the warlord. Hayward's own ideas of this warrior king would fluctuate wildly as his fortunes changed. Sometimes he would think of him as a 'wise and sage' ruler. At other times, fearing for his life, he would have good cause to call Yaqub Beg 'the greatest rascal in Asia'.

Notes

1   The real etymology of the name 'Taklamakan' is obscure and indecipherable. However, Hayward mentions that Eastern Turkestan as a whole – rather than merely the desert that defined it – was popularly known as 'the country from whose bourne no traveller returns'. This, it seems likely, was the source of the lurid 'go in, don't come out' mistranslation of Taklamakan. The inspiration for the original aphorism seems to have been human, rather than geographical, however – as both Hayward and Shaw would soon find out.

2   Rumours persist today of 'Jewish' villages, somewhere in the locked valleys in the foothills of the Kun Lun, south of Yarkand and Hotan. But if these lost Semites really do exist, Chinese sensitivities about inquisitive foreigners wandering in these mountains have so far kept them hidden.

6

THE WAY THEY TREAT THEIR GUESTS IN TURKESTAN

The echo of gunshots crackled off the rocky mountainsides. The hooves of sturdy Yarkandi ponies, going at full gallop, hammered on the mountain track as another long barrel was raised from the saddle, another report ricocheted off the slopes and a puff of yellow dust rose as the bullet found its mark. But the yells that came from the party of horsemen heading north at full tilt towards the Sanju Pass were not the cries of battle or fear; they were cheers of joy. And the shots they were unleashing with startling accuracy at some random point on the hillside as they galloped were fired in celebration, not in anger. George Hayward smiled at the delight of his companions – the same Turkis who until recently were his captors and pursuers. He was as happy as they were to be riding away from the dreary frontier post at Shahidulla, downhill towards Yarkand and the desert plains of Eastern Turkestan.

He must have been glad to be in the saddle instead of on foot too: it was less than twenty-four hours since he had shambled in from the mountains after his wild escapade on the Upper Yarkand

and his feet were surely still blistered and aching. In the bright light of the mountain morning, with the prospect of the great caravan towns ahead and of the High Pamirs beyond them, the excitement of the Turkis was infectious. Grinning at the Panjabashi, the senior Turki official riding beside him, Hayward clicked a round into the chambers of his revolver, kicked his own pony to a gallop, and joined in with the wild, whooping target practice.

It was 17 December 1868. George Hayward was finally heading into Eastern Turkestan. The Ladakhi caravan men had been paid off early that morning, given supplies and sent homewards across the mountains. Unlike Robert Shaw, who took a great deal of interest – albeit often mocking, contemptuous interest – in his Asian companions, Hayward was clearly not a people-person. Three of these Buddhist villagers had travelled with him during that gruelling twenty-day journey in the mountains; he had huddled with them under boulders in snowstorms; he had staved off starvation by partaking in gristly yak flesh with them; they had stood together at the source of the Yarkand River. Yet just one day after this ragged and remarkable expedition came to an end they were packed off home to Tangtse, their names recorded for posterity in no letter, book or journal.

This kind of attitude of apparent unconcern towards servants was hardly unusual amongst British travellers in the nineteenth century, but that Hayward made equally little mention of Shaw in his writings – indeed made equally little mention of anyone – suggests that it was not merely natives that he was unconcerned by; it was everyone. Hayward, intense, possessed and unsettling, had no interest in other people on an individual level. And as for the Ladakhis, trudging back across the Lingzi Thung, reflecting on what must have been one of the strangest episodes of their entire life in the Himalayas, no one will ever know what they thought of the tall, gaunt foreigner who had led them to the point of exhaustion and beyond for reasons that made no sense whatsoever.

As they picked their way along the road north out of the mountains, the Turkis lavished Hayward with every bit as much hospitality as they had offered to Robert Shaw, strongly suggesting that a softly-softly approach counted for nothing when it came to ensuring a smooth passage into Turkestan. In fact, Hayward's audacious and outrageous escape and twenty days spent on the run had gone completely unpunished.

Heading down through the sand-coloured mountains and across the Sanju Pass, along a trail littered with dead horses, they came upon camps of wandering Kirghiz and the first real villages Hayward had seen since Ladakh. Ahead only a sea of yellow haze showed where the hills finally gave way to the plains.

Even though it was now Ramadan and his Muslim companions were fasting during the mercifully brief daylight hours, at every lunch stop Hayward was presented with a gut-busting meal known as a *dastar khan* after the cloth on which it was presented – a formal symbol of Turkic hospitality. And the Panjabashi, Roza Khoja, did all he could to meet his every need. Hayward was genuinely impressed by the welcome he received. He was not, however, allowed to survey – though during wayside halts, he occasionally managed to sneak off into the bushes long enough to scribble down a few quick measurements.

On Christmas Day 1868 they finally left the mountains behind them. The plains on the southern edge of the Taklamakan are great swathes of grey, gravely desert, stalked here and there by a few feral twin-humped camels. Closer to the towns and villages irrigation ditches turn the country green and water the stands of tall poplars – bare and skeletal in late December – but the open country is stark and bleak. Moving away from the last foothills of the Kun Lun, the valleys and ridges seem to slot together, locking themselves closed. As Hayward rode away across the level ground, the great tangled mass of rock and ice that he had been deep within for the past weeks would have transformed itself into a single, impenetrable wall.

For the first time since leaving Leh, Hayward reached a town – the oasis of Karghilik. After three months in wild campsites or lonely villages the pungent smells and raucous noise of the bazaar would have been overwhelming. A mass of round Turkic faces, cropped heads bound under high white turbans or box-shaped skullcaps, would have stared up at him as he passed – the second inexplicable Englishman they had seen in as many weeks. This desert outpost must have seemed like a metropolis, and the carpeted chamber in which he slept like the plushest hotel room.

Here in the more sophisticated world of the town, the traditional Turki treatment of honoured guests was extended to its most fantastical extent. Hayward was welcomed by the governor of Karghilik, 'a fine-looking old man, by the name Ibrahim Beg', who 'exhibited the most unbounded hospitality'. His Christmas dinner, eaten alone, was the most lavish *dastar khan* yet: 'It comprised two sheep, a dozen fowls, several dozens of eggs, large dishes of grapes, pears, apples, pomegranates, raisins, almonds, melons, several pounds of dried apricots, tea, sugar, sweetmeats, basins of stewed fruits, cream, milk, bread, cakes, &c., in abundance.' It was, Hayward noted, enough to feed forty people. Less than a fortnight earlier he had been crouched under a boulder in a snowstorm, staving off starvation with a leathery strip of half-raw yak meat.

Belly bursting, Hayward clambered back into the saddle the following morning and continued westwards through the busy irrigated land around Karghilik, and out into the grey desert beyond. The mountains floated away to the south in a long ethereal line above the horizon. The next day, under a sky obscured by murky slabs of grey cloud, he reached Yarkand.

Today the town is a poor, scruffy and stupendously remote backwater at the very limit of China's vastness. It has been surpassed by Kashgar as the principal town of the southern desert, and the Chinese authorities, mindful perhaps of those easily besieged garrisons and the fates of their inhabitants, have moved the Xinjiang capital away from these wild frontiers, hundreds of miles north to Urumqi, a grey city of tower-blocks and flyovers. But in the 1860s Yarkand was a name to conjure with, a place as steeped in mysterious romance as Samarkand or Xanadu. It was one of the major cities of Central Asia, home to at least 120,000 people and 160 mosques, and was, whenever the country came under a single ruler, the capital of Eastern Turkestan.

In the depths of winter, under that cold, grey sky, Hayward's first impression of this fabled place was a little underwhelming. The packed earth ramparts of the city, a dirty grey-brown colour, rose from a plain studded with skeletal trees. Only a few minarets – and of course, the great set of gallows – showed from the jumble of houses within.

Hayward's party rode in from the east, passing through one of the great city gateways, and into the maze of narrow streets beyond. Houses rose on either side and pavements were lined with well-stocked hole-in-the-wall shops, most of them presided over by women with long white veils falling over their faces from high pillbox hats of sheepskin. This was a place of busy commerce, with traders hurrying back and forth from store to warehouse, and with the high chatter of bargaining rising on either side. And it was remarkably cosmopolitan. Hayward would have seen Afghans with hooked noses and pale eyes, lean Persians in long robes, stocky Kirghiz and wiry Tajiks. There would have been other strange men too that he could not place, and rising from the tumult of voices he might have picked out fragments of languages he half-recognised – Pushtu, Persian and even Hindi. There were, it seemed, more than a few Indians here. Though it had not yet been explained to him, those of them who were Hindu were the easiest to pick out, for they were forbidden to wear a turban and had to carry a belt of black rope around their waists to mark them out as infidels. Hayward might even have spotted tall, fiercely bearded men with angry eyes stalking the bazaar with long leather whips in their hands. These men, with their air of bullying, humourless authority, 130 years before the Taliban, were the religious police. They were charged with ensuring that every man prayed the obligatory five times a day, and that every woman was modestly shrouded in all-enveloping cloth. The whips were for transgressors.

This was also a military city in a country that had long been at war. As Hayward passed out through the opposite side of the old walled city and was led towards the fortified, Chinese-built garrison, he saw mounted artillery guns lining the road. Most of the pieces were manned by Indians, the more grizzled of whom, he guessed, might just have been fugitive rebels, forced to flee the subcontinent when the British regained control after the uprising of 1857. There were, it seemed, men from every corner of Asia in Yaqub Beg's mercenary military. It was just the kind of army that Alexander Gardner might have joined had he not been enjoying his Kashmiri retirement.[1]

The fortified new part of the town was the seat of government, and Hayward was led to a compound within its walls. For the next two months – though he didn't yet know it – he would hardly leave this little building with its smooth walls of creamy earth, its two small rooms carpeted with rich Hotani rugs and its roof of whittled branches and packed mud. The high walls of the courtyard offered no view beyond the tops of a few bare poplar trees and the empty Central Asian sky. Before long Hayward would hate this place with a bitter vengeance, and would feel no less confined within it than had he been tossed into the filthiest of dungeons. But for now, after months in the mountains, he was impressed by its comforts, and by the lavish *dastar khan* which was delivered as soon as he arrived. Once he had eaten and dressed in his best clothes, happily shedding his ragged, grubby travelling gear, he was led to an audience with the Shagawal, Eastern Turkestan's second-in-command:

> The room, to the entrance of which I was ushered, was a long, plainly decorated apartment, with a bright fire at the further end, in front of which two carpets were spread, covered with scarlet silk cushions. On one of these was seated a little man, plainly yet splendidly dressed in green silk cholah [robe] lined with fur, and a high fur and velvet cap.

This man, the Shagawal, welcomed Hayward graciously through a Persian- and Hindi-speaking interpreter (who, though Hayward didn't know it at the time, was a borrowed servant from Robert Shaw's party). He was, Hayward felt, 'a very pleasant, agreeable, and well informed man'. Hayward's impression of the Shagawal as 'well informed' was correct. He was apparently an educated man, and according to some reports Yaqub Beg, who was more skilled on the battlefield than in delicate diplomatic dealings, relied almost entirely on his number two for political advice.

The Shagawal made it clear to Hayward that he was an honoured guest, but he also told him that the king, Yaqub Beg, was still away campaigning on the slopes of the mountains beyond Kashgar and until royal permission had arrived for him to proceed, he would have to remain in Yarkand. The prospect of any kind of wait, as always, must have made Hayward twitch. But as he rose to take his leave and a fine silk robe – a parting gift offered at the end of every official meeting – was draped over his shoulders by some obsequious flunky, he felt sure that he would at least be treated well.

And as he made his way back to his allocated compound he must have felt at least some satisfaction at finally having reached Yarkand – scarcely more likely an event than the idea of getting to Atlantis today. To have arrived in a place 'so long deemed unapproachable and impracticable to Europeans' was no small achievement. But of course, Hayward's real goal – the Pamirs – remained skulking out of view somewhere beyond the western horizon and he had no claim to make on Eastern Turkestan itself; he was more than happy to be the second Englishman into Yarkand.

As Hayward settled down on the carpets of his new quarters, and began to pick at the dishes of yet another lavish *dastar khan*, the first Englishman into Yarkand was pacing his own compound, just 100 yards away across the fortress.

While Hayward had been blazing his trail along the Upper Yarkand and then making his way down to the plains, Robert Shaw had been sitting in his room eating frozen grapes. He had certainly received plenty of attention and lavish hospitality since reaching Yarkand – and as the first to arrive he had been housed in slightly larger quarters than Hayward. His horse and the flock of sheep he had accumulated as official gifts in every town and village between Shahidulla and the plains were stabled nearby, and he was still deluding himself that the soldiers stationed at the gate were 'appointed to remain in attendance on me' – humble servants rather than prison guards. On one occasion Shaw did make a gentle request to go out for a ride in the nearby countryside in search of fresh air. He was politely but firmly informed that 'It is the custom in this country that no guest goes anywhere out of doors before seeing the king'. In Eastern Turkestan it seemed 'guest' was a synonym for 'prisoner'. However, not wanting to shatter the illusion, Shaw made no more embarrassing requests to go out and explore, and settled down in his quarters.

His sense of self-importance was certainly flattered by the several audiences he had with the Shagawal. These meetings were elaborate exercises in mutual sycophancy. 'God has so created our two countries that we seem intended for mutual friendship … Your Mussulman faith is the string which binds the faggot, and I trust your present kingdom may hold together forever,' simpered Shaw. The Shagawal graciously concurred, before draping yet another silk robe over his shoulders and packing him off back to his quarters with an overflowing tray full of food.

Yaqub Beg, he was told, had recently shifted his seat of government to Kashgar, and would doubtless send for Shaw there whenever he finally returned from his campaigns and fort-building programmes on the western frontier. In the meantime, Shaw was to relax and consider himself an honoured guest. The Shagawal even had a search party sent out to try to track down the second string of Shaw's caravan, that which he had left in Ladakh in the charge of the 'Faithful' Arghon. Word had come that it had eventually departed from Leh but had never reached Shahidulla. It was presumed to have gone astray somewhere in the mountains.

The Yoozbashi who had accompanied him down from Shahidulla and a Yarkandi envoy, Mahammad Nazzar, who Shaw had met in Leh, came regularly to visit and to keep him sweet with their polite attention. Things would be much less cordial when finally he made it to Kashgar, but even so, boredom and suspicion began to play on Shaw's mind, and the very obvious fact that his Turki friends were priming him with misinformation made him a little nervous.

To kill time he did his best to rig up a thermometer in the middle of his courtyard in a thatched box built specially for the purpose. 'I intend to take two observations of temperature every day with this machine,' he wrote. This sudden attempt at fairly pointless scientific enquiry was all very well, but George Hayward had already been making such measurements three times a day for the past three months, even when subsisting on raw yak meat and adrenalin in the high mountains.

Shaw also spent a good deal of time bickering with his servants and taking them to task on theological matters. He was particularly eager to exercise his religious contempt for Indians of all faiths, and so was furious to overhear one of his Indian Muslim servants spreading amongst the dignified, fine fellows of Turkestan the garbled caste prejudices still common amongst communities long since converted from Hinduism in the subcontinent. The servant, Rahmet-Ullah, had told the Turkis not to risk the pollution of eating bread touched by the Hindus of Shaw's party, and Shaw disciplined him:

> I had him up, and held him by the ear (the native way of impressing a warning) … 'These people,' I said, 'are not half-Hindoos like you to have caste distinction in eating and drinking. If you ever again put such things into their heads, I will skin you'.

It was, unsurprisingly, 'the last I heard of such follies'.

Turkestan was ever a productive rumour mill, and Shaw learnt that the suspicions that had greeted his arrival at Shahidulla had a great deal to do with wildly exaggerated stories of a force of fifty Englishmen approaching through the mountains. There were also tales, the veracity of which was equally doubtful, that hundreds of Russians – or possibly just a larger than usual party of Kunjuti brigands – were massing on the western borders. Probably the rumour that he took most pleasure in was the Chinese whisper that seemed to confirm that Hayward had indeed been seized by bandits and dragged off to Afghanistan forever – though the moment of wicked delight soon passed with the news of his rival's arrival.

The Turkis would almost certainly have thrown polite obstacles in the way had Shaw and Hayward tried to meet in Yarkand. Yet as the Shagawal, the Yoozbashi and the envoy did seem to be taking a genuinely polite interest in their English visitors, and as Shaw's servants had been given permission to wander the bazaars unhindered, they could have communicated. In fact, in the calm quiet of the icy mornings, had both men stood in their court-yards and shouted, they could probably have managed a direct conversation. But at this stage, for Shaw at least, things still looked quite positive. Eventually, months later and in much less hospitable circumstances in Kashgar, mutual depression and desperation would force a covert correspondence of smuggled notes, but for the moment, they ignored each other.

Shaw had received good news from the Yoozbashi anyway: he would – probably, possibly, maybe – soon be allowed to continue to Kashgar. Shaw already knew enough not to get unduly excited – the endless excuses and delays from the Turkis had begun to make him a cynic and a pessimist. But for once the rumour proved to be true, and on 4 January 1869, Robert Shaw set out for Kashgar, 'delighted once more to be in motion'.

Hayward was left behind to fester. A guard was posted outside his door – and, unlike Shaw, Hayward had no illusions about their purpose. He too asked permission to go out in search of fresh air, and he too was firmly told that to do so before meeting the king would be to violate the 'custom of the country'.

He did what he could to put his time to good use, and at first it must have been an enjoyable novelty to eat well and sleep comfortably. *Dastar khans* were daily deposited before him, and whatever weight he had shed while slugging over the mountains must soon have been put back on. 'There is a saying in Turkistan,' wrote Hayward, 'that whoever has once tasted Turki hospitality is so charmed therewith, that he never wishes to leave the country afterwards, which means that he is not allowed to.' Still, Hayward continued, 'one could not but confess that however treacherous the Atalik Ghazee might be, he certainly had no intention of killing his guest by starvation.'

Belly ever replete, Hayward set about putting in order all the notes and observations he had made on his journey from Leh, tabulating the measurements and bearings and checking over the details. He also set to work writing up a full account of his journey as far as Shahidulla from the hastily scribbled notes in his diary. He filled the pages of a small notebook with what would eventually – in redrafted form with some of the more colourful digressions excised – form the first part of his official report to the RGS. He finished this account in the middle of January.

By this time his servants had been granted permission to go beyond the fortress and into the city proper, and they were able to bring Hayward titbits of gossip from which he could compile a general picture of life under the rule of Yaqub Beg. His most forthcoming informants were Hindu traders from India, who rather resented their discriminatory treatment at the hands of the Turki Muslims. He also made contact with an Afghan called Kureem Khan who primed him with tantalising information about the trade routes through the mountains to Chitral and Peshawar. Khan was a refugee from Kabul who had come to Eastern Turkestan in search of employment as a soldier. Other Afghans who had fallen into the same trap warned him off – there was no such thing as an honourable discharge from Yaqub Beg's army, they told him; if you came in to Eastern Turkestan, you didn't go out again, and a foreign mercenary would find himself as much a prisoner for life as any civilian guest. He was now stuck in Yarkand, desperately trying to devise a plan that would allow him to return home. He was quite happy to pass on whatever he knew to Hayward by way of a message-bearer.

Hayward also took a total of eleven separate sextant bearings for latitude to obtain a reliable average, and took the temperature of boiling water a number of times. In doing so he reliably fixed the position and elevation of Yarkand for British mapmakers.[2] He continued to take daily weather recordings (it was often cloudy, dipped well below freezing every night and snowed from time to time in January).

But all this could hardly keep frustration at bay. In almost two months in Yarkand Hayward was only allowed out of his quarters on the few occasions he was granted an audience with the Shagawal. For a man who had been in a state of energetic perpetual motion ever since leaving England over six months earlier, and who had lasted barely a week in Shahidulla before being driven to escape, this must have been excruciating.

Even Shaw, who was generally quite happy to idly bide his time, would later write of the depression that overcame him during his captivity in Turkestan. For Hayward, a much less passive man, it would have amounted to torture. 'The confinement was excessively irksome after such an active life amongst the mountains,' he wrote in his report, only hinting at the agonies of week after week in the same little mud-walled compound.

By the beginning of February Hayward was on the brink of losing control. Several times he attempted to repeat his Shahidulla escapade by confidently striding out of his quarters and setting out for a tour of the town. But Yarkand was no sloppily guarded frontier post in the high mountains; it was a large military city bristling with soldiers. Escape was impossible, though on one occasion he managed a quick circuit of the fort before being hustled back to the compound by the horrified guards.

A rumour eventually reached Shaw in Kashgar that Hayward had made this brief bid for freedom in a most aggressive fashion, chasing off his one-time companion, the Panjabashi, Roza Khoja, and storming furiously around the city in a state of near-hysteria. He was only finally brought back to his quarters after troops were mobilised to contain him. Such behaviour, Shaw snootily told the Turkis in Kashgar, was outrageous: 'In foreign lands one ought to follow the customs of the country, and obey the rulers,' he declared. According to Shaw, Hayward's repeated attempts at escape had forced the Shagawal to place a strict twenty-four-hour guard at his gate. At one point he heard that Hayward had proved so troublesome during his internment in Yarkand that the Turkis had bound him in chains.

Hayward himself only gave a few pages of his account of the journey to the two months he spent in Yarkand, and he mentions nothing of his dealings with the officials there beyond a description of that first meeting with the Shagawal. Shaw, meanwhile, later conceded that there was 'great exaggeration' in the stories he had heard of both Hayward's behaviour and his treatment in Yarkand, so we cannot know what really happened. But it is hard not to imagine tantrums, pacing, beseeching, more tantrums, pleadings, slumps into despondency, yet more tantrums and finally deep, acidic cynicism. In any case, it is fair to conclude that Hayward proved a much less compliant guest than the tea planter.

Perhaps the clearest glimpse into the state of his mind during this initial period of detention is found in a handwritten annotation on the back of a watercolour he painted of his quarters there, just two days before he finally left for Kashgar.

The temperature in the city was rather more clement than it had been at the source of the Yarkand, and Hayward had spare time in abundance, so this picture has a little more detail. The branches of the poplar trees, rising against the pale sky beyond the walls, have been drawn in close detail; the gloomy shade in the courtyard's corners has been effectively filled in, and the rough timbers of the roof beams and the uneven plastering of the walls are all clear to see. A door, half ajar, gives on to a pale alleyway beyond, and at the back of the courtyard a pair of miserable looking ponies, shaggy in their winter coats, munch at damp bundles of hay. In the foreground, rather spoiling the effect, is an amateurish rendering of a man with reddish hair, a long nose and a blue hat. He looks thoroughly unhappy – a self-portrait perhaps? Next to him are two very odd looking creatures with coarse, wiry coats. They could perhaps pass for some kind of half-wild dog from the Kirghiz herders' camps were it not for the double sets of curved horns rising from their heads.

On the reverse of the painting, once it had dried, Hayward wrote a sneering little note, full of bitter sarcasm:

> The house in which they entertain their friends so hospitably in the fort of Yarkand. First enticing them into the country as guests and then confining them like prisoners. Not to destroy the peaceful harmony of the scene a guard of 8 sepoys and a Panjabashi has been judiciously omitted. This is the way they treat their guests in Turkistan.[3]

The relationship between a man who would make such comments and his captors, no matter how generously they fed him, would likely be a little sour. Hayward did still manage to see the funny side of his own limited artistic capabilities however. 'As the animals in the foreground may be mistaken for hyenas, wolves or jackals,' he added, 'it is stated that they are meant to represent a species of 4 horned sheep met with in this part of Central Asia.'

Surrounded by such wolves in sheep's clothing, and in so caustic a mood, it is fortunate that the order to proceed to Kashgar came when it did: had Hayward spent any longer locked up in Yarkand there might have been some seriously ugly incident.

On 24 February 1869 George Hayward finally left for Kashgar. The relief at being on the move again after the weeks of confinement must have been overwhelming. He was accompanied by the usual guard of Turki soldiers. Their leader, an Uzbek mercenary called Mahomed Azeem Beg, was a fine companion. He had served in Yaqub Beg's militia since his earliest days on the banks of the Jaxartes, and he had a fine stock of blood-curdling war stories to tell. As they rode through the chilly countryside along lanes knee-deep in fine, clinging dust, he pointed out to Hayward the battlefields of Beg's ascendancy in Eastern Turkestan. The walls of the mud fortresses along the way were still scarred and scratched with the marks of musket-shot and cannonball.

And if fresh air and engaging conversation were not enough to lift Hayward's spirits, he must have been cheered to know that he was finally moving tantalisingly close to his ultimate goal – the Pamirs. Not far out of Yarkand a road branched away to the south. Had Hayward somehow managed to get away from his escort to follow it he would, in a couple of days, have reached the desolate fortress at Tashkurgan, which marked the northern gateway to the Pamir ranges.

Instead they continued westwards through stretches of bleak desert and through dusty, mud-walled villages in meagre little oases. Two days out of Yarkand they came to Yanghissar. Today it is a place of no significance whatsoever, a shabby truck-stop on the road between Kashgar and Yarkand. Then it was a sizable town with a bustling bazaar full of cramped little shops mixed in a wild confusion of trades and wares. 'Next to the shop of a vendor of silks and caps will be seen the stall of a butcher, reeking with horseflesh, which is the most popular article of consumption throughout Eastern Turkistan,' wrote Hayward.

He decided that Yanghissar was 'by far the most picturesque place which was seen in Turkistan'. This was not on account of that colourful bazaar or the ample supply of horsemeat however; it was because of the view. The weather at the end of February was fine and dry, and the dust and haze of the plains was cut by the winter cold. Yanghissar's greatest attraction was 'the magnificent view of the lofty Kizil Yart range of the Pamir, which is in full sight to the south-west and west'. Finally, after so many months, Hayward could actually see the object of his journey. The mountains floated above skeins of level desert and a few dusky foothills, ribbed with white ice and scoured with black valleys. The peaks looked vast, rising to well over 20,000ft, and dropping to the plains in a series of near-vertical ridges and spurs. The rumoured plateau and the 'lake-system' of the central Pamirs must lie directly behind this great bastion, Hayward decided, as he looked out from the upper levels of the royal caravanserai in Yanghissar in the weak winter sunshine, staring intently at the ethereal prospect drifting just beyond reach. Even in the depths of despondency in Yarkand he had clung to the possibility that, after meeting with Yaqub Beg, he would be allowed to continue to the Pamirs. Now, seeing how close at hand they lay, in a brief, illusory moment in the sharp sunlight of a Yanghissar morning success must have seemed almost certain.

After several days admiring the views, Hayward continued to Kashgar, and on 5 March the bulky fortress on the outskirts of the town, with its earth walls and its loopholes for the heavy guns of defenders, rose into view across the plains. Kashgar might have been smaller than Yarkand in the 1860s, but lying at the eastern promontory of the Taklamakan, deep between the jaws of the divergent eastbound mountain ranges, its geopolitical significance was unsurpassed. 'Although, perhaps, little known to European statesmen,' wrote Hayward, 'it must eventually play an important part in Asiatic politics'. He was right – by the end of the century the vast empires of China, Russia and Britain, the superpowers of the Victorian era, would converge within 100 miles of this lonely caravan town.

'Wonderfully well and centrally situated, it is a place of utmost importance both in a political and military point of view,' Hayward continued. 'Here all the roads from the Khanates of Central Asia converge.' Today the empires of two of the three great powers are no more, but roads still converge on Kashgar. The northern and southern branches of the old Silk Route, from Urumqi in one direction and from Yarkand, Hotan and Tibet in the other, come together here. The highest roads in the world lead over towering passes into other countries and other worlds; the Torugart and the Irkeshtam into Kyrgyzstan, and greatest of all, the Khunjerab into Pakistan. Eastern Turkestan's modern incarnation has borders with eight different countries (as well as with China, of course), four of them within a hundred miles of Kashgar. Arrival there is still an event to quicken the pulse.

But for George Hayward, riding into town and being led to a caravanserai between the fortress and the old city, this sense of excitement would be short-lived. The journey along the road through Yanghissar would turn out to have been merely a brief and temporary reprieve, and captivity in Kashgar would prove darker, grimmer and more soul-destroying than detention in Yarkand.

Had they been able to communicate, Robert Shaw already could have told him that it would be. The tea planter had arrived in Kashgar on 11 January in high spirits. The next morning, followed by some thirty servants bearing the gifts he had carried from India, he was ushered into the presence of the man who had loomed, abstract, omnipresent and ever-larger over his journey like some Turkic Mr Kurtz all the way from Leh. Having survived the complex formal greetings without faux pas, and after a little thoroughly British introductory small talk about the uncommonly chilly weather, Shaw engaged in diplomatic niceties in fumbling Persian with the Atalik Ghazi, the self-made King of Eastern Turkestan, Mohamed Yaqub Beg.

Shaw apologised for his limited ability in what was the official courtly language of most of Muslim Asia, and suggested they send for some Hindi-speaking interpreter. But the king dismissed such concerns with elaborate flattery of his own.

'Between you and me no third person is requisite,' he declaimed, 'friendship requires no interpreter.' And with that, Yaqub Beg dismissed Shaw with a cheery wave, telling him to enjoy himself and to 'see all the sights', while promising another meeting within three days. In fact, it would be almost three months before Shaw would receive the honour of a second audience, and far from enjoying the tourist attractions of Kashgar – its bustling bazaars, its ancient fortifications and the inlayed tombs of its former kings – he spent the entire period under house arrest.

Uncharacteristically, he sensed that all was not well from the very start. In Yarkand, despite being confined to quarters, he had been housed in very fine style. But in Kashgar Shaw and all of his servants were crammed together in one small courtyard house where there was a constant noise of comings and goings, and where privacy was a pipe dream. All of this was galling enough for a man with no small opinion of himself, but the worst blow came when Shaw's dinner was served after he returned from meeting the king. Used to extravagant *dastar khans* (and more than a few pounds heavier than when he first arrived in Turkestan as a consequence), Shaw was outraged when one of his servants scuttled sheepishly up to him with what the Turkis had offered for his meal. There were no whole roast sheep here, no overflowing plates of icy grapes and juicy melons, no eggs or nuts or cakes, and no elaborate ceremony of hospitality; instead the servant had been cursorily handed a tray of plain bread.

Shaw threw a tantrum. His munshi, who seems by all evidence to have been a very canny man and who was doubtless more conscious than his master of how dangerous a place Eastern Turkestan was for visitors, was horrified. He pleadingly suggested politeness – they really ought to be grateful that they were being fed at all, and refusing the food would be a deadly insult. But Shaw – the first Englishman into Yarkand and Kashgar no less – had puffed himself up into a self-important fury. A tray of bread was simply not good enough. To his satisfaction this petulant foot-stomping did finally produce a rather more expansive meal –still no feast by Yarkandi standards – but the affair left a nasty taste in his inadequately filled mouth. 'Of course, the thing was a mere trifle in itself; but in the East, want of respect is a precursor to danger,' he noted in his journal. Shaw must have slept uneasily that night, and it was not only the snoring of his servants, gratingly close at hand, that disturbed him.

Nothing in the next few days served to lighten his mood; no new call came from Yaqub Beg, and by the time a week had passed Shaw was beginning to suspect the worst. 'Although the King told me to go about and amuse myself, yet I am half afraid that it was only a figure of speech,' he wrote. By the following weekend Shaw had made a startling admission to his journal and to himself: it could no longer be denied – he was a prisoner.

The journal – which eventually formed the bulk of Shaw's book about his journey – downplays the very real anxiety he must have felt over the coming weeks and months. But something of the drudgery, the boredom and frustration, and eventually the paranoia that afflicted him, cooped up in his cramped Kashgar quarters, is conveyed. Shaw did what he could to pass the time, trying to teach arithmetic to the porters who had travelled with him all the way from Kangra, and having a set of dumbbells made up to keep himself fit (he had 'increased fearfully round the waist for want of exercise'). But being trapped indoors with the same people day after day soon began to wear him down. Shaw had long since run out of reading material, and whenever his servants were allowed out to wander in the bazaars he consumed any trivial news they brought back – a new corner of the market, a previously unknown gateway through the city walls – with pathetic eagerness:

> We linger reluctantly over each topic … we wring out of it each drop of subject matter which it will afford. We return to it again and again, like a dog to a bone which he has already gnawed clean. Meanwhile I pace up and down the verandah [sic], the only exercise I can obtain. At any sign of animated conversation, a raised voice, or a laugh, half-a-dozen heads peer out of as many doors all round the court, like marmots at their holes.

When the entire party was confined to the house – as they often were – Shaw's Muslim servants eked out what little novelty they could from the punctuations of the daily prayer routine, raising their heads from miserable torpor every few minutes to ask hopefully 'is it time to pray?', before dropping back into despondent boredom when the answer came – 'not yet'.

Though there were no high-level audiences, Shaw was not completely ignored by the Turkis, and his old friend the Yoozbashi was a frequent visitor. On one occasion Shaw, dignity long since abandoned, played a game of leap-frog on his veranda with this senior Turkic official, their long robes flapping wildly as they leapt over one another. But despite such diversions, as the weeks went on the strain showed more and more. Shaw engaged in a series of petty, ridiculous arguments with his erudite munshi, on matters of religion or over absurd hypothetical situations – arguments that usually ended with Shaw convinced that he had yet more evidence that the typical 'Oriental', besides being lazy, was 'generally a sharp-witted man, with a keen eye to personal profit in all the daily transactions of life, but beyond them as ignorant as a child, without the curiosity'.

Sometimes the Yoozbashi or some other gossipmonger insisted that the king was honoured by Shaw's presence in Kashgar, and that his lengthy confinement was, once more, merely the 'custom of the country'. For a while his spirits would lift; surely the promised second meeting was coming soon; perhaps the king had just been busy. But then the inevitable slump would come again. It probably didn't help that Shaw had essentially completed his mission. He had never intended to travel any further than Kashgar, and his stated aim was simply to see the country and deliver his gifts to the king. This he had done; if he was now allowed to return home he could consider the journey a success. *If* he was allowed to return home – but all the while that he was not, he must have wondered what on earth he was doing in this godforsaken place.

The Yarkandi orphan, Rozee, who had tagged along with Shaw's caravan since Kullu, was still hanging around, and was roaming the city on Shaw's behalf in search of gossip. The news that he brought was rarely good. One day he told his keenly horrified listeners in the courtyard that he had seen the body of a man lying just outside the main gate of the fortress with its throat cut. The unfortunate man in question had been a thief, it was said, and this grim reminder of Turki justice, slowly putrefying in full view of all passers-by, lay for days beside the road. Other rumours swirled in the cold Central Asian air – there were more stories of those invading Russians, of Yaqub Beg's brutality and of Hayward's escapades in Yarkand.

Unsurprisingly, paranoia began to creep into Shaw's journal entries. He had started to suspect that the king was using him as some kind of political tool – though he couldn't explain exactly how. One day one of his servants came back from the bazaar having met a Kashmiri there. There were thousands of these Indian hill men trapped in Kashgar, he had said, ready to rise against Yaqub Beg; all that was wanting was a leader. The invitation was obvious, but as Shaw gnawed it over, pacing his veranda or idly lifting his homemade dumbbells, he decided that surely this must be some trick, played by the Turkis to test their captive. If Shaw had responded with interest to the approach then wouldn't he too, faster than you could say *covert Kashmiri coup*, end up lying in a ditch with his throat cut?

Likewise, when on 11 February one of his servants brought him a concealed note from some new stranger, Shaw was full of suspicion. His stomach must have lurched with surprise when first he saw the letter – it was written in English. It was not Hayward's spidery scrawl, however; it had been signed by someone calling himself 'Mirza Shuja'. This Mirza claimed to be on an exploring mission, and asked, bizarrely, to borrow a watch – his own had broken – and to know exactly what day of the month it was, for he had been treated roughly and in the strain had lost track of the date. Shaw considered replying in Persian for a moment, then changed his mind – 'I have great doubts of his genuineness'. Surely this too was some devious trap laid for him by Yaqub Beg. Shaw sent back a brusque, dismissive verbal message through a servant to this supposed impostor: he had no spare watch (untrue) and he could not help the man. For Mirza Shuja the unexpected news of an Englishman in Kashgar must have seemed like the greatest of good fortunes, so this was a bitter blow – for he was entirely genuine.

Mirza Shuja, whose real name may have been Sajjad, but who was generally known simply as 'the Mirza' ('gentleman'), was a remarkable man on a remarkable journey. Shaw dismissively referred to him as 'one of the recent arrivals from India'. In fact, he was neither Indian nor was his departure from that country particularly recent. He had already been travelling for more than a year, enduring perils that would make Shaw's Turkestan jaunt, and even Hayward's hardy expedition, look utterly pedestrian. And while Shaw would repeatedly have to assure his captors that he came to Kashgar as a private citizen and had no official capacity (despite his eagerness to play at being an ambassador), the Mirza was, incredibly, an employee of the British – a secret agent no less. After all he had been through on his long journey, to have his ability to do his duty so dismissively thwarted in a verbal message from a pompous civilian tea planter some years his junior was the grossest of insults. And all he needed was a watch and the date.

The Mirza was something of an international man. Born in Meshed in Persia to a Turkish father and a local mother, he had led a strange and peripatetic life, orbiting Afghanistan and the North-West Frontier for decades. Before Robert Shaw was even born he had been in wild and outlandish places, and he had personally known Englishmen from an earlier, more romantic era of travel in Central Asia. In 1838 he had been in Herat, in Afghanistan, during a Persian siege, and had joined the service of the heroic British lieutenant, Eldred Pottinger, who defended the city on behalf of the Afghans. The Mirza had then travelled to Kabul during the disastrous British occupation, and despite his association with these infidel foreigners, he somehow managed to escape the bloody fate of 16,000 other soldiers and sundry camp-followers. Later he drifted east to Peshawar and there found employment, probably on the strength of his work with the British in Afghanistan a decade earlier, as an assistant to a military surveyor, Lieutenant Walker, later to become the Surveyor-General of India, the man in charge of mapmaking throughout the subcontinent.

Despite being 'incapable of field sketching or computing' according to Walker, the Mirza proved himself a useful junior surveyor. And more importantly, with his formidable language skills, his extensive travelling experience and his own Muslim faith, he could go deep into the lawless hills where – then and now – no Englishman could hope to survive. He stayed with Walker for several years, learning the tricks and techniques of the surveyor's trade. Had he remained, he would perhaps have achieved great things in the ever more important Great Trigonometrical Survey of India (GTS) – or at least as great things as any 'mere native' could ever hope to achieve. But the Mirza was clearly a man afflicted with wanderlust. Instead, with a firm grip of the basics of surveying, he abandoned his nascent career and drifted back to Afghanistan where he worked as an English teacher to the sons of the king. He was there for a decade, all the while that Hayward was seeing out his miserable military service, all the while that Robert Shaw was planting tea bushes and dreaming of Turkestan in Kangra.

While the Mirza was gone from British India, the survey had continued its work, filling in the blanks, pushing the maps high into the Himalayas. But as surveying work nudged beyond British territory, it became increasingly hazardous. In many places, not least Tibet and the wild country beyond the North-West Frontier, it was downright impossible – unless, of course, the mapmakers were not sweating, conspicuous Englishmen, but people like the Mirza.

The idea was hardly new – British soldiers, surveyors and politicians had, on an informal basis, been sending trusted agents into dangerous country in search of information for many years. But

it was the First Assistant on the GTS, Captain Thomas George
Montgomerie – a man with a hangdog expression, a broad
brow and a formidable beard – who first created an organised
body of native spies, men who could trace the sources of rivers
or the position of mysterious cities beyond forbidden frontiers.
Montgomerie's inspiration had come, appropriately enough,
when he was surveying in Ladakh in the 1850s. He had noticed
the unhindered traffic of local traders between Leh and Yarkand,
and decided that if amongst them 'a sharp enough man could be
found, he would have no difficulty in carrying a few small instruments amongst his merchandise, and with their good aid service
might be rendered to geography'. This canny observation led
Montgomerie to found the Pundits, a kind of geographical secret
service, the MI5 of mapmaking, and one of the most romantic,
mysterious and sadly little-documented episodes of British rule
in India.

The Pundits (the name means 'learned men') were brave and
talented men, carefully selected for their aptitude and intelligence – and for their prospects of survival beyond the frontier.
Montgomerie trained them in covert surveying techniques at the
survey's headquarters in Dehra Dun at the foot of the Garhwal
Himalaya. Here, in this dignified and orderly town of barracks
and exclusive public schools, in sight of the outer bastions of the
great mountain ranges, the Pundits were taught to pace out distances with an even stride and to secretly record measurements
and bearings. The places they would visit were exceedingly hostile to outsiders; anyone caught mapping out the country would
likely be put to death, so secrecy was essential. Equipment was
cunningly disguised – a compass hidden inside a Buddhist prayer
wheel; a string of beads numbered for counting out the yards of
a route march.

The Pundits were funded from the general budget of the
GTS, but the sensitivity of their work meant that they were little
known at the time, and few of the men have the dignity of a
real name in the history books. They went by enigmatic aliases

– the Havildar, the Mullah or, indeed, the Mirza. They did eventually receive a monument of sorts, however. Rudyard Kipling's great masterpiece *Kim* was clearly inspired by the exploits of the Pundits, and the book's Colonel Creighton is said to be based on Montgomerie. But the adventures of the real Pundits – not least that of the Mirza – were often far more wild and dangerous than anything that Kim, Mahbub Ali or Hurree Chunder Mookerjee ever achieved.

Montgomerie's protégés were mostly sent in the direction of Tibet, but by the late 1860s attention was beginning to shift west to 'the country beyond the North-West Frontier'. It is some signal of the Mirza's capabilities (which Montgomerie must have heard of from Walker) that even in 1862, when discussing possible explorations in Central Asia, he had stated that 'I know of but one man fitted for such work'. That man was at the time explaining irregular English verbs to Afghan princes; the course of the Upper Oxus was left uncharted, the passes of Kafiristan unmapped. But then in 1867 the Mirza re-emerged from Afghanistan. Whether he came unbidden, or whether word was sent for him from India is unclear, but he was quickly taken on by Montgomerie. His surveying skills were unsurprisingly rather rusty, but he was given a quick refresher course and then presented with his mission.

The Mirza's days of adventure should, by all rights, have been long behind him by 1867; he must have been about 50 years old. But 'from time to time God causes men to be born', says one of Kipling's characters in *Kim*, 'who have a lust to go abroad at the risk of their lives and discover news'. Clearly the Mirza was such man. It is hard not to suspect that he had much in common with George Hayward. Both men seemed to have that sense of dislocation that allowed them – or perhaps forced them – to wander. Whether the Mirza too was orphaned in his youth is unknown, but his lifestyle does not suggest a man with a wife, children or other close family ties. Like Hayward, the Mirza must have had some spark about him, some irresistible urge to move, for despite the meagre financial rewards, and despite his age, he was more than ready to take up the compass and sextant once more and to step forth into the wilds of Central Asia on behalf of the British – men with whom he shared neither nationality nor religion, and who were not even the rulers of his own country.

His mission was remarkably similar to that of George Hayward, though of course, the Mirza's was official, if secret: he was to visit Kashgar and Yarkand, and to explore the Pamirs and the source of the Oxus. But unlike Hayward, debarred by the Punjab Government from an Afghan approach, the Mirza was to follow a much more dangerous route – via Kabul.

The Mirza set out from Peshawar in 1867, twelve months before Hayward began his own journey. In fact, like Hayward, he was almost prevented from starting by the authorities. The viceroy of India at the time was Sir John Lawrence, an unusually dovish politician who believed in a policy of 'masterly inactivity' (or preposterous procrastination, fiddling while Rome burned, according to his critics) when it came to countering the Russian Threat. Mainstream civilian government in India in the mid-1860s frowned sternly on the kind of geographical black ops that Montgomerie organised. But a little frantic last-minute diplomacy cleared the way, and the Mirza slipped into Afghanistan disguised as a merchant.

He had tried at first to follow Hayward's own favoured route, due north through Chitral, but by the time he left Peshawar winter was fast advancing and the passes of the frontier were already closed by snow. He eventually managed to scrape through the little-known Mula Pass, far to the south, and headed for Kabul through a country in a state of civil war. Travelling across Afghanistan, even for a Pushtu- and Persian-speaking Muslim who knew the country well, was as dangerous then as it is now. It took the Mirza several perilous months to reach Kabul, where, to his great relief, he was welcomed by his old employers.

Afghanistan was in such a war-torn state that it was only in the autumn of 1868 that he was finally able to continue his journey, heading north to Bamian then onwards into Badakhshan.

On 24 December, while Hayward, footsore after his escape from Shahidulla was descending on Karghilik, and while Shaw was explaining the nature of Christmas to the Shagawal in Yarkand, the Mirza set out from Faizabad, the capital of Afghanistan's far north-west. He headed along the upper reaches of the Oxus, skirted the flanks of the Pamirs and slogged along the Wakhan Valley.

It was a stupendously tough journey for a man who was by no means young. Driving snow blocked passes and threatened avalanches; food and fuel was often hard to come by; horses died, men went snow-blind and altitude sickness began to take its toll. And there were all manner of human dangers too. The Mirza's caravan was robbed by brigands and threatened by locals; he faced mutinies from his own servants and was denounced as a spy and an infidel, often having to buy his way out of tight corners with his meagre supply of hard cash. And all the way, like Hayward, the Mirza was keeping a record of his route march and taking whatever bearings he could.

Eventually, crossing the height of the Pamirs in early January 1869, the Mirza descended on Eastern Turkestan, arriving in Kashgar on 3 February. Things did not go well. One of the senior mercenaries in Yaqub Beg's army was a man that the Mirza had known years earlier in Peshawar. Knowing all about the Mirza's past service with the British, this man stoked the usual smoulder-ing suspicions that attended the arrival of any outsider in Kashgar to a blaze of distrust. The Turkis housed the Mirza and his men in cold and shabby quarters, and demanded aggressively to know if he was connected to the two Englishmen whose arrival in the country was already causing them such headaches.

The Mirza, of course, had no idea who Shaw and Hayward were, but hearing that one of these men was already in Kashgar he was greatly relieved. Somewhere during his ordeal as he hauled himself over the mountains he had lost his watch and was no longer sure of the exact date. He needed both things to make accurate astronomical observations. Doubtless much cheered, the Mirza sent his note, asking a favour of the young tea planter. He must have been confident of help – after all, this Turko-Persian wanderer from the east of Iran had worked for Englishmen for much of his improbable life.

The rude, dismissive and singularly unhelpful message that came abruptly back from Shaw must have been sorely disappointing. And worse – so disheartened by it was the Mirza that when Hayward arrived in Kashgar three weeks later, he assumed that he would receive a similarly dismissive response from that Englishman too. He never even tried to contact him. This was a tragedy. Hayward might have at times seemed to have little interest in local people, but he lacked Shaw's bigotry and condescension. And more important, he was always eager to hear from local travellers. During his detention in Turkestan he compiled extensive accounts of the stages and way-stations of various trade routes through the mountains, information which could only have been based on local accounts. And when he came across a man with a story of wanderings in the vicinity of the Pamirs – the trader Mahamed Amin back in Murree and the Afghan Kureem Khan in Yarkand – he eagerly quizzed them.

No one he had met had a story that would have excited him as much as that of the Mirza. This man had followed the Oxus along much of its upper length (though he had never reached its source); he had stood on the watershed of the Pamirs; he had travelled through Badakhshan and must have known a great deal about all the routes through the mountains north of Peshawar. Had Hayward known this he would probably have done everything he could to communicate with the Mirza; the knowledge that such a man was in Kashgar would have sent him into a delighted frenzy. He would probably have been so animated by the rich potential of what he had to learn that he might have broken out of his quarters and gone to meet the Mirza in person. At the very least he would certainly have leant him a watch. But as it was, thanks to Shaw's snub, the two explorers, who it seems likely had more than an interest in the Pamirs in common, never even met, never communicated and knew nothing of each other's journey.

The day after he arrived in Kashgar George Hayward met the king. He was led into the inner court, carrying with him a rather more meagre array of gifts than the extravagant offerings Robert Shaw had presented. Yaqub Beg and his soldiers were true Turks, men of movement, not of calm courtly life. Installed in the Chinese-built fortress, where the unfortunate Manchu administrators had not long since been reduced to cannibalism, an air of the nomad camp still hung about them, and their formalities and extravagances had yet to take on the enervated air of debauched luxury that comes to all courts after a while. Hayward was impressed:

> Nothing could be more picturesque than the gaudy display, showing the outward glitter of Oriental pomp and splendour, in the courts where but lately all the horrors of siege and starvation had been endured by the ill-fated Chinese. Their Moslem conquerors had, however, effaced all traces of the tragedy, and if cruel and merciless in their religious fanaticism to their foes, their frank and manly courtesy, and warlike bearing, contrasting most strikingly with the degenerate and effeminate Chinese, win the goodwill as well as excite the admiration of the stranger.

Full of such thoughts of admiration for the Turkis and contempt for the Chinese (about whom he knew little but hearsay), Hayward entered an inner chamber and was led forward to meet Yaqub Beg himself. Unlike the bejewelled rajas of India, the Atalik Ghazi was simply dressed, and was apparently without pretension. Hayward guessed that he was in his mid-forties, and though he could hardly be called handsome, he was certainly striking.

Stocky and muscular, his broad, deeply lined forehead and sharp eye marked 'the intelligence and sagacity of the ruler'. Hayward continued with his rather overawed description:

the closely knit brows, and firm mouth, with its somewhat thick sensuous lips, stamp him as a man of indomitable will, who has fought with unflinching courage; and never sparing his own person, has, in the hour of success, been alike stern and pitiless in his hatred to his foes.

The impressive atmosphere of the court had perhaps clouded Hayward's usually cynical judgement, for he was quite prepared here to swallow the more romantic myths that surrounded the king:

Never so happy as when living the hard life of the soldier in camp, or assisting with his own hands to erect forts on his threatened frontier, it is not too much to predict, that were Asia alone in the hands of its native rulers, he would prove the Zenghis Khan, or Tamerlane of his age.[4]

In truth the uneasy world of Central Asia has long produced men like Yaqub Beg, who achieve great but ultimately transient success merely when the right circumstances meet with a somewhat more capable and determined than usual mercenary.

But the awe of this first meeting with the king was merely an incongruous precursor to all of the miserable frustration that Shaw was already experiencing – and worse. As soon as the audience was over Hayward was hustled off into captivity. Doubtless concerned that their new inmate would again make trouble and try to escape as he had done in Yarkand, the Kashgari officials installed him in a corner of the house of a senior Turki soldier. They would keep a very close eye on him, and they would not let him get away.

As with his stay in Yarkand, Hayward has little to say about detention in Kashgar, but we do know that he had been rapidly disabused of his plans to head south to the Pamirs: 'The Atalik Ghazee would not hear of such a step for one moment.' And even had he somehow managed to escape he was assured by reliable informants that the chances of even making it to the foothills were slim indeed. He might have been lucky enough to avoid an encounter with Kunjutis back in the mountains near Shahidulla, but the country between Kashgar and the Pamirs was swarming with murderous Kirghiz tribesmen. An Englishman without official protection would be lucky to survive long enough to see his first sunrise out there. This must have been an awful blow to Hayward. If he really would not be allowed to continue from Kashgar then all these months in Eastern Turkestan had, essentially, been a waste of time. The thought would have made him rage with frustration. 'The only alternative remained to endeavour to leave the country as soon as possible, and make the attempt to reach the Pamir by another route,' he wrote. For Hayward, with his sense of a ticking clock, of a desperate urgency, of a finite timescale, every day, every hour, every minute locked in a Kashgari townhouse, watched over by uncomprehending Uzbek soldiers, must have been agonising. If the more passive, less impetuous Robert Shaw had already succumbed to bitter ill-temper and increasing paranoia, Hayward must, quite seriously, have been driven half-mad.

We do know one thing about his time in Kashgar from his report. The Turkis permitted him one small, bittersweet liberty: he was allowed up the creaking wooden stairs and on to the flat, packed-earth roof of his quarters. In the chill of a clear evening Hayward would sit up there looking out across the jumble of flat rooftops under flocks of clattering pigeons turning in a sky where homemade kites dipped and tugged upwards at the end of coarse strings. Catching a smell of cooking smoke and grilled lamb and the chatter of women's voices from hidden courtyards; and hearing the uplifted voices of the muezzins of the multitude of mosques, rising from the pincushion of sharp minarets to call the evening prayer; Hayward would have looked out beyond the city walls, beyond the brown countryside to the distant wall of rock and ice, stark against a sunset sky:

> I could see the snow-covered peaks of the Kizil Yart Range of
> the Pamir in the distance, some 60 miles away, beyond which lay

the true Pamir, the 'Bam-i-duneeah' or Roof of the World, as it is called, the very name of which makes the mouths of geologists and geographers to water; while beyond that again lay Badakhshan – the ancient Bactria – and Trans-Oxiana, and the disappointment felt at being debarred from visiting all this unexplored ground was enhanced by its very proximity, after having succeeded in penetrating thus far.

Sitting on that dusty rooftop, mouth watering – and, you suspect, shedding a few frustrated tears – Hayward must have succumbed to bitter despair.

Somewhere across the city, bickering with the munshi perhaps, Robert Shaw would have been similarly despairing. He must have been lonely too. It was more than five months since he had left the pleasurable company of Dr Cayley in Leh, and almost as long since he had had any news of the outside world. Great developments could have taken place across the world; nations could have fallen; discoveries been made; and he would know nothing of any of it. At times his isolation must have seemed unbearable.

Hostages clutch at small things out of desperation, find comfort in trifles and seek out companionship with men they may otherwise have reason to despise – even with their jailors. So when, on 11 March, a letter from Hayward was smuggled to Shaw's quarters it gave him a great deal of pleasure. For all he had resented Hayward's presence in Eastern Turkestan, for all that he had needlessly considered him a rival and hoped fervently for his failure, it must now have been comforting to know that there was a compatriot, a fellow Englishman, enduring similar lonely torment in this hostile, remote and far from green-and-pleasant land.

He pored eagerly over the letter. It was long, and Hayward had written the first part back in Yarkand in what must, with hindsight, have seemed like a halcyon period of luxury and comparative freedom. He had written of all his adventures since their last, ill-tempered communication in Shahidulla. 'Apparently, he made a very laborious trip up and down the Yarkand rivers with valuable results,' Shaw noted in his journal. In Yarkand Hayward had praised the local hospitality and said that he would 'carry away pleasant recollections of the country'. But he had completed the letter in a much bleaker mood in Kashgar. Obviously, in little more than a week that awed first impression of Yaqub Beg had been forgotten, for now he declared that the king was 'the greatest rascal in Asia'.

From now on a desperate little correspondence continued between the two hostages: smuggled notes clutched in the greasy palm of the orphan Rozee, or some other servant, hurried through tangled alleys and passed from hand to hand in the shadow beneath dark archways. Both were free to express their fears. The fate of other Englishmen, imprisoned in other cities of Muslim Central Asia, must have played on their minds: of Alexander Burnes, hacked to death in Old Kabul; of the wandering veterinarian William Moorcroft, rumoured to have been poisoned on the banks of the Oxus. And both knew only too well the story of Arthur Conolly and Charles Stoddart, British emissaries who, two decades earlier, had been beheaded in the town square of Bokhara in Uzbek country. Before their deaths the two men had endured a long detention (they arrived there separately, with Conolly, in fact, on a mercy mission to seek freedom for Stoddart). Sometimes they were treated well and lavished with hospitality, sometimes they were kept in grim conditions – but neither of them escaped with their life. For both Shaw and Hayward, the parallels with their own situation were uncomfortably obvious. Indeed, Yaqub Beg had pointedly mentioned the fate of Conolly and Stoddart during his meeting with Hayward. It may have been simply a sinister joke on the part of the king, but it was a cruel one that must have played on Hayward's mind. Yaqub Beg had also mentioned the death of Adolphe Schlagintweit, in Kashgar itself.

Schlagintweit was one-third of a trio of polymathic German brothers who had sketched, measured and surveyed their way through the Western Himalayas in the 1850s. Eleven years before Shaw and Hayward, Schlagintweit had managed, after an audacious journey, to reach Kashgar – only promptly to have his throat cut at the city gate by the marijuana-crazed Wali Khan. That Wali Khan himself had long since had his own throat slit was hardly a comfort to Shaw and Hayward – the man who had wielded that particular assassin's knife was none other than Yaqub Beg. After eventually leaving Kashgar, Shaw actually met one of the unfortunate German's former servants. 'In this country,' the man told him, 'they have some compunction at killing a sheep, but none at killing a man.'

With the daily rumours of more executions, more brutality and more decapitated bodies lying at roadsides, the Englishmen's own prospects must sometimes have looked grim. At least once Hayward convinced himself that they were about to be executed and wrote to Shaw telling him as much. The tea planter, to his credit, kept a cooler head and tried to reassure his sometime rival.

This correspondence is long lost now, the hastily scribbled notes burnt in a campfire or stuffed into the mud mortar of some Kashgar townhouse, perhaps now demolished beneath the foundations of a modern Chinese supermarket. Shaw mentioned them briefly in his journal, and sometimes paraphrased them, but he never recorded the exact words – except once. On 24 March a note from Hayward was smuggled into Shaw's compound that was so striking that he copied part of it down. Hayward was, according to Shaw, 'in hot water' at the time. He had had a blazing row with his guards, complaining furiously about his treatment. He wrote to Shaw, telling him of this, and then, with grim, gallows humour, he penned the brief passage that stands out like a tall mountain on the far horizon from all the records he left:

And now I'll sketch your future for you. You will return to be feasted and feted, as a live lion fresh from Central Asia. You will

be employed on a political mission in E. Turkestan; you will open
out my new trade route with countless caravans; you will become
the great 'Soudagar'[5] of the age, and drink innumerable bottles of
champagne in your bungalow on those charming Lingzi Thang
[sic] Plains; you will write endless articles for the 'Saturday,' and a
work on the geology and hydrology of the Pamir plateau; you will
win three Victoria Crosses and several K.C.Bs, and live happily
ever afterwards.

This is all striking enough. There is, for all the facetiousness, a palpable sense of bitterness. Hayward clearly already knew that the odds
had always been on Shaw's side, that Shaw had men back across the
mountains championing his cause, while he would always have to
fight to be heard and struggle not to be cruelly dismissed.

But it is what comes next that makes you stop, blink to see if
you have read correctly, read again, and then pause for a long,
cold moment:

In contradistinction to all this, I shall wander about the wilds of
Central Asia, still possessed with an insane desire to try the effects
of cold steel across my throat; shoot numerous ovis poli on the
Pamir, swim round the Karakal [sic] Lake, and finally be sold into
slavery by the Moolk-i-Aman, or Khan of Chitral.

Again it is, it seems, meant to be bleakly funny. But in light of
what was eventually to happen, all the humour is lost to something much more startling – and much more disturbing. 'Still
possessed with an insane desire to try the effects of cold steel
across my throat': it seems like an open admission of a death-wish.
The predictions were, as Robert Shaw wrote in a footnote in
his book, published long after a fateful July morning in the Yasin
Valley had been and gone, 'very singular'.

It does have to be asked why Shaw bothered to repeat the
note in his book. He makes no other direct quote from Hayward
throughout, and he had, as we have already seen, made at least

a few allegations about Hayward's behaviour in Turkestan that somehow ring false. The original note and the man who had written it were both already lost to the Central Asian wilds when the Victorian reading public first got to tut and shake their heads over this strange little outburst, and the possibility that Shaw simply made it up, or at least embellished it, has to be considered. But something about the tone of the passage seems authentic; it echoes the stinging sarcasm in the note on the back of the watercolour of the house in Yarkand: the same sneer; the same hint of instability and fieriness. And it is utterly different in style from Shaw's own neat, jaunty prose. The tea planter certainly had a sense of humour (this was a 29-year-old man not averse to playing leapfrog after all), but not of cynicism or sarcasm. The words sound like Hayward's, and the fate he assigned for himself in them was unmistakably his.

As March rolled on the days lengthened and the night-time frosts vanished, but the correspondence continued and the rumours flowed. Shaw heard, with apparent unconcern, that the Mirza now had his leg bound to an enormous log – a punishment for failing to perform some glib trickery the Turkis demanded of him. But then, towards the end of the month, a whisper came from the Yoozbashi that sometime soon, perhaps, Shaw might be released. Then more notes started to arrive – written in English now, for apparently the Mirza was no longer chained to his block and was being used by the Turkis as an interpreter. These notes said that Shaw's long-awaited second meeting with the king would come soon.

Rumours now came thick and fast. Something had changed; the shift from chilly winter weather to warm spring sunshine had brought with it some alteration in the political climate too, though Shaw had no idea why. The king was soon leaving Kashgar, it was said, heading east towards Hotan; Shaw might travel with him, or in any case, leave soon afterwards. All this sense

of movement roused Shaw from his torpor. He became increasingly impatient. When the Yoozbashi urged calm, and told him
that all delays were the mysterious work of God, Shaw pointedly
replied that his impatience 'was God's work also'.

'I have just lost entirely three months, which are as it were
wiped out of my existence, and cannot be replaced,' he fumed.

The Yoozbashi, horrified at such sentiments, protested: 'No, no,'
he said, 'they are not lost; you will see that your residence here
has been productive of important results, and then you will look
upon these three months as one day.' Whether the Yoozbashi had
some kind of divine intimation of a future diplomatic career and
a bestselling travel book is unclear, but for Robert Shaw the time
he had spent in Turkestan was indeed to prove the making of him.

Finally, on 5 April 1869, at very short notice, Shaw was sent
for by the king. It was night when the order came, and Shaw was
hurried through the humming darkness to the palace, slipping in
through a side gate and into an inner courtyard strung about with
softly glowing Chinese lanterns. At the side of the courtyard light
flickered behind the latticework of a shaded pavilion. Shaw was
ushered to the threshold by a functionary and then left there. He
was alone with Yaqub Beg.

This time friendship did require an interpreter, and an Indian
mercenary was called for to translate. The king clearly intended
to make more than polite small talk. Still, he heaped praise on
Shaw – praise that all turned on his nationality. He had, he said,
heard much of the 'power and truthfulness' of the Englishmen;
they were a great nation, and his own insignificant strength was
but the tip of a little finger when compared to the great *Malika
Padishah* – the Queen of England. This was all rather startling to
Shaw. At their first meeting Yaqub Beg had made no such comments, and had seemed to know little of Britain or of its Indian
dominions. And at that time he had clearly never even heard of
the female emperor – perhaps fortunately, for he was a very conservative Muslim. In fact, Shaw reported, so little was known of
the British in Eastern Turkestan that it was widely believed that

they were some kind of vassal of the Maharajah of Kashmir – they must be, for reports said that that Hindu king ejected his British subjects from his realm every autumn.[6] But that had all changed now; the king had obviously been cramming up on his powerful southern neighbours. He wanted to send an envoy to England, he told Shaw, earnestly and honestly seeking his advice on how best to go about such an undertaking. Shaw, totally nonplussed by all of this, did his best to keep calm and to offer whatever suggestions he could. The king was leaving shortly on a tour of his possessions along the southern road toward Hotan, and Shaw, he assured him, would soon be leaving too, heading back to India.

After those three wasted months Shaw must have struggled to retain his composure at such delightful news, and must have struggled too to hide his utter bemusement at the king's sudden strange shift of attitude. Before they parted, with a promise to meet again in Yanghissar, Yaqub Beg, in excessively flowery language which the grizzled Indian interpreter did his best to render in polite Hindi, stated that 'The Queen of England is like the sun, which warms everything it shines upon. I am in the cold, and desire that some of its rays fall upon me.'

Shaw made his way back to his own quarters, his head spinning in the mild spring darkness. All his most overblown fantasies of success as an amateur ambassador seemed, after such long disappointment, to be coming true – the first Englishman into Kashgar and the man to open relations between Britain and Eastern Turkestan, and he was about to be released!

The truth, of course, was that Shaw was merely the smallest of pawns in the Greatest of Games. His imminent release, and all the attention the king was suddenly paying to both him and his country, was the result of developments of which he knew nothing at the time.

Like the Afghan Taliban more than a century later, Yaqub Beg had quickly discovered that to form a militia and seize a country was significantly easier than getting the rest of the world to recognise the legitimacy of your rule. Like those late twentieth-century upstarts, Yaqub Beg had brought to an end a bloody civil war and wrought a rough sort of order over former chaos on one hand, and on the other put men with whips on the streets to enforce Sharia law and made the all-covering burka mandatory – a move which, according to the Mirza, 'the women particularly dislike'. But in the mid-nineteenth century his problem was hardly with liberals and feminists.

The Chinese, as they always would, still regarded Eastern Turkestan as theirs; to make himself a real king rather than just a successful insurgent Yaqub Beg needed a great power to acknowledge him. British India was little known and far away, but there was another mighty, ascendant nation in Central Asia that everyone from Kashgar to the Caspian knew only too well – Russia. Britain had, it seemed, remained safely on the other side of Afghanistan and the Himalayas for decades, but the Russians were storming through the steppes at a formidable pace. Within a few years they would even take Yaqub Beg's own Kokandi homeland. Recognition from the tsar would be the only obvious guarantee for independent Eastern Turkestan's survival. Without it, even if the Chinese didn't eventually return, the Russians themselves would before long simply add Kashgar and Yarkand to their own ever-growing Central Asian property portfolio. Stories of a massive Russian invasion force loitering in the Tien Shan were exaggerations, but the rumours of Cossack-manned frontier posts in the mountains close to Kashgar were true.

With this in mind – like the Taliban sending their ragged delegations to Washington for talks with oil men and energy secretaries – Yaqub Beg had dispatched an emissary to Moscow with a returning Russian envoy who had departed Kashgar, and about whom Shaw had heard rumours, shortly before the Englishmen arrived. Refusing ever to let guests depart was a long-established Turkestan tradition, but the king had more reason than usual to keep his English inmates festering on the back burner: he was waiting to see what word would come from St Petersburg. Had a favourable response arrived then things may have looked very grim indeed for Hayward and Shaw. But they were lucky. The word, when it came from Russia, was that there was no word at all; Yaqub Beg's emissary had never even been received by the St Petersburg court. Russia, it seemed, wanted to avoid offending its nominal Manchu allies and at the same time to keep open its own option to annex Eastern Turkestan for itself. Yaqub Beg's hand was rapidly narrowing so he hurriedly turned in search of recognition to the only other significant power he had heard of in Asia – the British.

Robert Shaw knew nothing of this as he paced his Kashgar courtyard in a much brighter mood. Spring was coming, the poplars that just a month earlier had loomed like grim skeletons in the frigid air were now blurred by new green leaves, and it was warm, even late at night. Best of all, he really was about to leave Kashgar. He had another meeting with the king, who was every bit as friendly and genuinely interested as in the last. The conversation once again, Shaw noted, 'fell chiefly on his own insignificance compared with our Queen'. Bags loaded with gold and silver were delivered to Shaw's quarters for his 'private expenses'. Shaw guessed they must be worth nearly £700. Even the munshi was given a none-too-small bag of silver, and both he and Shaw were given new robes, 'gorgeous with gold and embroidery'. A magnificent horse with the finest of embossed saddles was hustled into the courtyard and presented to the increasingly bemused tea planter. Clearly Yaqub Beg saw no point in subtlety: he was a desperate man.

On 7 April the king left for Yanghissar and Shaw was told that he would be allowed to depart in the same direction within two days. The courtyard house that for so long had been a slow-moving pit of despondency was now all a-bustle as saddlebags were loaded with sagging pouches of gold coin and silk robes were bundled into rolls for the journey. In all this excitement, Shaw had probably completely forgotten about George Hayward. There had been no mention of the other Englishman in his meetings with the king, and no smuggled letter had come for several days. Then, on the same day that the king departed the city, a panicked note

arrived at Shaw's quarters. While gold and good wishes had suddenly begun to flow freely in one part of Kashgar, in a corner of a
soldier's house with a rooftop view of the mountains nothing had
changed. Hayward had heard all the rumours of Shaw's imminent
departure, but nothing had been said about him. He suspected,
he wrote to Shaw, that they had no intention of letting him join
the departure.

The Turkis had clearly always recognised Shaw as the more
senior man. He had, after all, come with a large caravan and elaborate gifts for the king, whilst Hayward, with his ragged little
party and makeshift presents, could be dismissed as an oddity
and a nuisance like the Mirza. It is back to our old comparison between the backpacker and the tourist once again, but this
time the Gortex trekking boot is on the other blistered foot. The
threadbare backpacker, with his pretensions of getting really to
know the Himalayan villagers finds that they are largely ignoring
him, lavishing attention instead on the man with the panama hat,
and – quite obviously – the money.

Hayward's alarm was well-founded this time, for that same day
Shaw heard 'an ugly rumour'. The gossip said that Shaw was to
be sent back to India with an envoy from Yaqub Beg; Hayward,
meanwhile, was to be kept a hostage for the envoy's safe return.
This information must have rather spoilt the party atmosphere
in Shaw's house, and perhaps the tea planter slumped down on
his veranda amongst packing cases and abandoned dumbbells at
the news. Months earlier the idea that Hayward might be swept
away by an avalanche, detained forever in Shahidulla or locked
in a dungeon in Yarkand might have appealed to him immensely.
But now things were different; Shaw's mission was over; he had
achieved success. As an honourable Englishman he could hardly
leave Hayward to rot in Kashgar while he rode home to glory. He
must have thought uncomfortably for a moment on Hayward's
'singular prediction', and perhaps too, having read enough of
his notes over the previous month, he might have realised that
Hayward would never have survived in Kashgar for the many

months it would take an envoy to return without losing his mind
or provoking his own execution. Above all, Shaw had no option
but to do something. Conolly had gone to Bokhara to try to free
Stoddart; that was the kind of manly behaviour and Newboltian
fair play that Victorian England demanded. If Shaw had ridden
out of Kashgar leaving his countryman behind he would have
been ostracised on his return.

Perhaps with the last flicker of a conflict in his conscience,
Shaw, for the first time, acted decisively on Hayward's behalf. He
sent a stern message to the Turkis. 'As long as an Englishman is
kept here against his will, it is quite useless to expect any good to
come from sending an Envoy,' he stated, 'if they are not going to
allow Hayward to depart, they may save themselves the trouble of
entering into any communication with our Government.'

The message had the desired effect; somewhere in Kashgar
a door creaked open and a deeply depressed man who had
been wondering what was to become of him was told the
news, while back in Robert Shaw's compound the messenger
returned with the Turkis' reply. Shaw, his packing complete,
scribbled in his journal the last entry for Kashgar, dated 8 April:
'Both Hayward and Mirza Shuja shall be sent back in my company from Yang-Hissar.'

On 31 May 1869 George Hayward waited in the soft spring
morning sunshine in the garden of a farmhouse in the rich, irrigated countryside east of Yarkand. He had left the city the day
before and ridden through what seemed like an entirely different
country from the bleak, stony wasteland he had passed through
on the way down from the mountains in December. Now the
trees were in leaf and the orchards were full of pale pink blossom.
The withering heat of high summer had yet to raise its dust devils
and desiccation, and for once Eastern Turkestan really did seem
like some kind of Eldorado.

The farmhouse, property of some local landlord, was a fine building surrounded by groves of fruit trees and with a shady courtyard
with smooth yellow walls and a mesh of vine-covered trelliswork.
Arriving at dusk the previous evening, Hayward had been shown
to quarters in a far corner of the house. He had seen the pack
animals and the bundles stacked outside; he knew he was sharing
a house with Robert Shaw. Both men must have been strangely
nervous. After only that brief and ill-tempered meeting, long ago
and far away in the Chang Chenmo, each had surely completely
forgotten what the other looked like, yet both must have developed
a strong sense of the other's identity. It might even have occurred
to each man that the other had more than a few reasons to be furiously angry. Now, finally, it seemed that they were going to meet.
How would they react to one another? Would there be more of
that chilly distance? Would there be harsh words or even blows?
During the mild spring night, trying to sleep in separate corners
of the same farmhouse, both men must have wondered. But in the
gentle warmth of the morning, while Arghons, Ladakhis and Turkis
busily packed for the onward journey towards Leh, with both men
heavily bearded and doubtless rather sleek from the *dastar khan* diet,
they probably just laughed and embraced. It was, wrote Shaw, 'great
pleasure to meet with an Englishman again'.

Inevitably, even in the exuberant good mood of burgeoning
Anglo-Turki friendship, things had not unfolded exactly as promised. The envoy had been sent on alone, and Shaw had ridden
in style out of Kashgar on 9 April without either Hayward or
the Mirza. But after a final farewell interview with Yaqub Beg in
Yanghissar – which was a veritable orgy of effusive flattery on
the part of both men – Shaw heard that Hayward too was on the
road. He was, needless to say, completely unconcerned about the
fate of the Mirza.[7]

Hayward's own departure from Kashgar had come in the bright
sunlight 'so characteristic of the climate of Eastern Turkistan' on
13 April. The Kun Lun and the Pamirs were razor sharp against the
clear sky, and 'the grand display of mountain-masses around offered

an ample compensation for the long detention and delay which had been experienced'. It must have been a bittersweet view though: those were the very mountains that Hayward had come so far to explore; he had never reached them and now he was moving away in the opposite direction. He had far from abandoned his plans of 'penetrating to the Pamir', but he would have to go the long way around.

Still, 'It would be impossible for any scene in nature to surpass the vast grandeur of these mountains', Hayward wrote, 'as seen towering up like a gigantic wall, with the well-defined outline of their lofty summits cutting the clear azure of the sky'. That alone was surely worth something.

Making his own separate way east, Shaw too had felt that he seemed 'to have re-entered the world again, after our long seclusion'. His journal takes a jauntier note – though the rose-tinted spectacles he had worn on his outward journey had been lost somewhere during the months of detention. On the way into the country he had seemingly missed the large tracts of desert, so busy was he recording the bountiful fields of the oases; he had even claimed that there were 'no rags or appearance of poverty anywhere'. Now, a little jaded perhaps, he could see the dozens of beggars who lined the roads quite clearly.

Both Shaw and Hayward were delayed again in Yarkand, and once more they were not allowed to meet. But this time the delay had a comprehensible justification: the passes on the road up to Shahidulla and beyond towards Leh were still snowed up and passage for loaded animals was impossible. This outbound wait was much more bearable than the long weeks of uncertainty earlier in the year. The travellers were treated with civility and lavished with food and gifts. There was finally even some news of the missing half of Shaw's caravan – it had miraculously turned up in Shahidulla after apparently rattling around the Karakoram for the best part of six months.

Finally, at the beginning of May, word came that the passes were open. Caravans were reloaded, leave was taken of the Shagawal, and two parties set out from Yarkand on the same day, just a few hours apart. And then the next morning in that lovely farmhouse, they came together as one party.

East to Karghilik, south across the rising shingle plateau and into the camel-brown foothills, George Hayward and Robert Shaw rode together, filling in the long gaps in each man's knowledge of the other's experiences and sharing perspectives on incidents and happenings of the past months. They picnicked together and doled out medicine to sick villagers they met along the way, while the Yoozbashi – still accompanying them – told them tales of Turkic history.

One day the Yoozbashi peered over Hayward's shoulder as he was reading a book. He was, of course, unable to make any sense at all of the roman script, but he spotted one of the plates. It was a picture of a woman, some literary lovely. The Yoozbashi pointed to the image with a grin. 'This is some daughter of a Lord Sahib whom the Captain Sahib wanted to marry but was disappointed of,' he said. 'That is why he keeps her portrait.'

Whether Hayward appreciated the joke or not is unknown; perhaps he went off in a huff to do some surveying – for he was now hungrily taking all the bearings he had been unable to obtain in the more suspicious atmosphere of his first journey along the same road. The Yoozbashi seemed unconcerned about the Englishman apparently mapping out every inch of the country. He and Shaw would ride on ahead while Hayward scaled some ridge and fiddled with his compass. 'There he is, off again after some new road,' the Yoozbashi would say.

At the foot of the Sanju Pass on 18 June the Turki escort left them. They clearly had had enough of the mountains and had no intention of trudging all the way up to Shahidulla with their English charges. But the farewell from the Yoozbashi was a touchingly tearful one, and both Hayward and Shaw's last memory of Turkestan was one of kindness and generosity rather than of malicious prevarication.

The two men had been travelling together for over two weeks now, and perhaps, once the novelty of English conversation had worn off, a hint of the old animosity returned. Possibly Hayward's ceaseless surveying began to grate with Shaw, reminding him uncomfortably of his own lack of scientific credentials. Or perhaps the lumbering pace of Shaw's huge baggage train frustrated the fleet-footed Hayward. On 26 June, after passing quickly through Shahidulla, where Shaw picked up his stragglers, and heading due south along the Karakoram Pass road, they shook hands and went their separate ways at the junction of some narrow eastbound side valley near a campground called Chadartash.

Hayward suspected the side-pass would lead back to the valley of the Upper Karakash – the scene of his first real bout of exploration. Crossing it would let him link up all the country that he had mapped in these mountains. Shaw, meanwhile, simply wanted to press on as quickly as possible over the Karakoram Pass on the main summer trade route to Leh. In the event, as soon as he was free of Shaw's cumbersome caravan Hayward was travelling once more at his familiar scorching pace. He soon reached the Karakash, and within a couple of days was camped out in his old Happy Valley, Khush Maidan. He surveyed everything in sight, marched his best horses to death, blazed back across the Lingzi Thung in an unseasonable blizzard, and was actually back in Leh – and indeed gone from it on the road to the Punjab – before Shaw had even made it down from the Karakoram Pass.

But what the two travellers said to each other as they parted at Chadartash, or what they really thought of each other, remains in the realms of imagination and conjecture. That parting of the ways on that bright June morning – in a spot every bit as wild and desolate as that where they had first met a lifetime ago – brought to an end one of the strangest episodes, and one of the most strained relationships, in the history of British exploration in Asia. Two men, as radically different in background, outlook, aims and attitude as the luxury tourist and the backpacker, had by sheer chance entered the same unknown country at the same time, and had endured the same trials and uncertainties – together, but apart.

As their paths diverged Robert Shaw was riding towards a future that bore a startling resemblance to that that which Hayward had sketched for him in his caustic prediction in Kashgar.

Everything had changed in India while Shaw and Hayward were locked up in Turkestan. The masterly inactive Viceroy Lawrence had retired, and in his place had come the gruff Irish Conservative, Lord Mayo, a far less dovish politician. Missions and explorations beyond borders were suddenly in vogue once more, and Turkestan and the wildly romanticised person of Yaqub Beg had become topics of discussion in parliament and over suburban breakfast tables. Shaw – a live lion fresh from Central Asia no less – was all set for celebrity and riches.

The mid-nineteenth century was a boom time for travel writers. Anyone having completed a journey far less daring and dramatic than Shaw's was virtually guaranteed a bestseller, and every petty explorer on every glorified shooting trip was keeping a rather self-consciously publishable journal. Shaw did hurry back to England for a quick round of lionising and backslapping – but the bestseller would have to wait a year. First he had to fulfil another facet of Hayward's prophecy. Barely twelve months after his return, Shaw was heading back to Yarkand and Kashgar. This time he was not alone; Douglas Forsyth was with him, his official status no longer confining him under the new viceroy, as was a doctor called George Henderson. They were on official business – the first British envoys to the court of Yaqub Beg. Shaw had indeed been 'employed on a political mission in E. Turkestan'.

The mission was actually a failure politically; nothing was achieved, no treaties signed, no new trade mart founded. They never even met the king, but even if they had it is doubtful that they would have achieved success or made history. Yaqub Beg was, after all, merely a mercenary upstart, a warlord whose kingdom was built – quite literally – on sand. Serious negotiations with such people – as the Americans would find out in Afghanistan more than a century later – were worthless.[8]

But Shaw, still perhaps stung that the presence of the professional explorer, George Hayward, had exposed him as a total amateur during his first visit to Turkestan, had learnt to survey properly. On this second trip he mapped the head of the Shyok River. He had also learned how to travel hard and light, and the journey was a tough one. He won the RGS Gold Medal for the feat; his book was published to great acclaim – and he would always be 'the first Englishman into Yarkand'; no one could take that away from him.

For all his pomposity and occasional ridiculousness, for all that he could exaggerate, for all that he was bigoted and for all that he had treated Hayward unreasonably at times, little, puffing, wheezing Robert Shaw the tea planter had achieved remarkable things and made remarkable journeys. As well as recognising the need to know how to survey properly, perhaps he had learnt something else from George Hayward: that time is short, and that you must make the most of it. Shaw's time was not as short as Hayward's, but he was not destined for a venerable old age. In 1879 the 'rheumatic fever' finally caught up with him. He died in another outlandish and exotic country – Burma. He was just 39.

But leading his sluggish caravan onwards towards the Karakoram Pass that bright clear June morning, glancing back perhaps and seeing the smaller, leaner party bearing away uphill to the east, shifting gear, slipping into a faster pace, Robert Shaw still had a decade to live. George Hayward, hell-bent on fulfilling his own part of the prophecy, had little more than a year.

Notes

1 Incredibly, five years later, the crumbling Alexander Gardner, then in his very late eighties, did manage to get himself involved with Yaqub Beg. He was somehow tangled up as a facilitator in a dubious plot to covertly run rifles over the Himalayas from Srinagar to Kashgar, rifles that might just

have tipped the balance and made Yaqub Beg the founder of a lasting independent nation, rather than the flash-in-the-pan that he ultimately proved to be. However, the plot was scuppered at the last minute by a nervous British Government. It was a suitably murky end-piece to Gardner's life of remarkable roguery.

Even more incredibly, the late Victorian editor of Gardner's cursed journals reveals that sometime in this same twilight period of his shadowy life the old colonel fathered a daughter named Helena – though with whom he does not explain. Years later Helena returned to Kashmir for a holiday – as Mrs Botha – and was welcomed by her late father's old comrades. By then she apparently had a child of her own, a little boy who she had named Alexander. Somewhere out there the direct descendants of Colonel Alexander Gardner may still survive.

2   In fact, some five years before Hayward an Indian Muslim named Abdul Hamid working for the British Great Trigonometrical Survey of India had reached Yarkand in disguise and made what eventually proved to be a very accurate reading of its latitude. However, George Hayward was the first Englishman to have taken bearings in the city, and in the Victorian era that counted for everything.

3   Turkestan is generally spelt with an E these days, but in the nineteenth century there was no consistency. Robert Shaw had some sensible ideas about how to spell foreign words: deliberate alphabetical exoticism – *djinn* for *jin* and so on – was, he felt, pointless affectation; better to go for whatever most closely matched English standard spelling. He used 'Turkestan'. Hayward, however, like many others at the time, alternated between 'Turkistan' and 'Turkestan'.

4   Shaw too had heard this dubious legend and repeated it verbatim.

5   Large-scale merchant or trader – perhaps 'tycoon' is the best
     translation.

6   The Turkic conception of Britain as a compliant Kashmiri
     vassal was an amusing, if natural, misunderstanding, obviously
     based on authentic reports. While treaty-bound under the
     British, Kashmir was technically independent; and as a major
     princely state with ill-defined borders, the maharaja – as we
     shall see – was able to act with impunity in the more remote
     reaches of his territory. There were also still some restrictions
     on travel there for British citizens, and special dispensation
     was required for an Englishman wishing to stay year-round
     in the kingdom. And of course, there was something of an
     exodus of foreigners from the Vale of Kashmir in the autumn
     – it was the end of the tourist season.

7   With both Englishmen gone, the Mirza was left in misery.
     Like all the other travellers who arrived in the country, his
     chances of leaving were slim, and if Shaw wasn't going to save
     him then no one else would. However, the Mirza eventually
     managed to make a direct petition to the king, who appar-
     ently rather liked him. Finally, on 7 June, he was allowed to
     leave. He returned to Leh in the company of a band of would-
     be Hajj pilgrims, heading for the ports of India. He finally
     reached the GTS headquarters, and a delighted Montgomerie,
     in the early autumn. He had been away for over two years,
     had covered over 2,000 miles, surveying the entire route with
     remarkable accuracy, and had brought back insights about the
     state of Eastern Turkestan that benefited from the perspective
     of a Muslim who knew the culture of Central Asia well – far
     better than a tea planter or a Yorkshireman. It was an incred-
     ible achievement. When the write-up of the Mirza's journey
     was read at a meeting of the RGS, his 'pluck and endurance'
     was warmly praised. Had he not been a 'mere native' he
     would certainly have earned the society's Gold Medal.

After such a feat the Mirza might have been expected to
retire to some modest little house among the pine trees on
the ridges beyond Dehra Dun, but his own flame of insane
desire still burned. Three years later, well into his fifties, the
Mirza set out on another of Montgomerie's missions. This
time he was to plot the route to Bokhara. He passed through
the frontier and Kabul without incident, but sometime in
early 1872, somewhere on the road beyond Herat, he was
murdered in his sleep by his own guides.

8   Though Yaqub Beg would eventually extend his realm all the
way to the marches of Gansu, the Chinese pushed back just
as quickly. In 1877, while desperately trying to organise resist-
ance to the advance of Manchu armies back into the towns
on the northern side of the Taklamakan, Yaqub Beg died – by
poison, the rumours said. He had come a long way from a
petty fortress on the Jaxartes, and for a decade his star had
burned brightly. But by December 1878 the court in Kashgar,
where ten years earlier Shaw and Hayward had been received
and heard triumphant stories of Turkic victory, was full once
again of Chinese soldiers, reclining in their boots and eating
noodles with chopsticks.

1 'In the costume of a Chitral Chief Moda of Yassin': the only known photograph of George Hayward, more like some Greek god of carnage than a foppish Victorian dandy. The picture was presumably taken in Kashmir in early 1870 in the turbulent weeks before his final departure into the Western Himalayas. *Image courtesy of the Royal Geographical Society (with IBG)*

2 'From long habit a complete Oriental': the gloriously disreputable Colonel Alexander Gardner in old age, dressed in all his peculiar finery.

3 'The house in which they entertain
their friends so hospitably in the fort
of Yarkand': Hayward's watercolour of
the building in which he was confined
during his stay in the desert outpost.
On the reverse he scrawled a note, full
of bitter sarcasm, describing 'the way
they treat their guests in Turkistan'.
*Image courtesy of the Royal Geographical
Society (with IBG)*

4 'The greatest rascal in Asia':Yaqub
Beg, self-made King of Eastern
Turkestan who toyed with George
Hayward and Robert Shaw, keeping
them under house arrest in Kashgar
during the bleak winter of 1869.

| Mirza Beg, an Astori, (Sunni Muhammadan). | Ghulâm Muhammad, a Ghilghiti, (Shiah Muhammadan). | Dr. Leitner's Hindustani Munshi | Dr. Leitner | Kásim, from Skardo, (Little Tibet) | A Ghilâsi, (standing) Botchi, (a Bashgwit Kafir, sitting) | The man in the white dress is Mûlck, also a Kaldsha Kafir, subject of Chitrâl; the last man on the right is Ghafib Shah, a Ghilâsi. |

GROUP OF DARDS, &c.

5 Dr Gottlieb Leitner Etc. with his ragbag of Dardic house guests. A formidably talented linguist, passionate champion of the people of the Western Himalayas and an unbearable public nuisance, Leitner was the one man to back up Hayward's claims for the people of Yasin against the expansionism of the Maharaja of Kashmir. *Image courtesy of the Royal Geographical Society (with IBG)*

6 Modern Indian buses grinding over the Zoji La, the 3,528m pass that marks the gateway between Kashmir proper and the upland deserts of Ladakh and Baltistan. Hayward crossed it heading north towards Turkestan in 1868, and again a year later as he set out on his first winter journey towards Gilgit.

7 The Ladakhi capital, Leh. In the 1860s it was a key staging post on the India–Turkestan trading routes, the place to fit out a caravan and to bargain over camels and horses. While Robert Shaw frittered away the whole of the summer of 1868 in town, George Hayward was in and out inside a week.

8 'An interminable mass of mountains': the high peaks of the Kun Lun beyond the valley of the Tiznaf River. The Upper Yarkand, scene of Hayward's wild twenty-day escapade out of Shahidulla, lies beyond the first ridge of mountains. Today, as a sensitive Chinese borderland it is strictly off-limits for wandering foreigners.

9 'Just like public schoolboys, of boisterous spirits, but perfectly well bred': Uighurs, the descendants of Robert Shaw's fine Turki fellows, in modern Kashgar.

10 The author at Hayward's grave in the tiny Christian cemetery in the Pakistani mountain town of Gilgit.

11 A ramshackle city of wild polo matches and endless cups of tea: Gilgit in the twenty-first century.

12 The last remaining tower of Gohar Aman's fort in Yasin village, seat of Mir Wali. Hayward camped out in the garden beside the fort on both his visits to the valley.

13 'The Foreigner's Valley': the spot where George Hayward died. Fifth from left: Abdul Rashid; sixth from left: Mohamed Murad; fourth from right (holding baby): Badal Beg; and an assortment of young Darkotis at Feringhi Bar.

14 Darkot at the head of the Yasin Valley, as close as George Hayward ever got to the High Pamirs. The road to the Darkot Pass branches away to the right and Feringhi Bar, the spot where the explorer was killed, lies at the base of the steep slope on the left.

7

THE ROAD IS FULL OF STONES

The hall was noisy with the chatter of earnest voices, the rustle of papers and the screech of chairs shifting on a polished wooden floor. Outside the damp cold of a December evening in London would have cleared the streets of all but a few hackney cabs rattling through the smog, but here the lamps mounted on wood-panelled walls cast a warming glow on the bearded faces of the Fellows of the Royal Geographical Society, gathered for the fortnightly meeting. At the head of the great echoing room the dais was ready with chairs for the president and vice-president and a lectern for the speaker. In the audience respectable gentlemen in evening dress leafed through the programme and eagerly discussed pagan tribes in darkest Africa and 20,000ft Himalayan passes giving on to forbidden kingdoms. By the door the newspaper reporters shifted on their benches, polished their battered eyeglasses and fiddled with their notebooks. In another corner Dr Gottlieb Leitner, the diminutive German egomaniac with the etcetera after his name, was busily explaining the history and cultural particulars of Eastern Turkestan to anyone who would listen.

Every meeting of the RGS was an opportunity for Dr Leitner to pontificate, but this evening was a particularly exciting one for him. The meat of the proceedings would deal with territory that

he considered part of his own immodestly broad field of special-
ity. On the basis of his one forty-eight hour visit to Gilgit three
years earlier, Dr Leitner had appointed himself the pre-eminent
authority on all things Western Himalayan. He had, it must be
said, done a great deal to bring a very little-known corner of High
Asia to the attention of the British and Indian publics. He had
given a popular name to the knot of mountains west of Kashmir
and east of Afghanistan: Dardistan (a term borrowed and modified from ancient Greek geographers) and he had christened its
diverse peoples 'the Dards'. The terms are still used today, though
mostly only by linguists, which is appropriate enough for Leitner
could without doubt claim to be the first serious scholar of the
so-called Dardic languages.

Despite having barely dipped a toe into actual physical exploration of the region, he was, by the end of the 1860s, well on his
way to thoroughly demarcating its linguistic geography. He made
his Asian headquarters, the University of the Punjab in Lahore,
into a sort of YMCA (the C in this case standing for Central
Asia) for any wandering native who emerged from the mountains. By interviewing this ragbag of house guests tirelessly, he
not only knew precisely which languages were spoken in which
wildly remote valleys, he could actually speak many of them himself. Shina, Burushaski, Khowar – Dr Gottlieb Leitner Etc. could
quote native proverbs and folk songs in all of them.

But Leitner did not restrict himself to linguistics alone. He
considered himself the go-to man for any authoritative statement
on the history, culture or politics of the Western Himalayas. For
the next three decades he would continue to brew up this heady
cauldron of very real knowledge and expertise mixed with unrestrained and spectacular self-importance. As the century wore on
and the floodlights of the Great Game were cast ever more on
the mountain country around Gilgit he would make himself a
very public nuisance, firing off unsolicited letters to newspapers
and unrequested reports to politicians, and making enraged statements in meetings of the various societies of which he was a

member. Why were the authorities not listening to him? If only the Government of India would take his advice, then their dealings with the Dards would run a lot more smoothly.

The sad truth is that he was probably right, but on 13 December 1869 the RGS met in London, the Raj had yet to deal with Dards. Instead the evening would be, Dr Leitner surely hoped, another opportunity for him to demonstrate his wisdom. Eastern Turkestan was by no means part of the doctor's Dardistan and nor were its people Dards, but such considerations mattered little. Leitner was perfectly happy to regard anywhere that bordered on or shared some loose connection with the Western Himalayas as coming under his self-granted remit. Afghanistan, Kashmir, the Pamirs and the Kirghiz country, even, by way of some tenuous suggested link, the mountains of Lebanon: you need look no further than Dr Leitner for anything you wanted to know. And of course, he had a great deal to say about Eastern Turkestan. In fact, just a couple of weeks earlier he had actually presented a real live native of Yarkand, plucked from his Lahore menagerie, to another meeting of the RGS (presenting baffled Central Asians to equally baffled English audiences was one of Leitner's specialities). To be fair, on that cold December evening in London he probably did know more about Yarkand and Kashgar than anyone else in the room, for the real hero of the hour was absent, thousands of miles away in Asia.

But now the meeting was about to begin; the conclusion of Dr Leitner's detailed explanation to some unfortunate Fellow of the precise difference between the Dardic and Turkic language groups would have to wait. With a final shuffling of papers and squeaking of chairs, the secretary declared the session open. Notices were read, a few procedural matters taken care of and an overview given of the latest news from various RGS-sponsored expeditions currently in the field. And then it was time for the highlight of the evening, something the Fellows had been eagerly anticipating for more than a year. The secretary took to the lectern, read an introductory letter penned in Murree three months earlier, and then, with a sip of water and a gentle clearing of his throat, he announced that he would now read a most interesting report that the society had recently received from one of its men in the field. The audience edged forward in their seats; the secretary began:

> I arrived at Leh, the capital of Ladak, on the 21st of September 1868, having left Murree in the Punjab on the 26th of August …

It was heady stuff, and the Fellows listened, rapt. Intensely cold winds whipped across elevated plateaus; temperatures dropped far below zero; pack animals died; unknown passes were crossed; a promising new trade route scouted out; and the work of a previous mapmaker politely discredited. Suspicious Asiatics were encountered; an unmapped river mapped to its source; unapproachable cities approached; and, ultimately, a successful return made from the country from which no one returns. Even the sparse, restrained prose read in the clipped tones of the secretary could not hide the excitement of it all, and when the author allowed himself some full description of the mountain scenery his enthusiasm and his intensity showed through. In the final excerpt he even let the visage of the high Kun Lun prompt him to quote the flowery eighteenth-century poet Alexander Pope:

> Eternal snows the growing mass supply,
> Till the bright mountains prop the incumbent sky
> As Atlas fixed each hoary pile appears,
> The gather'd winter of a thousand years.

Such an indulgent digression was not the stuff of serious geography, but so impressed were the Fellows by everything else they had heard that they hardly cared. George Hayward had done the RGS proud; he had exceeded expectations, and any doubts that had been raised twelve months earlier about his lack of qualifications and his questionable background would have been roundly quashed.

When the secretary had finished and meekly stepped down from the spot-lit lectern, the president, Sir Roderick Murchison, rose to address the sea of geographers. This, he said with utter conviction, was 'a communication of the very highest merit'. Hayward had achieved remarkable things 'under the greatest difficulties in the wildest and most inaccessible of countries, inhabited by Mussulmen, many of whom would have put him to death had they detected him making astronomical observations'.

Who, Murchison asked the appreciative hall, when thinking back on earlier tentative expeditions into the Karakoram, 'who, I say, could then have thought that the day would soon arrive when these savage territories, extending northward from the frontiers of Kashmir, would be so thoroughly explored and surveyed as they have now been by Mr George Hayward?' The president was in a state of geographical ecstasy. The High Pamirs were, for the moment, completely forgotten. Even if Hayward never mapped another valley, never surveyed another peak, he had 'already entitled himself to the highest honour we can bestow upon him'. Murchison even gave way to ludicrous hyperbole and described Hayward's very ordinary watercolours as the 'most exquisite artistic sketches' – though rather more reasonably he also said that Hayward was a 'ready and attractive writer'.

The mood of the evening was celebratory, Murchison's speech was gushing, and there was every reason to hope for more great things from George Hayward in the future, for he was still in the field. But in expressing this last sentiment, Murchison said a very strange and slightly unsettling thing: Hayward's courage and ability were great, he said, 'and I firmly believe that if his life be spared, he will terminate his researches by a thorough delineation of the geography of the wild Pamir Steppe'.

If his life be spared …

Of course, all the explorers who ventured into the wild in Asia or Africa were taking enormous risks: disease, accident, a poisoned arrow or sharp spear; there was no comprehensive travel insurance policy in the nineteenth century. But this was an era when upper lips were at their stiffest – you simply didn't mention such dreadful possibilities. Britannia ruled the waves and a good deal else besides; an Englishman's life was sacred, and even to suggest otherwise was to indulge in that most unmanly and Cassandraesque of crimes – 'croaking'.

But, if his life be spared, even this early, thousands of miles away in London, something, some hinted scent of disaster, some ghost-touch chill down the spine lingered around the letters and papers that Hayward had sent back to the RGS. For it was true that from the moment he returned to India from Eastern Turkestan a dark shadow seemed to hang over him; his insane desire had intensified, tightened its grip, and bared his throat for the waiting cold steel. The months in the mountains had left him leaner and gaunter than ever, and when he left the room in Murree where he had hurriedly written up the report and finished his maps and route tables, those who can sense an aura – dogs and children and some holy men – would have crossed the street to get away from him as he approached. George Hayward was a dead man walking, and perhaps, just perhaps, Sir Roderick Murchison suspected as much.

But if any of the Fellows glanced uneasily at one another as they heard the president's ominous remark nothing was said to spoil the mood. When Murchison stepped down from the podium his deputy, Sir Henry Rawlinson, rose and gave some equally complimentary if slightly less effusive comments of his own about Hayward's paper. A few queries rose from the audience, and then, before anyone could escape, Dr Leitner came strutting to the stage to offer his authoritative and exhaustive explanation of the manufacture and use of several Yarkandi trinkets that Hayward had sent back to England. And with that the meeting was adjourned until January. A hubbub of voices rose, chairs scraped again against the floor, the Fellows wished one another season's greetings and traipsed out of the hall and on to the cold, damp street where the lamps of the hackney carriages gleamed in the heavy mist.

That same evening, thousands of miles away to the east, George Hayward himself was camped out in the bitter cold, somewhere in the wild mountains that surround the upper reaches of the Indus River, on his way to his own fateful dealings with the Dards.

It had been late summer by the time Hayward had made it down to the Punjabi plains from Ladakh on his return from Eastern Turkestan. Winter, with its snowfalls and closed passes, was already preparing to descend on the Western Himalayas, and though the brief, copper-gold Indian summer is the most heart-breakingly beautiful time to travel in the high mountains, it is a time of transience and no season to be setting out on a lengthy expedition. Hayward knew this, and he must have realised that he had little realistic chance of advancing on the Pamirs until the early summer of the following year. He also had to spend time putting his papers in order and forwarding them to the RGS. He would have been quite justified in booking himself a passage to Southampton and spending the winter months being celebrated by an adoring British public and writing a bestselling travel book before returning to India in the spring with, in practice, no time wasted. But such a course of action was for Hayward unthink-able. An endless round of lavish, celebratory dinners in London clubs – 'Another brandy old chap? Now tell me again about these Mohammedan customs' – would have gnawed at his impatient soul every bit as much as house arrest in Kashgar. His consuming sense of urgency, his ever-faster ticking clock would have allowed him no such interlude. And what was more, despite the celebra-tions of the RGS, for Hayward the Eastern Turkestan journey had been a failure. He was clearly concerned that Rawlinson and Murchison too might be disappointed with him for having failed to reach the Pamirs, and in the letters he sent back from India in 1869 he was ever anxious to assure them that he really had tried his best.

'It was simply not possible to get to the Pamir from the plain country though you will no doubt be struck with the fact of my having got so near and not attempted to do so,' he wrote apologetically in his very first letter back to Rawlinson. 'Had the slightest opportunity offered itself I should at once have availed myself of it,' Hayward assured him, but even had such a chance arisen he doubted that success was possible thanks to the hordes of marauding Kirghiz who haunted the north-east flanks of the Pamirs. Two months later he was still needlessly pressing the same apologetic point to Sir Roderick Murchison. 'I have been much disappointed in not being able to effect my original intention of returning to India from Yarkand via the Pamir and Chitral. I found every effort to get away in that direction quite useless,' he wrote in early September. Even Murchison and Rawlinson's repeated assurances that he had acquitted himself admirably were of little comfort; as far as George Hayward was concerned he had failed, and failure only doubled his determination. The Pamirs and the source of the Oxus were still waiting; they had to be conquered, and nothing so trivial as a Himalayan winter could be allowed to get in the way.

Coming down through the Chang Chenmo towards Leh in July, the next course of action seemed to crystallise in Hayward's mind. Trudging south he had obviously remembered the legendary journey that Colonel Alexander Gardner claimed to have made in the same direction forty years earlier. When Gardner reached Kashmir after crossing the Karakoram, instead of going south to India, he had blazed due west through the mountains, beating the bounds of Baltistan, grappling with Gilgit and charging through Chitral. True, from the pagan uplands of Kafiristan[1] Gardner had branched away towards Kandahar in Afghanistan, but Chitral and Kafiristan were within striking distance of the Pamirs. This, then, was where Hayward would go.

By the time he reached Leh the plan was already fully formed and he wrote to Rawlinson from there:

> I am now advancing for a fresh start for the Pamir via Gilgit and
> Chitral, or Hunza and Nagar … I am very sanguine of succeeding
> in my next journey. After crossing the Hunza passes I believe that
> reaching the Karakul[2] is simply a matter of supplies and perseverance.

Hayward had perseverance aplenty, and he headed south through
Kashmir in August, passing the junction of the road to Gilgit
across the Burzil Pass and the bleak Deosai Plateau. He realised
that snow would have blocked this route long before he had time
to complete his reports and maps and get back to the mountains,
and frustration must have knotted in the pit of his stomach. Had
he had no other responsibilities he would have headed that way
immediately. But as it was he hurried on down through the foothills and reached Murree at the end of August. He had no time
for fraternising with old army comrades and instead got straight
to work. By 11 September he was ready to send his maps and
papers to London. In the accompanying note to Murchison he
explained the seemingly patchy appearance of the map:

> No attempt, as you will observe, has been made to fill in the country
> situated at any distance from the line of route which has not been
> personally explored and surveyed … I wish to be able to maintain
> its general accuracy, in preference to filling in uncertain details of
> country, which might be found incorrect by future explorers.

Hayward would not repeat Johnson's mistakes. He also let the
RGS know that he had made his journeys 'with a thorough liking
for the work in hand, and a determination to do my best', and he
assured them yet again that he was still doggedly heading for his
ultimate prize – the Pamirs.

Two days later he penned another note to Murchison, this one
determinedly political. News of the turn of events that had actually prompted his and Shaw's release from Kashgar – the Russian
snub of Yaqub Beg – had by now reached India. With this devel-
opment, and with the ever-increasing Russian dominance in

Central Asia, Hayward felt sure that the tsar's troops would soon sweep down into Eastern Turkestan. 'There can be little doubt that we shall soon have the Russians for our neighbours across the Karakoram,' he wrote. This all gave an extra impetus to his urgency: from Kashgar Russian mapmakers would surely lunge determinedly at the Pamirs, Kirghiz bandits notwithstanding.[3] 'Hoping a Britisher may yet be the first to bag the Bam-i-dunya,' Hayward wrote with a certain degree of jaunty arrogance.

While he was in Murree Hayward also opened his first – and his last – friendly dealings with the British Government of India. With Lord Mayo newly installed on the viceroy's throne, the political climate had changed: there would be no more 'masterly inactivity', and there was a great deal of new interest in Eastern Turkestan and the Western Himalayas. At the request of T.H. Thornton, secretary of the British Lieutenant-Governor of the Punjab, Hayward drew up a memorandum giving details of all the major trade routes across the Karakoram towards Yarkand. He also provided copies of his maps and route tables. Thornton forwarded these to the viceroy, who then passed them on to an even higher authority – the Secretary of State for India in London, the Duke of Argyll.

Hayward had long complained of the scant assistance he received from the government. His lack of status in Eastern Turkestan had been the source of many of his problems there, he believed, and on his next journey too a little official support would serve him very well indeed. 'A friendly letter from the Indian Government to the Emeer of Badakhshan without expressing the slightest political import would enable me to explore the whole of the Pamir and dispel much risk and anxiety,' he had written to Rawlinson in July, though he added that he was deeply pessimistic about obtaining such a missive.

Now he applied again to the government for some kind of official backing. Again his request was declined, but he was graciously thanked for his maps and memorandum, and the viceroy, Lord Mayo, quietly let him know that while Hayward could never expect open support, he himself would look favourably on a successful exploration by a civilian of the mountains of Central Asia. Hayward had also written to Thomas Montgomerie of the Great Trigonometrical Survey, spymaster of the Pundits and employer of Mirza Shuja. Montgomerie, always a maverick as a state employee, let Hayward know that he too would look very favourably on such a journey, though there was little he could do actively to help: he had enough trouble steering his own local explorers through provincial obfuscation and bureaucracy to get across the frontier.

Still, even without the direct backing of the government, Hayward had his own stock of intense determination to rely on. And he also hoped that he would be able to gain support from another quarter – support that would have a much more direct bearing on the immediate success of the early stages of his planned journey. On 21 October, with news of the first snows already coming down from the mountains, Hayward wrote a quick note to Murchison from the garrison town of Rawalpindi (today the unruly sibling of the modern Pakistani capital). He was about to leave for Kashmir, he said, where he hoped 'to be able to obtain the assistance I wish from the Kashmir Government'.

Over the coming months Hayward's letters would take on an almost schizophrenic tone. His opinions of the Indian Government, of the Maharaja of Kashmir and of his own prospects of success would lurch back and forth from bright optimism to bitter pessimism. Sometimes he felt assured of success and support; at other times it seemed that everyone was out to get him – and always the Pamirs loomed darker and darker on the northwest horizon. But for now things looked reasonably bright. He made no mention of the advancing winter or the vexing question of how exactly he would get to Gilgit at such a late season – even if Kashmiri permission was forthcoming. The difficulties were no doubt great, he wrote to Murchison, 'but still success is very far from impossible'. And with that Hayward headed for the hills, just as the last of the holidaymakers and sportsmen were coming down in the opposite direction.

Autumn days are clear in Kashmir. As Hayward made his way up through the Siwalik Hills, across the roaring grey gorge of the Chenab River and onwards and upwards to the cusp of the Vale of Kashmir, there would have been frosty mornings and snatched glimpses of high snow peaks, blazing to the north in the light of dawn. And then, dropping from the heights into the vale itself, the wheat fields would have been a buzz-cut of golden stubble and the roads burnished with stands of yellowing poplars. Srinagar would have been deserted of Europeans except for the handful with dispensation for permanent residence: Colonel Alexander Gardner, the Resident and a few others. Dal Lake would have been a shining mirror, reflecting the dustings of new snow on the mountains that ringed the valley; and in the Mughal gardens the flower beds would have been bare, the great chenar trees beginning to shed their coppery leaves. Even the maharaja would have been preparing for the shift to his winter seat in Jammu, though for now he still idled in his summer palace on the banks of the Jhelum River.

Hayward knew Srinagar well, and had of course travelled extensively in Kashmir long before he ever presented himself to Henry Rawlinson in search of active employment. But he had never tried to venture into such testy territory as that towards which he now aimed, and he had never had to appeal directly to the maharaja for protection before.

The man enjoying the last days of the fading summer in that palace beside the Jhelum was the second Maharaja of Jammu and Kashmir, Ranbir Singh. Tall and bearded, he had been placed on the throne a decade earlier by his own dying father, Gulab Singh, to avoid any succession disputes. Ranbir Singh was reputed to be thoroughly chauvinistic about his Hindu faith. On hearing from various temple priests that his father had been reincarnated as a fish – surely a massive karmic downgrade for a maharaja – Ranbir ordered that no fish were to be killed anywhere in the kingdom. In a land of lakes and rivers fish was a staple food; every morning for generations boatmen had paddled out over the waterweeds of Dal Lake to cast their nets in search of *mahseer*, the succulent, white-fleshed carp of the Himalayan waterways. The ruling – which came on top of a Hindu ban on cow-killing that applied even to beef-eating Muslims – caused enormous distress amongst the peasantry. On seeing that what they may have meant as a subtle criticism had sailed way over the royal head, the priests hurriedly declared that Gulab Singh had already shed his scales and moved on to some other body.

This was a particularly extreme example, but the lot of the maharaja's Muslim subjects was not a very happy one. The ruling coterie were Dogra Hindus with ancestors from Rajasthan. They shared no common heritage, culture, religion or indeed sympathy with the Kashmiri masses. The journalist Andrew Wilson, who visited Kashmir a couple of years after Hayward, noted that 'every common soldier of the Maharaja of Kashmir felt himself enti-tled to beat and plunder the country people'. Several decades later, under the third maharaja, things would be little different, and another British visitor would note that the only people in Kashmir who approved of the situation were 'that small body of Hindoos from which the officials are selected – corrupt even for Oriental officials – who grind down the unfortunate Mussulman peasantry with their outrageous rapacity and with the forced labour which they extract'. More than a few Kashmiris would argue that nothing has changed even today.

All of this did prompt a fair amount of criticism from British visitors to the valley in the nineteenth century. But the usual bug-bear for Englishmen holidaying in the Himalayas was not the abuse of the inhabitants, but what they viewed as the far more outrageous mistreatment of their own sacred selves. The maharaja was a treaty-bound British vassal, yet British citizens visiting his kingdom found themselves tangled in the kind of red tape that blights foreign tourists in despotisms and communist relics today. There was even a printed list of unhappy restrictions for tourists hoping to take in the beauty of the Kashmiri lakes and mountains. No Englishman could own property there; no one could stay year round. While Asians of all types could come and go as they pleased, British visitors could only enter the valley by four of the many available routes; could only camp at precisely defined spots; and could not engage mules or porters along the way. According to Rule XV: 'Officers are not allowed to take away with them, either in their service, or with their camps, any subjects of the Maharaja, without obtaining permission and a passport from the authorities.' A well-worn story in Punjab mess halls told of how a smitten British soldier found perhaps one of the last true beauties in Kashmir not sold to down-country brothels and harems, and attempted to smuggle the damsel in question out of the valley in a wicker basket. The kohl-eyed contraband was unfortunately detected at the border and the young officer went back to the plains alone with a broken heart.

Another rule, number XVI, stated that a British visitor was responsible for any debts incurred by his servants, while Rule XVII declared that 'Presents of every description must be rigidly refused'. Anyone who transgressed against this raft of regulations and took so much as a single souvenir from a well-meaning Kashmiri could be summarily expelled from the kingdom.

For many of India's British residents this was all utterly outrageous. According to his treaty terms the maharaja was to 'acknowledge the supremacy of the British Government', yet British citizens were treated like some kind of criminal pariahs in his realm, and worse yet – the rules in question were actually drawn up and administered by the British Government of neighbouring Punjab. True, the maharaja was one of the grandest and most important of all British signatories, but even those other twenty-one-gun salute-worthy Indian royals like the Nizam of Hyderabad would not have been allowed such liberties. The truth, of course, was that the maharaja's territory was not only one of the biggest of India's princely states; it was also by far the most geopolitically important. For the British rulers of the Raj keeping the Dogra sweet was far more important than soothing the sensitivities of a few blustering holidaymakers.

George Hayward had never had cause to complain about the maharaja in the past. He had never tried to buy a lakeside villa in Srinagar or to smuggle a Kashmiri maiden out of the country in a basket; permission had always been granted for shooting expeditions, and the Kashmir Government had thrown no obstacles in the way of his previous journey north through Ladakh. But now he was hoping to travel in far more troubled country.

West of Kashmir lay Dardistan, intellectual property of Dr Gottlieb Leitner. It was all wild country which, when every blank space on the map was filled in, would eventually prove to hold eight of the world's twenty highest mountains. The people who inhabited the deep valleys between these soaring summits were Muslims almost to a man, but they were not Kashmiris. They spoke a great diversity of languages and were much given to warfare. To the north their country was bounded by Yaqub Beg's Turkestan; to the south-west by the Pashtun hills of the frontier; and in the far west by pagan Kafiristan and the Pamirs. Within Dardistan lay such fearful fiefdoms as Hunza and Chitral, but in the east Dardistan ran into Kashmir.

Gulab Singh had seized Baltistan (the people of which had a much-diluted Tibetan language and ethnicity but a Shia Muslim faith) to the immediate north-west of the valley even before he had been granted Kashmir itself. Now his son was apparently extending his territory further west into Dard country. Gilgit, a much chewed-over bone of contention on the brink of terra incognita, was home to a Dogra garrison.

The cause of the problems and later controversies in the west of the Kashmiri realm was that no one, least of all the maharaja himself, knew where his official border was supposed to lie. According to the terms under which the British had handed him the country, Kashmir consisted of 'all of the hilly or mountainous country, with its dependencies, situated eastward of the River Indus and westward of the river Ravee'. This all sounds quite reasonable until you glance at a modern map and realise that for much of its course through the mountains the Indus flows east–west, not north–south. Deciding what lay 'east' of it was largely impossible.[4] This made the maharaja's claims to Ladakh and Baltistan – through which the Indus flows towards the sunset – difficult to argue against on treaty grounds, but the Indus did make an abrupt southern turn just before Gilgit. Gilgit lay indisputably on its western shore. The maharaja clearly shouldn't have been meddling there, and it seemed rather unlikely that he would be enthusiastic about a wandering Englishman going through that way and seeing what his soldiers were up to. The last foreigner to do so had been Dr Leitner, and he had done little but complain about Kashmiri policy ever since.

But perhaps the benign autumn weather had dulled the usually prickly senses of the Kashmiri court, or perhaps the maharaja was preoccupied in pondering the current transmigratory location of his deceased father's soul, for to Hayward's delight the Dogras seemed to offer all the help and enthusiasm that had been so aggravatingly unforthcoming from the British. He met Ranbir Singh in his riverside palace, and the maharaja insisted that he was welcome to travel to Gilgit and could be assured of royal protection as far as there. He did make it clear that beyond that final garrison Hayward would be on his own, and amongst tribes with the most atrocious reputation, but the maharaja would not stop him trying to go there.

Hayward had already heard all these bloodcurdling stories of dastardly Dards from other Kashmiri officials, and plenty of people in Srinagar had done their best to dissuade him from travelling that way. One of the maharaja's English employees, the state geologist Frederick Drew, a man who Hayward got on with well and who would later play a key role in the sad epilogue of his story, had introduced him to Kashmiris who claimed knowledge of the Dards of Yasin and Chitral and had cautionary tales of treachery to tell. But what none of these naysayers realised was that for George Hayward danger, near-impossibility and prophesies of doom were encouraging rather than disheartening. And in any case, he could see no other possible route to the Pamirs. They were, he had written, a 'closed letter' from the plains of Eastern Turkestan; the direct route through the frontier north of Peshawar would remain off limits and short of somehow getting into Russia and approaching from the west, there was no other option than to go through Gilgit. At least the maharaja would help him get that far.

He had had other help too. The RGS were so delighted with his work in Turkestan that they had voted him another £300, and the Indian Government, in gratitude for the map and memorandum, had given him a bursary of a further £100. These were serious sums of money and would be more than enough to see him to the Pamirs and beyond. The government had also agreed to provide him with a full set of new surveying equipment, complete with spares. If he was to drop another sextant on some high ridge in the Hindu Kush, and be less fortunate than he had been at Khush Maidan, then there would be a replacement waiting back at camp.

While he waited for this equipment to be sent up from the Mathematical Instrument Department in far-off Calcutta, Hayward fitted out his expedition. It was slightly better equipped than the Turkestan foray: for one, he now had a tent and some folding camp furniture, and he carried sundry gifts and trinkets to appease any suspicious tribal chiefs met along the way. But it was still no grand caravan, and Hayward's permanent staff (as opposed to local porters recruited along the way) amounted to only five men. Once again, as with his first journey, Hayward felt it completely unnecessary to record the names or natures of any of these companions in his letters. Hayward's munshi was apparently Kashmiri (which would, of course, have necessitated special permission from the maharaja's government under Rule XV of the travellers' regulations), but at least two of his other staff were Pashtuns.

The Pashtuns, known to the British as Pathans, were the men of the North-West Frontier. The 'worthy adversaries' of the young British soldier, they were subdivided into warring clans with piratical names: the Afridis, the Mahsuds, the Yusufzai, the Wazirs. Today their country sprawls across the imaginary border of Afghanistan and Pakistan and from their ranks rise the Taliban and the other wolves that harry the fringes of the subcontinent. They were, according to Mirza Shuja – himself a Central Asian Muslim rather than a British bigot – 'a very lawless race, and much addicted to highway robbery'. They were also often claimed to be among the least trustworthy people in Asia. 'Trust a Brahmin before a snake, and a snake before an harlot, and an harlot before a Pathan,' says Kim, the namesake of Rudyard Kipling's novel. Many would have agreed, but the Pashtuns were also bound by a fierce honour code in which pride, bravery, hospitality and revenge were the central tenets. And they were very tough. Clearly the Pashtuns were George Hayward's kind of people (he had started his first journey disguised as one after all); he just never bothered to record their names.

We do have one tantalising – and alarming – glimpse of the identity of one of these wild frontiersmen who were with him on his last journeys. A couple of years earlier, before the Mirza had abandoned his teaching post in Kabul and returned to India to join the Pundits, Montgomerie and his superior at the GTS, General Walker, had recruited several men from the Peshawar region for possible explorations in Afghanistan and beyond. One of them was handed over for training to the greatest of all Montgomerie's Pundits, Nain Singh from the Kumaon Himalayas. At first all went well and the Pashtun seemed to have some aptitude for surveying. But then, giving in to that 'addiction to robbery', he stole the gold watch which the RGS had awarded to Nain Singh for his travels in Tibet.[5] The Pashtun was abruptly kicked out of the survey's headquarters, and according to General Walker, 'the last thing we heard of him was that he had attached himself to the unfortunate Mr. Hayward'; he was with him until the end. With this party of rascal Pashtuns, one of them a known criminal, and with Hayward himself still lean and bearded from his earlier journey, never had a more disreputable looking party of explorers set out into the Western Himalayas.

Finally, in mid-November, the surveying equipment arrived from Calcutta and Hayward was ready to start. Winter was far advanced in the mountains and the journey was sure to be a dreadful one. But the insane desire was burning, and Hayward was full of enthusiasm. On 17 November, the day before he set out from Srinagar, he wrote to Sir Roderick Murchison at the RGS.

'I am leaving here for Gilgit to-morrow, in the hope of being able to penetrate to the Pamir Steppe and the source of the Oxus from that frontier,' he wrote. He had, he assured Murchison, had much assistance from the Kashmiri Government, and 'great credit will be due to the maharaja for his kindness and consideration'. Within a couple of months Hayward would be talking of his 'bitter enmity' for this same ruler, but for now all was well despite the fact that 'the officials here maintain the risk to be great, and give a very bad character to the tribes inhabiting the head of the Gilgit and Yassin valleys'.[6] Hayward accepted that there might be some truth in these wicked rumours, but nothing would stop him trying:

> Although not so fanatical as the Mahomedans further westward,[7] they are sufficiently untrustworthy to render success very doubtful, and it is quite possible that I may be a second time foiled in my attempt to penetrate to the Pamir … The danger is certainly great, but I trust that, by taking every precaution and feeling the way carefully before advancing, it may be reduced to a minimum.

Hayward also had warm words for the Indian Government. Someone had obviously gently explained exactly why they couldn't offer him their open backing: 'It would be impolitic to accord me any official recognition and sanction, and so run the risk of complications with the frontier tribes.' But Hayward was delighted with the £100 and the equipment they had given him; he could ask for nothing more. He admitted to Murchison that the season was now very late, and was quite prepared for the possibility of a winter in Gilgit waiting for the onward passes to open

– not that he would idle away any time he had to spend there: 'Much ground might be accounted for between the Indus and the passes.' He still believed that reaching Lake Karakul would be 'a comparatively easy task', and had high hopes of making it that far by early May. From there, 'alone in the heart of Central Asia', he might continue towards Russian territory, or perhaps swing back east through Afghan country. He was, he told Murchison, confident of 'securing valuable scientific results'.

He signed off the letter asking to be remembered to the Fellows of the society, and warning that postal communication from Gilgit and beyond would likely prove impossible. It was, all things considered, a remarkably positive letter. For once Hayward felt that people were behind him; the maharaja and the government had taken a positive interest, and the funds he had received counted for more than a little.

Such happy considerations should have provided a warming glow to see him through the snows as far as Gilgit, but then something happened. Sometime later that same day, as final preparations were being made for a morning departure, as bags were being packed and bundles tied and the afternoon sun was slanting west across the Vale of Kashmir, someone must have come to see him. Someone must have summoned him back to the palace, where the maharaja and his officials seemed suddenly to have woken from their lackadaisical slumbers. When Murchison received the letter in London, weeks later, he found a single extra sheet, written on both sides in a tight, urgent hand, clipped to its final page:

> The Kashmir Government is trying to dissuade me from going via Gilgit, not wishing an Englishman to see the exact state of that frontier. The dangers are, I think, exaggerated by the Kashmir officials, and I feel certain that every obstacle will be thrown in the way of proceeding beyond the Gilgit frontier. I shall find it very difficult to communicate with the Yassin or Hunza and Nagar people. The maharaja has himself told me that only lately the Hunza people have made a raid and burnt some of his villages, and

yesterday the news was received here that the Kashmir commandant of the Gilgit district had caught half-a-dozen of the Hunza
folks, had mutilated them and then killed them, so that reprisals
seem certain. It is impossible to say how an Englishman may be
received, or even if they would allow him to come on. Even then
he might not be allowed to proceed beyond Yassin or Hunza, and
thus the prospect of being able to penetrate to the Pamir seems
limited … I believe that I shall eventually succeed in the object of
my labours, but it may take months, nay, years, to do so.

And with that ominous note, Hayward and his Pashtuns disappeared into the mountains.

In a favourable season the standard journey time from Srinagar
to Gilgit was twenty-two days. Hayward, with his penchant for
double marches and disregard for sleep, could probably have done
it in little more than a week. He wrote nothing of his outward
journey from Srinagar late in 1869 so there are none of the hints
of hardship that pepper his report of explorations on the Karakash
and the Upper Yarkand. But that the usual three-week journey
took him well over two months says enough: this would have
been another horrific ordeal in murderous conditions.

By the time he set out on 18 November the Burzil Pass was
barred with huge drifts of icy snow and the Deosai Plateau, a
Sound of Music upland of butterflies and wildflowers in summer,
was now a blizzard-swept waste. Hayward would have to go the
long way round, a journey of 383 miles – and not one of them
easy. He headed north out of the Kashmiri capital, leaving the lake
and the dissuasive courtiers behind, and skirted the valley's eastern
mountain wall. Beyond Manasbal Lake he turned east, following
the same mountain route he had taken to Leh in an easier season
the year before. Even in August it was a wildly exposed road; in
late November it would have been positively evil.

Crossing the Zoji La, Hayward and his men slipped beneath the trans-Himalayan rain-shadow. There were no more fading chenars or golden wheat fields; this was a broken, up-thrown desert of fractured rock and jagged peaks. Hayward dropped towards the icy upper reaches of the Indus. Here in the high country west of Ladakh the great classical river that gave its name to the sub-continent is a grim torrent full of glacial dirt, the colour of old bathwater. Here and there it manages to push the mountains back far enough to allow a few relaxed meanders between empty banks of dust and shingle, but for most of its course the Indus roars furiously between sheer flanks of cold rock. A journey this way often entailed as much rock-climbing as trekking, but with ever heavier snowfalls higher up, cleaving to the river was the only way Hayward could see through the mountains.

The course of the Indus bore him into Baltistan, sometimes known as Little Tibet. Here there were white villages with flat roofs and ibex horns above the doorways in a landscape like broken builder's rubble. On the northern shore the snouts of great glaciers – the longest in the world outside Antarctica – pushed down towards the river. Beyond them rose a great army of monstrous peaks with evil names, towering to 25,000ft: Gasherbrum and Masherbrum, which would kill dozens of climbers in the future years of mountaineering. Hidden amongst them was the huge 'Snowy Peak' that Hayward had spotted twelve months earlier from a chilly outcrop far to the north: K2.

Struggling into Skardu, the capital of Baltistan with its forbidding fortress on a high outcrop, the going would have eased for a few days. Here the mountains fell back a little and the Baltis – once an independent people, but long subjugated by the Dogras – scraped out an existence along irrigation channels over the grey alluvium left by the Indus' wanderings. Hayward would have found a few meagre supplies in the bazaar, a little gritty flour and stale rice, and perhaps he could have slept for a few nights under a roof rather than beneath flapping canvas. But Skardu was still a grim place where dirty snow would have fallen most days, and when it didn't grey dust-devils would have come pirouetting over the barren floodplain and along the frozen alleyways of the town.

Beyond Skardu the geography was even more extreme. After its meandering interlude, the Indus plunged again into the narrowest of gorges. No one lived here; no one travelled here. Walls of rock, sometimes extending improbably beyond the vertical, loomed on either side, rising on the left towards the Great Himalaya's monstrous western buttress, Nanga Parbat, the Naked Mountain, and on the right towards Hunza's huge attendants. As Hayward and his men scrambled along ledges less than a hand's breadth across they would have often had to avoid showers of pebbles, rocks and even huge boulders pouring from the unstable slopes above. Elsewhere they would have found the cliff face simply too sheer to continue, and would have been forced back in search of some other goat's trail to follow. And on top of all of that it would have been bitterly cold, and finding a ledge or a patch of gravel wide enough to pitch the tent would often have proved impossible.

Christmas and the closing of the decade were passed uncelebrated somewhere along the way, and finally, on a bitter day in late January, Hayward reached the meagre hamlet of Haramosh, huddled in the cold shade where a cobalt-blue side stream met the main grey torrent and the Indus made its sudden southward turn. Following the eastern shore the next day, 25 January, Hayward passed the mouth of the Gilgit River, roaring in through a cleft in the opposite bank, and came to Bunji. This spot, in a barren valley with huge mountain walls skirted with vast debris flows and capped with a chaos of broken ice, was where the Treaty of Amritsar stated that the maharaja's territory should have ended – and sometimes it did. When Dr Leitner had come here in 1866 most of the Dogra soldiers – who must have resented this spectacularly inhospitable posting every bit as much as the modern Indian and Pakistani troops on the Line of Control today – had temporarily retreated across the river and Gilgit was virtually a no-man's-land.

Despite the Kashmiri occupation, Bunji was well within Dard country. It lay on the northern marches of Chilas. The Chilasis occupied perhaps the most wildly inhospitable of all the cold corners of Dardistan – the narrow gorge of the southbound Indus under the looming wall of Nanga Parbat where the valley is at its most barren. Nothing grows there, nothing, it seems, should live there, and in this vicious environment the Chilasis live up to their icy name. In Dr Leitner's primer of useful phrases in the Chilasi language there are all sorts of alarming utterances. 'Beat him now, kill him afterwards', was apparently a common saying in Chilas. To questions about the condition of routes out of the country the reply was invariably negative: 'How is the road between this and there? Very bad and dangerous.' And the portentous: 'The road is full of stones.' In demonstrating the imperative 'Bring him at once or else I shall be angry' and 'Shoot him the moment he comes near' were appropriate examples, while 'This man is treacherous' hardly needed saying at all. And another favourite Chilasi phrase was 'We kill all infidels', to which Leitner's feeble reply appears to have been: 'I have come to learn the language.'

This then was wild country, and the road was indeed full of stones. But Hayward had made it through the mountains in the worst of seasons along a route most would have considered impossible; he was surely up to its challenges. The following morning he crossed the Indus below Bunji on a raft of slimy sheepskins inflated beneath a mesh of poplar branches, and two days later on 29 January 1870 he arrived in Gilgit, now back in the hands of the maharaja's Dogra troops.

Gilgit was the crux of the matter, the hub of Dardistan. To its south lay Chilas and the Indus Valley; east lay Baltistan and the glacier country. To the north Hunza and Nagar feuded across their narrow gorge and scouted far and wide in search of plunder; while in the west lay Yasin, and beyond it across the Shandur Pass was Chitral, current big fish in Dardistan's small pond. Gilgit had long fallen through the cracks between these mountainous puzzle pieces, and it had a turbulent history.

The pre-Islamic past of this stony valley, and even its post-conversion history until the 1840s, is clouded with myth. Long ago Buddhist pilgrims came this way, for just outside the headquarters of the infidel-slaying Chilasis a seated *bodhisattva* is carved into the yellow rocks, and another monumental Buddha gazes blindly out of a cliff face west of Gilgit. In the more recent past the people of Gilgit were claimed to have been Hindus, but the dateless ibex carvings scratched into roadside rocks throughout the region, the megalithic stone platforms in high pastures and the lingering shamanism in lost side valleys suggest that whatever world religions came this way, none laid down anything more than the shallowest of roots in mountain villages. Until the army of the Sikh Maharaja Ranjit Singh captured Gilgit in the 1840s many people there were still burning their dead – an absolute travesty of orthodox Islamic practice. It was actually claimed that it was a Punjabi Muslim commander in the Sikh army, Nathu Shah, who converted the Gilgitis from such heathenish practices and made them 'good Muhammadans'.

Long before that, at some unspecified date, the last entirely non-Islamic King of Gilgit was said to have been a brutal monster named Sri Badat. In legend he was a cannibal. According to a story still told in Gilgit today, the king was once given a meal of roast lamb in one of his villages. The meat was the sweetest, tenderest he had ever tasted, and on enquiring of his cringing host he learnt that the animal had been fed on the breast milk of the lady of the house – a disturbing enough story in itself. From that day on Sri Badat ate nothing but the flesh of breastfed babies kidnapped from the terrified farmsteads of the Gilgit Valley. Beyond this gruesome point the legend breaks down in mythical confusion and borrowed narratives, with a pair of superhuman brothers from Hunza, arrows fired over impossible distances and conversion to some kind of compromised Islam all thrown into the mix.

A change of religion did not free Gilgit from tyranny, however. Though there was a rather feeble dynasty that claimed true right to the throne, the valley's most recent ruler before the arrival of the Sikhs had been a man named Gohar Aman.[8] This rampaging warlord – according to some sources a minor prince of the Chitrali royal family – seemed to be largely responsible for Dardistan's recent dreadful reputation. He had seized Gilgit some time in the early nineteenth century and ruled it brutally until the Sikhs made their audacious advance through the mountains. The Sikhs had, in fact, invaded partly at the instigation of one Karim Khan, the son of the former Gilgit chief that Gohar Aman had deposed. Of course, once Ranjit Singh's forces had gained their tenuous toehold in Dardistan they had no intention of leaving, though they did install Karim Khan as a puppet raja.

With the collapse of the Sikh Empire little changed in Gilgit and the territory was simply handed over to the newly invested Maharaja of Kashmir. The same occupiers – a mixed army of Sikhs and Dogra Hindus – remained in the town, and the same simmering resentment of these occupying infidels festered in the surrounding valleys. In 1852 this resentment boiled over. Gohar Aman, who had been skulking somewhere to the west, returned and chased the Kashmiri troops back across the Indus to Bunji. According to one British champion of the maharaja, Gohar Aman had 'no right at all to Gilgit, only the power of acquiring it'. This may well have been true, but he was a Dard and he certainly had more right to the place than the Kashmiri troops. Until the end of the 1850s he remained there, Dards and Dogras eyeing each other coldly across the Indus, while hundreds of miles away in India the 'Mutiny' against the British came and went unnoticed.

In 1859, the year that George Hayward joined the British army thousands of miles away to the west, Gohar Aman died. With Ranbir Singh now having gained Kashmir from his father, the Dogras surged once more across the Indus and the unhappy history of Gilgit continued. Throughout the 1860s there had been a string of bloody Kashmiri excursions up the valleys towards

Hunza and Yasin, always followed by a retreat to Gilgit, and on one occasion, with a force of Chitralis on their way across the Shandur Pass, a brief return across the Indus to Bunji. This had been the unfortunate moment that Dr Leitner had chosen to make his little foray into Dardistan.

With his very real passion for the Dards, who he rather liked to think he had discovered, Leitner had been noisily championing their cause against the Kashmiri Dogras for the three years before Hayward's visit. But no one was listening. Mutual atrocities committed against one another by Hindus and Muslims in a place so remote that it was almost impossible to reach even in a time of peace were not a major concern of the British. The only vaguely known quantities in Dardistan – Chitral and Hunza – hardly had reputations to elicit tender sympathy, and of course, the Maharaja of Kashmir was a sensitive British ally. Nothing was done, and as George Hayward shambled wearily into Gilgit in the new year of 1870 he found a miserable, brutalised place.

The sky would have hung filthy grey over dark, treeless mountains. It was bitterly cold, and here and there Sikh and Hindu soldiers – far from pleased to see an English stranger in town – trudged through the muddy, slushy snow towards draughty barracks with rifles over their shoulders. Almost every day there were rumours of skirmishes and atrocities in outlying hamlets, and all the countryside around Gilgit was a wasteland of untilled fields and burnt-out villages. It was, in short, a war zone. The miserable townsfolk, who had known nothing but occupation and violence for decades, would have scurried back and forth along dirty lanes between their grubby, smoky, stone-and-mud dwellings and the dreary bazaar with its meagre selection of rotten vegetables and greasy goat meat. Gilgit consisted of only 200 houses, but there were at least 1,000 Kashmiri Dogra troopers in town.

Hayward realised immediately that communicating with the tribal chiefs in the valleys beyond Gilgit and plotting his onward journey would be even more challenging than the outrageous journey he had just made along the Indus. It would be like turning up in Indian-occupied Kashmir today and trying to make enquiries about a trekking expedition with villagers on the other side of the Line of Control. For once George Hayward would not be able simply to put his head down and plough blindly onwards; for once he would have to play a diplomatic game.

Three years earlier, when Dr Leitner had wanted to make it known that he wished to meet the locals, he had simply ordered a large drum to be noisily beaten on Gilgit's main street. Sure enough, turbaned tribesmen soon filtered down out of the hills and beside a roaring fire that evening Leitner had presided over a wild party with roast sheep, a band of local musicians and the jerking, foot-stomping dancing of the Dards. But Gilgit had then been virtually deserted with no one in obvious control. In January 1870 things were very different.

Hayward was in Gilgit for three weeks. The nervous, hostile Kashmiri troops did not want him there, but were reluctant to kick him out. Meanwhile, the tribes in the surrounding valleys were intensely suspicious of any approach from Gilgit by a foreigner. 'In this,' Hayward wrote, 'has lain the great difficulty – to go through either hostile camp, as it were, and still keep friends with both.' Here there could be none of the tantrums he had thrown in Turkestan.

Gilgit was a place of intrigue. At least one former ruler of Yasin – and one-time furious enemy of the Dogras – was now installed in a bungalow in the town on a Kashmiri pension, and there were spies and agents from the surrounding valley fiefdoms loitering in the bazaar. As a cold February advanced, Hayward and his Pashtun staff made quiet enquiries at tea-stalls and horse yards. They learned two things of interest: that all of the high passes that led on towards the Pamirs were totally snowed up and would remain so until much later in the year, but also that the very best route out of Dardistan in the direction of the Oxus lay over the pass beyond the village of Darkot in the Yasin Valley.

As soon as he had arrived in Gilgit Hayward had begun to send messages into the mountains by way of the bazaar spies. Small gifts and requests for an approach were smuggled across the front line, but there was no reply. The rulers of Hunza and Nagar were so intensely hostile towards the Dogras that any gift or message from Gilgit would have been regarded as poison. Isa Bagdur, the petty Raja of Punial, an area which bordered on to Gilgit itself, would have been more forthcoming, but he had capitulated to the Dogras several years earlier in return for being reinstated in territory previously seized by Yasin. He was now a subservient vassal of the maharaja and Hayward took an instant dislike to him. In any case, Punial offered no viable route to the Pamirs, even in better weather. To the west the Mehtar of Chitral, Aman ul-Mulk, the greatest of the Dard chiefs, was far away and out of reach beyond the snowbound Shandur Pass, and from Yasin came only silence.

Hayward began to suspect that his cause was hopeless. Camped out in some cramped and filthy quarters in Gilgit, hissed at and eyed suspiciously by Dogra troopers in the muddy streets, and always beneath the grim grey shadow of the ragged mountains around the town, depression must have begun to creep in. Those 383 miles along the sheer banks of the Indus had, it seemed, been for nothing. But then, finally, in mid-February, came the reply that Hayward had been waiting for. A message arrived from Yasin: its ruler, one Mir Wali Khan, was ready to welcome him. Hayward was elated, and even if he realised that his would-be host was the second son of the tyrannical Gohar Aman, he would still have thought warmly of him. He slipped out of Gilgit, passed the last of the ruined villages and the last Kashmiri sentry post, and headed west along the Gilgit River, passing skeletal stands of poplars and bare fields between dry-stone walls.

Yasin, a long valley branching to the north of the main Gilgit–Chitral route, had a history almost as convoluted and conflicted as that of Gilgit itself. Gohar Aman had used it as a base for his attacks on Gilgit; since his death it had been tussled over by the multiple sons of his three marriages. About two years before

Hayward arrived on the scene, the old tyrant's first son, Mulk Aman,[9] and his second son, Mir Wali, had had some kind of a falling out. With the aid of the Mehtar of Chitral, to whose daughter he was married, Mir Wali kicked his older brother off the throne of Yasin and clambered on to it himself. It was Mulk Aman who was now collecting his Kashmiri pension in Gilgit, clearly having decided that small fry in the bloody streams of Dardistan had to throw their lot in with one or other of the two big powers in the mountains – Kashmir and Chitral – to survive. With Chitral on the side of his traitorous brother, there was only one way for him to go. He was almost certainly banking on one day being reinstated as a Kashmiri vassal – like his neighbour Isa Bagdur. Meanwhile, a third son of Gohar Aman, a feisty teenager named Pahlwan, was waiting in the wings as Governor of Mastuj, just across the Shandur Pass in the upper reaches of Chitral.

Hayward was stepping into a family quarrel played out on a grand scale by a clan with a history of violence. But none of that mattered to him as he made his way west, past Isa Bagdur's seat at Sher Qila, past Gakuch and the mouth of the Ishkoman Valley. The streams were full of ice, and an upwards glance at the state of the surrounding mountains revealed that there was only so far that he could go at this time of year. But finally it seemed that the Pamirs, surely brooding just beyond those northern ridges, were almost within reach.

On 27 February,[10] camped out at a hamlet called Roshan, Hayward wrote a letter to the serving soldier Colonel Showers, who had expressed an interest in his explorations while he was back in India. Hayward knew that he would not be able to post the letter any time soon, but here in this high, wild and achingly beautiful valley he simply had to express his excitement to someone.

'I am on the point of entering Yassin,' Hayward told Showers. Mir Wali had sent out an official to meet him on the road, and this man had already confirmed the tales Hayward had heard in Gilgit about the Darkot Pass, and how it led directly towards the Pamirs. 'There should be no great difficulty in penetrating to the Karakul,' he wrote.

The Yasini official had also let him know that the following morning Mir Wali himself would ride out to join him for the last part of the journey. Hayward was just hours away from meeting the man who held the keys to the High Pamirs, the man he would soon consider a friend, the man on whose behalf he would detour hundreds of miles back to the east and in voicing whose complaints he would earn the wrath of the Indian and Kashmiri governments. And this same chieftain, riding a sturdy Afghan pony down the valley towards the fateful rendezvous, was also the man who would be directly responsible for Hayward's murder.

Notes

1   'Kafiristan', the Land of the Unbelievers, is now the Afghan province of Nuristan, the Land of Light. Until the beginning of the twentieth century this was the last bastion of non-Muslim culture in Central Asia, its people following an ancient religion that, while showing a few hints of Zoroastrianism and primitive Hinduism, was mostly indigenous to the mountains. With their complex concepts of purity and impurity, of sacred high pastures and guardian spirits – not to mention their propensity for banditry – the Kafirs of the Hindu Kush had long had a strained relationship with their Muslim neighbours. Finally, in the 1900s the Afghan King Abdurrahman stormed into the mountains and forcibly converted the Kafirs to Islam, piously renaming their country 'the Land of Light'. A handful of 'non-believers' survived, however. By that stage the Indo-Afghan frontier had been arbitrarily defined, and three remote Kafir Valleys had found themselves lumped in with Chitral at the very top of the North-West Frontier.

Remarkably, a few thousand of these original non-Muslims, who refer to themselves as the Kalash rather than by the derogatory 'non-believer' designation, still maintain their beliefs, customs and, in the case of the women, their dress, in the heart-breakingly beautiful valleys of Birir, Rumbur and Bumberet.

Rudyard Kipling's most famous short story, *The Man who would be King*, is set in Kafiristan.

2 This was the Pamir lake Hayward suspected was the source of the Oxus.

3 Of course, the Russians never did sweep down into Eastern Turkestan, though both they and their British rivals eventually established consulates in Kashgar. Robert Shaw's nephew, Francis Younghusband, maintained the first British post there.

4 According to some conspiracy theorists, the apparent 'mistake' in the Treaty of Amritsar may have been deliberate. Knowledge of the geography of the Western Himalayas was shaky to say the least when the British signed their agreement with Gulab Singh, but they should at least have been well aware that the Indus flowed west through Ladakh. By making the definition of the new maharaja's territory as vague as possible, the argument goes, the rulers of the Raj left open the possibility for mountainous expansionism by proxy.

5 The award of a gold watch alone was a remarkable gesture from the RGS in an age of racial supremacism, and some indication of Nain Singh's stature as an explorer. In fact, several years later in 1876, after a great deal of controversy and argument, Singh was actually given the Founder's Gold Medal. This was groundbreaking stuff – the award had never before been granted to an 'Asiatic' and there was plenty of disgruntled muttering amongst the Fellows, including from Sir Henry Rawlinson, then the president. Had Nain Singh been a European he would have been given the medal years earlier, of course. Instead he had to wait until it was hard to dispute, in the words of the great geographer Henry Yule, that

'His observations have added a larger amount of important knowledge to the map of Asia than those of any other living man'. Hayward's Pashtun stole this watch.

6   In the colonial era the name of the valley was usually spelt with a double S – this is how Hayward spelt it in all of his writings. Today, however, it is usually rendered in the roman script with a single S, not least by the modern Government of Pakistan.

7   By which he meant the Pashtuns of Swat and the surrounding hills – then as now renowned for their religious extremism.

8   Another example of the intricacies and inconsistencies of trans-literation – the name is sometimes written as Gohar Rahman, and alternative spellings include Gauhar and Gaur. 'Gohar Aman' seems to be the most commonly used version today.

9   Mulk Aman is not to be confused with Aman ul-Mulk, the Mehtar of Chitral, a much more important figure in the mountains. The ul-Mulk family had already been ruling over Chitral, a country as big as Wales, for almost two centuries, and were related by blood or marriage to just about every clan in Dardistan, including the feuding brethren of Yasin. Although their royal status has long since been removed, the ul-Mulks are still by far the most influential family in Chitral today – though their evil reputation no longer applies and they are very nice people indeed.

10 There is a little confusion over this date: the letter – both Hayward's handwritten original and the published version in the Journal of the RGS – is clearly dated 17 February. However, in his tables of instrumental observations Hayward first records being out of Gilgit – at Bargo, some way east of Roshan – on the 21st. According to these records he reached Yasin on the 28th. Hayward, in his excitement when writing to Showers, seems to have got the date wrong by ten days.

8

SPEAK, OR DIE
BURSTING WITH RAGE

The steep, stony hillside was white, as if covered with snow. To the south the broadest part of the Yasin Valley lay bleached of colour at the end of winter; to the north the valley narrowed towards Darkot and the Pamirs. The surrounding mountains were certainly crusted with ice, and the high passes were still blocked – they would be so for another three months yet. But here at Madoori – an outcrop of iron-coloured rock standing over the hamlet of Sandhi, close to the Yasin River a few miles upstream from the fort and the main village – temperatures rose well above freezing in the March sunshine. It was not snow that coloured the hillside at this lonely, abandoned spot.

George Hayward squatted down and looked out over the horrible scene. He glanced at the men who had brought him here, Yasinis with heavy robes and roll-edged caps. They looked grimly back. There was nothing that could be said.

Hayward had already heard of the atrocities committed by the Maharaja of Kashmir's Dogra troops even before he left Gilgit; he had seen the wasteland of burnt-out villages that surrounded the town; and he had heard tale after tale of massacres and brutality by the foreign invaders since arriving in Yasin a fortnight earlier. But none of that had prepared him for the stark shock of this place: the hillside was covered with human bones, bleached by the sun of six summers and the frost of seven winters. Slender thighbones and cracked pelvises, pale and smooth and growing a little green algae on their edges, were half buried in the thin soil; vertebrae were scattered amongst the rocks like the lost playing pieces of some macabre board game. But worst were the skulls. There were dozens of them, smooth and clean like giant field mushrooms, or cracked and smashed like hollow eggs. Eye sockets gaped; fractured jawbones leered. Many of the skulls were tiny, with paper-thin craniums. Children – very small children, babies even – had been killed here.

George Hayward began to count the skulls. It was merely a reaction to the horror, a hopeless attempt to make some kind of order and logic out of what was clearly disordered and illogical. He scrambled over the slope, trying as best he could not to tread on and smash a fragile arm bone or shoulder blade. Up above, the mountains rose beyond the last of the willows that lined the irrigation ditches, beyond the pines and the goat pastures, and into rock and snow. The sun was warm on his brow and the back of his neck as he counted, and the stream below, a tributary of the main river running west from the Asumbar Pass, was busy with the first of the meltwater. There were birds singing in the bare branches of the poplars. But Hayward could see and hear none of that; he only counted. Ten, twenty, fifty, eighty and then, with grim inevitability, past 100 onwards and upwards.

He counted 147 skulls, many of them obviously those of children. Something awful had happened here. One hundred and forty-seven people had been slaughtered on this hillside. Hayward came slowly back down over the snow-white ground to where his Yasini guides were waiting. He told them his grim tally, but the men only smiled bleakly and explained the true, unimaginable scale of the massacre: after the killing was over the people of Yasin who had escaped, those who had bolted for the high pastures or hidden amongst the fields and ditches, crept back down to bury their dead. The 147 skulls that Hayward had counted belonged only to those who had had no one left to bury them; those whose entire families had been killed. In all, they guessed, perhaps 1,200 or 1,400 people had been slaughtered here. Still others had been carried off alive by the invaders and never seen again.

It had happened seven years earlier in 1863. Yet it was not the Dogras' first attack on Yasin. Back in 1860, after retaking Gilgit following the death of Gohar Aman, they had stormed up the Gilgit River valley, and into Yasin. They had actually taken the little capital and installed in its mud-walled fort a puppet leader of their own choosing – some loyal lickspittle who had been loitering in Gilgit. The Dogras had then for some reason retreated. By the time they arrived back in Gilgit they found their traumatised puppet already there ahead of them. His rule had lasted barely a few hours. He had fled along some mountain shortcut in his desperation to reach the safety of Gilgit after being toppled by Mulk Aman, the elder brother of Mir Wali, Hayward's host in Yasin.

Mulk Aman was still on the throne when the Dogras returned in 1863 under a colonel, Hoshiyara, with a reputation for bravery bordering on rashness. They took Yasin itself; Mulk Aman fled to Chitral, and his villagers retreated up the valley to a second fort at Madoori. The details of what happened next are far from clear amid the conflicting accounts, but it was definitely something very bad. Some people seem to have escaped into the mountains, but others, including most of the women and children and those too old to bolt up sheer Hindu Kush hillsides, were left hiding in the fort. It was an impressive defensive spot, rising sheer from the valley below, but occupied mainly by old women, grandfathers and children it could not hold out for long. The maharaja's troops broke into the fort – either by force or by treachery, depending on who was telling the tale. Carnage ensued.

In a remote, sparsely populated valley 100 dead would be devastating enough; 1,000 was almost genocide, and seven years later the memory of the trauma still haunted Yasin. The death toll and the lurid tales that Hayward heard – and believed – of babies tossed in the air and hacked in half as they fell and of unborn foetuses ripped from their mothers' wombs may have been inflated by anger and outrage. But that the maharaja's Dogras (Hayward called them 'employees'; they were 'not worthy of the name "troops"') had done something terrible in Yasin was undeniable. The 147 skulls still littering the Madoori hillside were proof enough of that.

For George Hayward the visit to the scene of the massacre, sometime in mid-March 1870, was to prove decisive, tragic and ultimately fatal. It enraged him; it left him disgusted with the British Government of India. The behaviour of the Dogras was, he would repeat over and over during the last months of his life, 'a disgrace to a feudatory of the British Crown'. But looking back from the viewpoint of 140 years, the same moment also redeemed George Hayward as a human being. Without it he would have left only traces of selfishness and, with his apparent disinterest in his local companions, of a complete disregard for others. But hearing and seeing what had happened in Yasin – a place that no other European had ever visited; that had not been placed accurately on any map; and that only the tiniest handful of outsiders had ever even heard of – showed that George Hayward had a profound sense of justice and was capable of furious compassion. And, incredibly, it even drew him briefly and disastrously away from his consuming passion: for the sake of the Dards of Yasin, and for his newfound friend Mir Wali, George Hayward was prepared temporarily to turn his back on the High Pamirs. It was a decision that would kill him.

Had it not been for that grim charnel house, waiting on that Madoori hillside to direct him towards disaster, the weeks George Hayward spent in Yasin would have seemed like a halcyon interlude. Far from the 'very bad character' ascribed to the Dards by just about every non-Dard who had ever heard of them, Hayward found them warmly welcoming. He wrote that he had been 'most well received and hospitably treated'. And it was true that if there was one defining characteristic of the Dards, besides a tendency for internecine warfare and treachery, it was hospitality. Almost anyone who went amongst them without wishing to colonise or subjugate them came away impressed and a little beguiled. Forty-eight hours was all it took for Dr Leitner to fall head over heels in love with the Dards; Hayward was in their Yasin heartland for almost three weeks.

At the tail end of winter the valley would have been a pleasant place. The snow would have cleared from the lower slopes and dripped away from the drooping branches of the pines and junipers; the very first tiny, swelling buds would have been beginning to show on the branches of the willow trees. In the little fields beside the noisy streams, grey with meltwater, smallholders would have been driving pairs of yoked black cattle, turning clods of pale soil ready for planting with wheat and corn. The villages would have been full of happy noise – cockerels crowing, donkeys braying, children shouting and squabbling, and women calling from kitchen to smoky kitchen.

It is tempting to suspect that among the charms of Yasin that appealed to Hayward were the good looks of its women. They were said to be – along with the fair maidens of Chitral, just to the west – the most beautiful in the Western Himalayas. The previous year Hayward had certainly commented favourably on the women of Eastern Turkestan, though considering that he was mostly kept under house arrest while there, and that Talibanesque dress codes were enforced on the streets, it is hard to see how he could have actually seen many – unless, of course, some extra-special Turki hospitality was laid on from time to time.[1] 'They have not the fine eyes and gait of the Cabul and Chitral women,' he had written in his report (not explaining what exactly was lacking in their 'gait', nor where he had seen these 'Cabul and Chitral women', never having been to either place), 'but are certainly handsome, with round, pleasant faces, rather low in stature, and robust, while their complexion is of the healthiest.' The Dard women were more beguiling yet, with 'a more English cast of countenance than any I have yet seen in Asia'. Then as now in the villages around Gilgit, it was not uncommon to come across people with strikingly European features. 'Light and dark brown hair, with grey, hazel, and often blue eyes are seen,' wrote Hayward, and indeed, 'Black hair is the exception amongst them'.

Throughout the high mountains of Asia, from Tibet to Tajikistan, pale eyes, fair hair and freckles crop up unexpectedly in remote valleys. Wherever they do there are far-fetched ancestor myths surrounding them – almost always relating to a Macedonian adventurer from the fourth century BC. The Kalash survivors of Kafiristan, the Drokpa nomads of Ladakh, the Hunzakuts, even a few of the Pashtuns: all of them like to ascribe their fair complexions to lost battalions of the army of Alexander the Great or even, in more fanciful moments, to the notorious homosexual militarist himself. It's an enticing story, and when Hayward heard the Yasinis claim their own Alexandrian ancestry he was impressed.

But the truth is that the great knot of mountains at the heart of the Eurasian landmass has seen myriad peoples wash back and forth along its flanks for millennia, leaving remnants and throwbacks marooned in isolated valleys like rock pool fish trapped by the receding tide. If there are Mongolian-featured peoples in the fastness of Bamian in Afghanistan, and even further west among the nomads of southern Iran, then it is hardly surprising that the occasional redhead crops up on the marches of Tibet. Any wayward soldiers who dropped out along Alexander the Great's route march would have been but droplets in a genetic ocean. But in any case, whatever their ancestry, the women of Yasin were very attractive, and indeed their resemblance to English women made the tales of Dogra atrocities committed against them all the more upsetting for George Hayward.

Hayward was soon writing of his 'friendship with the Yassin people'. Though he had sometimes been admiring of the Turkis of Kashgar and Yarkand, and had – in between throwing tantrums about his captivity – praised their hospitality, he had never spoken of 'friendship'. But as far as he was concerned the Yasinis were real friends. The feeling was apparently mutual, for in spite of all that was to happen within a few short months, fifteen years later Hayward was still remembered fondly in Yasin, particularly for 'his pleasant manners and courteous ways with the poorer classes'.

It was not merely the beauty of their women, the charms of their homeland or their general hospitality that had drawn George Hayward under the spell of the Dards of Yasin; it was also their leader. Mir Wali, the man who had ridden out to meet Hayward on the road from Roshan that morning at the end of February, had impressed him from the start. Despite his terrible family background, the chief's 'courtesy and bearing', Hayward wrote, 'were quite beyond what I expected to meet with in Dardistan'. Mir Wali not only welcomed him and let him wander wherever he chose in his little mountain kingdom (then comprising the Yasin Valley itself as far as the head of the snowbound Darkot Pass, the neighbouring valley of Ishkoman and the country leading up to the Shandur Pass); he also agreed to help him with his journey to the Pamirs in any way that he could. Hayward was soon pinning all his hopes of success on this one wild chieftain so it was understandable that he leant a sympathetic ear to Mir Wali's complaints about the excesses of the Dogra forces, and even to his own claims to Gilgit.

This may all seem hopelessly naïve with hindsight – a quick glance over Mir Wali's recent résumé of treachery suggested that he was not a man to be trusted – but considering Hayward's past experiences with the rulers through whose country he had travelled, it is perfectly forgivable. From the very start, from that first return to Murree with Sir Henry Rawlinson's mission in his hand, Hayward had been baffled by authority. The British had turned him away from the Peshawar–Chitral route and refused him official support; Yaqub Beg's Turkis had definitively closed the letter on the Pamirs and made him a prisoner to boot; and the Kashmiris, despite their initial friendliness, had seen him off into the mountains with a chorus of sinister naysaying. By contrast, Mir Wali even offered him an armed escort to accompany him out of Yasin and through the lawless country on the banks of the Upper Oxus, which, Hayward was assured, lay just a few short marches beyond the Darkot Pass. Hayward felt that finally he had found not just a friend and a supporter, but someone who could – and would – do something actively to help him.

But for now the passes were still well and truly blocked. Hayward had pushed as far north as he could up the Yasin Valley, as far as a lonely campsite at Darkot where he would pass a bleak vigil four months later. But even for a man who had crossed the Karakoram in midwinter without a tent and traversed the howling Indus Gorge in a highly unsuitable season, it was obvious that he could go no further. 'It was most tantalizing to get to the foot of the Darkote [sic] Pass to know that the commencement of the Bam-i-Dooneah (Roof of the World) lay just beyond the pass, and to be unable to get there yet on account of the snow,' he wrote. He also explored a side valley, branching north-west from Yasin, which ended at the Moshabur Pass. This pass too was thoroughly snowed up, not that Hayward would have been entirely happy about crossing it in any case; it led into Upper Chitral.

Barely 100 miles to the west, over the Shandur Pass, down through Mir Wali's baby brother Pahlwan's domain of Mastuj, along winding valleys beneath the great glowing ice-tower of the Hindu Kush's highest peak, Tirich Mir, lay Chitral. And ensconced in the mud-walled fort beside its glacier-fed river was its ruler, the mehtar, Aman ul-Mulk. Hayward was rightly nervous of this powerful chieftain. He knew that there were fine passes leading from Chitral towards the Pamirs – indeed, the Peshawar–Chitral route had been his original choice of approach eighteen months earlier. But he also knew Chitral's atrocious reputation for slavery, violence and treachery. Even for a man as obviously brave – and possibly foolhardy – as Hayward, the discovery that there was a direct route from Yasin to the Pamirs that bypassed Chitral had been a great relief.

When two letters addressed to Hayward, signed by the mehtar, arrived in Yasin (some hardy postal runner must have been slogging through 12ft of snow on the windswept saddle of the Shandur) he was suspicious. The letters seemed to be friendly enough: the mehtar was delighted that an English guest had made the acquaintance of his son-in-law, would like cordially to invite the same honoured foreigner to visit his own country and would be happy to help to facilitate any onward travels the explorer had in mind. But Hayward, with an insightful clarity that seemed to be lacking in his dealings with the Dards of Yasin, suspected an ulterior motive. 'The Chitral ruler would probably like to get an Englishman into his power, to be able to play him off against the aggressions of the Dogras in the Gilgit Valley,' Hayward wrote astutely, though the idea that this was also exactly what Mir Wali was successfully doing seems never to have occurred to him.

In the aftermath of what was to happen in Yasin the coming July, as rumours and theories whistled back and forth over mountain passes, plenty of people claimed that Mir Wali was essentially a loyal vassal of the Mehtar of Chitral, and that Yasin was Chitrali territory in all but name. It was certainly true that Mir Wali was married to a daughter of the mehtar, and that the mehtar had backed him in his family coup against Mulk Aman two years earlier. But Dard chiefs were forever marrying each other's daughters and forming insincere alliances even while intriguing against one another and plotting treachery. Mir Wali ruled over a small and vulnerable kingdom, squeezed up against Chitral by the advancing Dogras; he had little choice but to turn to his father-in-law from time to time, but he was probably also very glad that a decent amount of snow cut him off from the mehtar's meddling for at least a few months each year. When the letters arrived he strongly advised Hayward to ignore them and to steer well clear of Chitral – and Hayward was happy to take his friend's advice. He put the letters aside and went off shooting.

The stark slopes that rose up towards the snowline on all sides were a happy hunting ground, and Hayward had 'capital sport' stalking ibex and markhor. Scrambling over stony ridges, peering over blinds of dripping ice or from behind stunted bushes, time and again he lined up magnificent mountain goats in the sights of his rifle. He shot one huge ibex with great curved horns measuring 54in across. Even the shooting to be had in Kashmir, which he had compared favourably to the unchallenging business of slaughtering cumbersome wild yak in Chang Chenmo, could 'not be compared with the sport met with across the Indus'.

All this bloody fun on the mountainsides only heightened Hayward's excitement about what lay beyond the passes to the north. He had been told by old men with sun-scarred faces and cloudy eyes in the villages around Yasin that 'the Pamir Steppes swarm with game'. The greatest of its beasts, a prospect almost as thrilling as the true source of the Oxus itself, was the magnificent *ovis poli*, the Marco Polo sheep. It was the biggest of all the mountain ungulates in Asia, and as far as Hayward knew no European had ever killed one; hardly any Europeans had even seen one since the Italian for whom they were named.[2]

But Hayward's time in Yasin was not spent entirely in killing wild animals. He also surveyed and scouted side valleys and ridges, delighted to be able to make measurements with impunity in a mountainous Muslim country. He had already concluded that once again existing British maps of the region were hopelessly inaccurate. Valleys ran in the wrong direction; watersheds lay hundreds of miles out of place; there were even towns marked on the current cartography that had never existed. Hayward set about putting all this right. He spotted giant 20,000ft peaks and charted the course of the tumbling streams that gushed between boulder-filled ravines to feed the Yasin and Gilgit rivers. In doing so he collected the data for the first accurate and comprehensive map of the country across the Indus, work that could be connected to the Grand Trigonomical Survey's extensive measurements in Kashmir.

Hayward also interviewed any local with a wandering urge and a history of travel in the mountains. He put together rough outlines of routes north-east through Hunza, south through Swat and west through Chitral. He was also taking an interest in the languages. Quite what language Hayward would have spoken with his Yasini hosts is not entirely clear. It is doubtful that they would have known any Hindi. After travelling for months with a posse of Pashtuns, the smattering of Pushtu that Hayward had set out with in 1868 had probably developed to a very firm grasp of the frontier language, but that would unlikely be of use with anyone besides a few traders in Yasin. Hayward did have a Kashmiri munshi with him to translate and to write letters to local rulers (speaking a language with a modified Arabic script is one thing; writing it quite another), but he would have known no Dardic dialects. Persian was in theory the lingua franca of Muslim Asia (the letters from Chitral would almost certainly have been written in Persian) and if he had had any kind of formal schooling Mir Wali would probably have had a basic understanding; it seems most likely that it was this that he and Hayward spoke together.

But Hayward also turned an ear to what he heard in the villages and bazaars. For the first time in his travels he put together word lists in various local dialects. These lists ran to six pages and several hundred words from 'anybody' to 'Yesterday evening' in the languages of Gilgit, Chilas, Hunza, Yasin and Chitral. From a few old wanderers he even scraped together a more limited vocabulary for Wakhan, Shignan and Roshnan – wild countries beyond the northern passes on the flanks of the Pamirs. Months later, when the word lists finally reached the RGS, Dr Leitner, with a lordly stroke of his chin and a 'well, I suppose …' whiff of faint praise, declared them reasonably accurate, but took serious issue with Hayward's chaotic system of transliteration.

Whatever the doctor thought, it is hard not to scan the language tables in search of some kind of significance – and there is plenty of Freudian fun to be had: A includes the words for Anger and Annoyance; there are Bridges of both rope and wood, and Beards and Breasts (the latter is apparently *diling* in Yasin and *paz* in Chitral). D's grim listings are Darkness, Desire, Door, Distant, Death, Defeat and Difficult. There is only one J, a doubtful Justice (*isaf* or *insaf*, borrowed from the Arabic, in all the languages); but it is followed immediately by Kill and Knife. It is by no means a cheerful vocabulary, but that probably says more about standard topics of conversation in Dardistan than about Hayward's state of mind, for it seems that for once, for one brief interlude, he was happy in Yasin.

Perhaps it is best to grant him that, to hope that those forays in pursuit of ibex and markhor really were the finest sport he'd ever had, to hope that March 1870 was particularly mild in the Hindu Kush and that the mountains were at their most beautiful. Perhaps it is best to hope that in the company of the Dards, and in the friendship of Mir Wali – whenever the Dogra atrocities were not allowed to cloud the conversation – Hayward found real companionship, and that in his decent dealings with the common Yasinis he found humour and ready smiles. Perhaps it is best even to embark on a truly wild flight of fancy and hope that somewhere in one of the valley villages there was a particularly fine pair of blue eyes … For from here on in, from the moment George Hayward turned east, away from Yasin at the end of March, nothing would be good; everything would be bad.

On 14 March Hayward wrote from 'Camp, Yassin' to Sir Roderick Murchison. As with the letter to Showers – which must still have been tucked away in his baggage – Hayward knew that he would probably have no chance to post it for weeks, but he filled the RGS president in on the details of his travels during the winter months. He also gave vent to his sense of angry injustice over the treatment of the Dards by the Maharaja of Kashmir and his Dogra troops. They were, inevitably, 'a disgrace' and a prime example of the 'foulest treachery and cruelty'. Virtually every letter he wrote from now on would sizzle with similar sentiments and, embarrassed by their unashamedly and unrestrainedly political nature, the RGS stopped reading his correspondence in their fortnightly meetings. Yet by the standards of his later furious missives this letter was positively mild, and he gave only a few lines to outrage and human rights abuses. What was more, with Mir Wali on his side he was thoroughly optimistic: 'I am very sanguine of being able to thoroughly explore the Pamir Steppe during the summer of 1870, for everything promises well for the eventual success of the expedition,' he wrote. If only that were true.

By the end of the year many were claiming that Hayward had lost all sense of judgement while he was in Yasin, blindly accepting the word and the faith of a lying, cheating traitor. But his March letter to Murchison makes it very clear that he knew only too well that he was treading deep waters. It would still be months until the passes opened, and pleasant as Yasin was he had no wish to outstay his welcome there. 'I may find it advisable to return to Gilgit and there wait for the proper moment to advance,' he wrote, 'for a prolonged stay here is, to say the least of it, somewhat risky.' It was not just the danger of stretching the limits of Yasini hospitality that was troubling George Hayward; with the steady melting of the snow the Mehtar of Chitral, beckoning with a sinister leer and a hollow protestation of friendship, no longer seemed at such a safe distance.

In the event Hayward lingered a few more days in Yasin after writing his letter to Murchison, and then, with genuinely fond farewells and promises of a reunion in early summer, he rode out of the valley, turned left, and headed for Gilgit. His departure came not a moment too soon: had he waited any longer disaster would have overcome both George Hayward and his Dard hosts, for back at the Dogra frontier a wicked plan was about to be put into action.

After the weeks in Yasin, crossing the frontier and passing again through destroyed villages and a cowed and traumatised country-side would have been depressing enough. After the hospitality of Mir Wali and his people, the cringing of the subjugated Gilgitis and the narrow suspicion of the Dogra occupiers would have created a tense and unhappy atmosphere. And after all he had heard and seen of massacre and mayhem in Yasin it was probably all Hayward could do to stop himself from dragging out his revolver and shooting the first Kashmiri soldier he came across. But what he found when he returned to Gilgit was much worse than all that.

His sudden, unexpected arrival must have caused excruciating embarrassment and all kinds of frantic scrambling in the Dogra garrison. Finding that the entire body of the Kashmiri army based on the western fringes of the state, including the 2,000 men usually stationed at Astor and Bunji, were in town polishing their sabres and preparing for perfidy, Hayward demanded to know what was happening. The sniggering explanation made him rage. Clearly assuming that the explorer had settled down to see out the rest of the winter amongst the Dards – or possibly had somehow got away across the passes – the maharaja's officials had concocted a scheme to justify another attack on Yasin. They had spread an outrageous rumour that Hayward had been attacked and robbed by the Yasinis and had summoned reinforcements from across the Indus to avenge this imaginary crime.

Yasin was not that far from Gilgit, and the news that the English explorer had been well received there would certainly have been current in the bazaars; it is impossible to give the Dogras the benefit of the doubt and accept that they could have believed such a wicked rumour. However, it should be noted that the maharaja himself could not have had an active role in developing this scheme: in March Gilgit was still cut off by snow; the garrison there was left to its own devices and there would be no communication with Srinagar until May.

Regardless of whoever had actually devised the plan, it was clear that had Hayward idled away a few more days in Yasin to explore one more side valley, shoot one more ibex or go back for one more look at the snowy heights of the Darkot Pass, the invasion would have been unleashed. There would certainly have been more atrocities, and perhaps, with the Yasinis completely unprepared, this time the occupation would have been permanent. For George Hayward it would have been catastrophic. 'Such

an act would have been fatal to the whole Pamir expedition,'
he wrote, with a certain amount of understatement; such an act
would indeed have been fatal – in a very literal sense – not just
to the expedition but also to its leader. The Dards, ever suspicious
of outsiders, would almost certainly have assumed that Hayward
had been party to the Dogra plans (Kashmir was known to be a
British ally after all). As news of massed troops storming up the
valley from Gilgit arrived and panic spread, Mir Wali and his men
would have guessed that Hayward was a devilish traitor, that he
had come on ahead to scout out the ground for the attack (they
had seen him scrambling around the slopes with his compass and
sextant), and they would have dealt him a suitable punishment.
Hayward suspected that this eventuality might actually have been
part of the Dogra plan all along, and perhaps he was not giving in
to paranoia when he suggested this.

It was certainly true that the Kashmiris had resented Hayward's
presence on the frontier from the very start. Far from Srinagar
and further still from British territory, they had long been able
quite literally to get away with murder in the mountains around
Gilgit. They knew all about the English tendency, hypocritically,
to huff and puff about fair play and decency, and were right in
thinking that Hayward's visit could lead to a certain amount of
trouble. If an invasion of Yasin would result in Hayward's death at
the hands of the Dards, then such an action would, so to speak, kill
two birds with one stone. No one would have been able to challenge the trumped up charges of robbery (any protesting Yasinis
would have been roundly disbelieved), and indeed the maharaja's
commanders would likely receive warm congratulations from the
Indian Government for so promptly avenging the murder of an
Englishman. It was, it must be said, a very cunning scheme.

With Hayward's return it all fortunately fell apart; the reinforcements went scurrying back across the Indus and the Gilgit
commanders simply shrugged and made their excuses. Hayward,
however, was furious – and with very good reason. It was probably the discovery of the Dogra plan that decided him to return

to India. His visit to the scene of the old massacre at Madoori had already convinced him of Kashmiri cruelty, and he had already promised Mir Wali – with protestations that he was only a civilian with no official influence – that he would do what he could to make the plight of the Yasinis known in India. But though he had mentioned in his letter to Showers the possibility of a return as far east as Kashmir to see out the winter, just few days before leaving Yasin he had written to Murchison only of waiting in Gilgit for the passes to open.

But now he was determined: he had at least three months to spare before any attempt could be made on the Pamirs; he was confident of his own speed and knew that he would lose no time in hammering back towards British territory. In any case, spending several months in the overtly hostile atmosphere of Gilgit, surrounded by its bleak stony mountains, would have been thoroughly unpleasant – especially after his discovery of the plot. He was already 'entertaining a feeling of bitter enmity' towards the Dogras, and was now determined that the world should know of their dastardly doings. If George Hayward had been on course for disaster for a long time, he was about to make the final, fatal step.

On 21 March, leaving his horses, his tent, most of his baggage and at least some of his Pashtun staff in Gilgit, George Hayward temporarily turned his back on the High Pamirs. His insane desire was burning brighter than ever, but for the moment its caustic glow was shining in another direction. He crossed the Indus to Bunji, probably scarcely able to muster basic politeness to the Dogras on duty there, and stormed up the steep grey gorge towards Astor. Today Astor is a wild outpost at the end of a terrifying road, a scrappy bazaar of piratical Chilasi traders under the northern flanks of the monstrous Nanga Parbat, known by mountaineers, without hyperbole, as 'the Killer Mountain'. One of the supply lines to the icy army posts on the Line of Control between Pakistani and Indian occupied country runs through the township, but it has a decidedly end-of-the-world feel. In the mid-nineteenth century it was all the more isolated, but it was even then a key staging post on a military supply line: it was the first significant settlement reached on the western side of the passes between Kashmir and Gilgit.

In theory the route beyond Astor over the Burzil Pass and the Deosai Plateau to Srinagar should still have been firmly closed in late March. No supply trains from the east would make it to Gilgit until the middle of May. In fact the Burzil Pass was still firmly closed, but so consumed was George Hayward that he would move mountains – or at very least clamber over them in suicidal conditions – to get where he was going. For five days skeins of filthy cloud lashed Nanga Parbat and its attendant peaks; for five days Hayward paced furiously in Astor, scowling at Dogra soldiers. Then, when the sixth morning showed aching blue skies streaked with thin white mares' tails, he launched himself at the western wall of the Great Himalaya.

George Hayward had already made some ridiculously risky journeys – the tent-less crossing of the Karakoram, the escape from Shahidulla, the traverse of the Indus in midwinter. But this brief, blazing attack out of Astor was perhaps the most insane of all. The snow was waist-deep on the Burzil, and Hayward, without a tent or snowshoes, waded through 50 miles of it in the searing light of the high mountains. For three freezing nights he slept outside amongst the drifts. He had no high-factor sunblock and no reflective sunglasses. Hands, nose and ears would have been scorched to a stinging scarlet; lips would have dried to a mess of oozing cracks; and the sheer intensity of the glare of a world where all was white would have left dark shadows drifting across his vision. Hayward didn't care, and when he stumbled into Srinagar in the middle of April he took only a grim satisfaction in having crossed a pass that no one else would even consider attempting for weeks.

He was still snow-blind and horribly sunburnt when he dropped in on his old hero, the disreputable mercenary Colonel Alexander Gardner. The ancient adventurer was doubtless delighted by Hayward's tales of travels in a style very much his own. Mumbling in that curious Irish accent, he assured Hayward that he was on the right track by attempting to reach the Pamirs through western Dardistan – he had been through that way himself after all, he claimed.

Hayward rested a mere three days in the Kashmiri capital. Anyone else coming to the end of a trek only half as arduous as that which he had just completed would surely have taken weeks, nursing their blisters in a Dal Lake houseboat, or easing their snow-scarred eyes in the cool shade of the chenars in the Mughal Gardens. But Hayward had no wish to linger under the auspices of the Maharaja of Kashmir, a man whose former 'kindness and consideration' now counted for nothing. His vision not yet recovered from the high snowfields, he hurried out of the valley and pressed for the Punjab.

On 23 May 1870 the Royal Geographical Society held its annual Anniversary Meeting in London. Outside the English spring was advancing and the trees in Hyde Park would have been bursting into fresh green leaf. Ducks and swans would have been milling on the waters of the Serpentine and ladies in frilly white would have shaded their delicate heads from the gentle sunshine with parasols as they promenaded. But inside the society's headquarters men who had made journeys in far less benign conditions were being celebrated, for the Anniversary Meeting was the day when the RGS dished out its accolades.

The Patron's Medal was handed to a French sailor, Lieutenant Francis Garnier, who had explored Cambodia and the Yangtze River and whose English was so limited that he had to give his acceptance speech in French. But the highest honour of all, the Founder's Gold Medal, was received by the Vice-President Sir Henry Rawlinson on behalf of an Englishman whose current location was then a mystery to the president and most of the Fellows.

Rising to the lectern, Sir Roderick Murchison spoke with an enthusiasm that matched that with which he had praised Hayward's report back in December. 'The Founder's Medal for the year 1870, has been awarded to Mr G.J.W. Hayward,' he told the audience, not only for his remarkable geographical discoveries in the Karakoram, the Kun Lun and beyond, but also 'in acknowledgement of his zeal and energy in entering at the present time on another perilous expedition for the same purpose'. The importance of Hayward's mapping work in Eastern Turkestan could not be underestimated, Murchison said. He was even prepared to stray just beyond the boundaries of the society's strictly apolitical remit in his praise. 'The Council of the Royal Geographical Society, as a scientific body, can take cognizance officially only of geographical services,' he said, but still, the journeys to Kashgar of George Hayward and Robert Shaw had been 'at least as valuable in a public as in a scientific point of view'. They had eased suspicions about the character of Yaqub Beg; they had opened a great new field for British trade; and had 'laid the foundation of what may prove in the sequel to be a valuable political alliance'. In short, Shaw and Hayward had all but conquered Kashgar for the Crown. Such wildly optimistic pronouncements were, it should be said, entirely the product of Robert Shaw's unashamed over-egging of the 'Turkestan trade' during his visit to England the previous winter. Hayward had already voiced some quiet dissent to the ludicrous claims being made for British prospects beyond the Karakoram. 'I am afraid the Yarkand trade has been very much exaggerated,' he had written, 'and will not fulfil the expectations formed of it.'

But no matter – Turkestan had never been Hayward's main concern anyway; that, Murchison explained, had always been the Pamirs. 'With regard to Mr. Hayward's present position, nothing positive can be announced,' he said. All that was known was that Hayward had been 'stimulated rather than disheartened' by his initial failure, and was right now in the midst of another attempt to scramble up on to the Roof of the World. Once he got there,

Murchison now told the audience, his adventures would still not be over. The president had brought all his influence to bear and had, remarkably, received permission from St Petersburg for Hayward to return to Britain through the new Russian acquisitions in Central Asia once he had finished his explorations in the mountains.

With that Sir Henry Rawlinson stood up to accept the medal on the absent explorer's behalf. He spoke of his own pride at this marvellous moment; it had been he who had introduced Hayward to the society and who had shoved him in the direction of the Pamirs. And how he had been vindicated! Hayward had 'fairly earned the distinction which has been conferred upon him'; he would be a towering inspiration to other would-be travellers and at least some of that glory ought to be reflected on to Rawlinson himself, he modestly suggested. After all, 'I was instrumental in sending this promising explorer on his travels'.

Rawlinson went on to speak of Hayward's 'indominatable will', his 'fertility of expedient', his 'disregard of dangers and hardships' and his 'iron constitution'. He also praised the explorer's 'tact, temper and diplomatic skill', and was happy to predict great future successes. 'If any Englishman can reach the Pamir Steppe, and settle the geography of that mysterious region, the site of the famous Mount Meru of the Hindoos, and the primeval paradise of the Aryan nations,[3] Mr. Hayward is the man,' he said.

Rawlinson also, like Murchison, professed ignorance of Hayward's current location. Whether he was telling the truth here is unclear. Hayward had been back in India for a month and had been making a thorough nuisance of himself from the very start. That cables to this effect had already reached the India Office seems likely, and if Rawlinson was feeling a little uncomfortable about his protégé's recent behaviour it was understandable if he kept it from the Fellows of the RGS. If he could hope to bask in the reflected glory of Hayward's triumphs, then surely he would share some of the embarrassment when he misbehaved. Rawlinson may even have already heard about Hayward's latest indiscretion. A fortnight before the RGS awarded him their highest honour he had done something that demonstrated an absolute absence of all 'tact, temper and diplomatic skill', something that had thoroughly embarrassed the Indian Government and something that, considering Hayward's plans for continued exploration in the high mountains west of Kashmir, seemed downright suicidal.

The Calcutta *Pioneer* was one of the most influential Indian newspapers of the nineteenth century. Calcutta was still the administrative capital of British India at the time. Bombay and Madras were distant places given soullessly over entirely to trade; Delhi, meanwhile, was simply unspeakably hot; the last embers of its Mughal soul had been thoroughly doused in the bloody post-Mutiny reprisals, and it had only its relative proximity to Shimla and Kashmir to recommend it. For an Englishman in India only Calcutta had a serious intellectual life; only in Calcutta were decent books published; only in Calcutta were some of the locals reasonably well educated by English standards; and only in Calcutta was there a serious and vibrant press. Some of the newspapers of the day – including the *Pioneer* – are still publishing now in the twenty-first century, though Calcutta itself has long since been left behind by other Indian cities to stagnate on the banks of the Hooghly River.

In 1870, however, Calcutta was still very much at the heart of things, and when on 9 May the *Pioneer* appeared carrying a particularly shocking and aggravated letter, there was plenty of noisy discussion in the polite drawing rooms of Bengal. The letter was the furious outpouring of a very angry man. It gave graphic and upsetting details of atrocities committed by troops of the Maharaja of Kashmir in a remote mountain valley at the far top-left corner of the Indian subcontinent, a place that very few of the *Pioneer*'s readers had ever heard of:

They threw the little ones in the air and cut them in two as they fell. It is said the pregnant women, after being killed, were ripped open and their unborn babies hacked to pieces. Some forty wounded women who were not yet dead were dragged to one spot, and were there burnt by the Dogra sepoys. With the exception of a few wounded men and women who ultimately recovered, every man, woman and child within the fort, and, in all, 1200 to 1400 of these unhappy villagers, were massacred by the foulest treachery and cruelty. After plundering the place Yassin was burnt and all the cattle carried off, together with some 2,000 women and men.

The author, crackling with unrestrained indignation, explained exactly how he knew all this:

I have visited Madoori, the scene of the massacre, and words would be inadequate to describe the touching sight to be witnessed on this now solitary and desolate hillside. Even after a lapse of seven years since the tragedy, I have myself counted 147 still entire skulls, nearly all those of women and children. The ground is quite literally white with bleached human bones ... I have written all this in the hope that the Indian public may be made aware of what our feudatory the Maharaja of Kashmir has perpetuated across the Indus. Apart from the infringement of any treaty, and putting all political motives aside, I trust that every Englishman and Englishwoman in India will join in demanding justice upon the murderers of innocent women and children.

The letter went on forcefully to argue for radical changes in the way that Kashmir was dealt with. For a start, the Treaty of Amritsar had to be enforced; the maharaja must be hustled back to where he belonged: the east bank of the Indus (where such a place existed). As for what would then become of Gilgit, it should be returned to its 'rightful owner', one Mir Wali of Yasin (that there were several other potential 'rightful owners' was not mentioned). To stop the maharaja's general excesses a permanent British Resident with full powers ought immediately to be installed in Kashmir, with the authority to boss the Dogra royal around. All this was essential, the author of the letter stated, to save British India from all kinds of trouble. The maharaja, if left unchecked, would only continue in his westward expansion, bringing India into conflict with bigger, more powerful neighbours. He even invoked that ultimate bogeyman – the Russian Threat. There were, the letter claimed, already agents of the tsar intriguing with the Kashmiris. This last accusation was unfounded, but no matter; the writer was on a roll.

It was all delivered in the sizzling syntax of the fieriest of public speakers. The writer was aiming to whip up the readers of the *Pioneer* into a frenzy of righteous outrage that would quite spoil their breakfasts. He even appealed to the latent racism of the average Victorian. The readers could not comfort themselves with the thought that the horrors he had described were merely one set of swarthy savages brutalising another set of swarthy savages; far from it: 'The English public must not think that these innocent women' – he was ever keen to press the innocence and womanliness of the victims – 'were "niggers" as they might choose to term them. They were descended from the ancestors of the true Aryan stock and had eyes and tresses of the same hue as those of their own wives and children.' If that didn't get them spluttering over their toast and marmalade, then nothing would.

The letter would certainly have been a major talking point in Calcutta that morning, and then throughout British society in India when the late editions arrived. The misdoings of the maharaja were a favourite newspaper correspondence topic for Outraged of Ooty and Disgusted of Darjeeling, but this took things to a new level. At the bottom of the column it was attributed to Mr George Hayward, though anyone in India who was remotely well informed – not least the viceroy and the Maharaja of Kashmir – would have guessed that long before they reached the final furious flourish. Here certainly was 'indominatable will' on proud display; without doubt there was blatant 'disregard for danger', but as for 'tact and diplomatic skill', George Hayward had clearly abandoned it.

From the moment George Hayward burst snow-blind from the mountains in mid-April he had made a nuisance of himself. He covered the ground from Srinagar to Murree in a mere four days and set out in pursuit of the viceroy, Lord Mayo, waving his written report of the Dogra atrocities like the worst kind of irate constituent. After chasing the viceroy back and forth between Murree and Rawalpindi, Hayward finally caught up with him at the end of the month.

Lord Mayo was a very busy man, and he had much more important things to be dealing with than the rantings of a troublesome private explorer. The first official mission to the court of Yaqub Beg under Douglas Forsyth (with Robert Shaw in tow) was about to depart; there were military matters to contend with, and all the other administrative duties that came along with the colonial rule of 'one fifth of humanity'. Mayo had also probably already heard – from Shaw and Forsyth if no one else – that George Hayward was a troublesome, unstable man, and probably best avoided.

But the viceroy was a man of tact and charm, and he was quite used to gently fobbing off petty complainants against the maharaja's tourism policies.[4] He listened politely while Hayward fumed, and took his written report with assurances that he would give it his full attention. Hayward raged, as usual, about innocent, fair-haired women and children; he quoted the Treaty of Amritsar and then explained the precise geographical location of Gilgit. He cited the 'abominable treachery' of the Gilgit garrison and their evil plot to invade Yasin while he was there. He demanded the instalment of a proper Resident in Kashmir, and the ceding of Gilgit to Mir Wali. Then he stretched credibility with confident claims that, were all this to be done, the entire North-West Frontier would instantly subside into benign tranquillity. The Pashtuns, at seeing British justice granted to their co-religionists to the north, would lay down their arms at once and return forever more to their other passions – roses, poetry and pederasty. The fanatical Akhund of Swat would take inspiration from the example and become a champion of world peace, and the Mehtar of Chitral would hand over the keys of his kingdom to the British. If Hayward's recommendations were not put into practice, however, then there was always the Russian Threat.

The viceroy made soothing noises. He sympathised greatly with Hayward's position and truly felt for the suffering of those poor women and children – 'Blue eyes? Really? How fascinating'. But with so much action around the frontier regions – the Forsyth Mission would rely on Kashmir for safe passage, for example – now was not the time to get tough with maharaja. One day, he said, there would indeed be a fully-empowered Resident in Srinagar; one day perhaps the western borders of Kashmir might even be properly defined, but not just now. However, he would be having an official meeting with the maharaja at Sialkot a few days later, and he promised to have a quiet word about the behaviour of the Dogras in Gilgit.

Mayo also firmly suggested that Hayward abandon his plans for a return to Gilgit and Yasin. On discovering just what a troublemaker Hayward was he seems to have forgotten his earlier privately favourable opinions about exploration of the Pamirs. In light of his current ranting, Mayo probably thought it best to keep Hayward well away from remote valleys where dirty little wars were fought while no one was looking. He knew the reputation of the Dards, and probably had grave doubts about the explorer's judgement, but he also knew the less than savoury reputation of the Kashmiri court. There were any number of reasons to fear for Hayward's safety if he returned to the mountains, and though the viceroy may well have been harbouring 'who will rid me of this troublesome traveller' type considerations, a riding accident in Rawalpindi or a bout of malaria in Murree would have been more suitable. A shadowy demise on the fringes of Kashmir would have been exceedingly unhelpful.

Naturally Hayward took no notice of the latter warning, but he did seem briefly to be mollified by Mayo's assurances and feigned sympathy. He described the meeting as 'very satisfactory', took his leave of the viceroy and departed immediately for the viper's nest itself – Srinagar – to prepare for his next assault on the Pamirs. As soon as the door was closed Lord Mayo must have breathed a sigh of relief, filed Hayward's report in the corner of his brain marked 'forget', and hoped that the matter was settled. Naturally, when he met the maharaja at Sialkot he made no mention of any of the explorer's complaints.

Really, what had Hayward expected? That the viceroy would instantly dispatch a crack squad of policemen to arraign the Dogra chief? His passionate concern for the Dards was admirable but it was also stupendously naïve, and his claims that the settlement of the Gilgit issue would lead instantly to the pacification of the entire frontier were ridiculous. In the grand political scheme of things Dogras counted for far more than Dards, and Yasin was but an ill-defined dot on an incomplete map, no matter how blue the eyes of its womenfolk.

Back in Srinagar, with spring rapidly advancing and preparations underway for his next journey, Hayward would have been well placed to hear rumours of the details of the maharaja's viceregal encounter in Sialkot. There was no mention of the atrocities. He should now have paused, taken some long and lonely walk by Dal Lake and carefully considered his position. For two years he had been trying to reach the Pamirs; until he arrived in Yasin it had been his only all-consuming passion. Now, finally, he seemed to have a very real chance of getting there. He surely ought not to do anything to jeopardise that. What had happened to the women and children of Yasin, what he had seen with his own eyes at Madoori, was unquestionably deeply upsetting, but Hayward had done all he could for the moment; now was not the time to pursue it further. Were he to wait, perhaps just six months, there was every chance that he would finally become the first Englishman to reach the High Pamirs and definitively map the Oxus – a far greater prize than the Yarkand River – to its source. He would be a hero. Then he would have real influence; then, not now, would be the moment to unleash his shocking revelations about the Kashmiri killings.

But George Hayward had never had a level head. He had never thought calmly about the future. This was a man who had launched himself on at least three spectacularly dangerous mountain journeys without a care, and most crucially of all, this was a man who seemed totally incapable of waiting. He was possessed with an insane desire, and he was very, very angry.

One of Dr Gottlieb Leitner's favourite pastimes was collecting the proverbs and idioms of Dardistan, and rendering them into English by way of two steps. First the doctor made a direct, word-by-word translation, which generally produced nothing but an incomprehensible and ungrammatical mess; then he would bring his formidable intellect and capacity for lateral thinking to bear on the conundrum and drag out from it an ordered version. Many of these finished translations remained unintelligible to anyone but Leitner himself, but a few were neat, profound and universal. One of the best was the story of a frog, squatting on the bed of a fast-flowing river:

> So said the frog: 'If I speak the water will rush against my mouth, and if I keep silent I will die bursting with rage'.

In Srinagar in May 1870, on realising that the viceroy had done nothing on the Dards' behalf, George Hayward shared the plight of the frog. It must have been in this state that he mailed that letter to the editor of the *Pioneer*. The day before it appeared he wrote to Colonel Showers that he was 'determined the public at home should know exactly what our loyal feudatory is doing'. Within a few weeks, clearly realising the terrible gravity of what he had done,

Hayward was claiming that the letter had been printed against his wishes; it contained statements always meant to be private and he had never wanted his name to appear in connection to it. The last is just credible – though everyone would have known that such a letter could have come from one of only two men: Hayward or Leitner, and to Leitner anonymity was anathema. But you simply do not write letters to major national newspapers, addressing them directly to the readership and stating that you 'have written all this in the hope that the Indian public may be made aware of what our feudatory the Maharaja of Kashmir has perpetrated' purely for the private and strictly confidential enlightenment of the editorial staff. That the editor of the *Pioneer*, knowing that Hayward was still planning to return through Kashmiri territory to the Pamirs, should have realised how very detrimental to his safety the publication of such a letter would be is a separate issue; 'ethical journalism' has always been an oxymoron.

The letter caused a good deal of disgusted headshaking from the British public in India – 'eyes and tresses of the same hue as those of our own wives and children, don't you know?' – but the viceroy was furious. The maharaja, a man who had banned the killing of fish to save his deceased father's soul, obviously had delicate sensitivities. To keep him on side was a troublesome task, and the appearance of such a venomous attack in the press was a diplomatic disaster. Clearly Mayo had underestimated George Hayward if he thought a few soothing words would be enough to placate him; clearly the man was insane. And worse yet, he still seemed hell bent on returning to Gilgit and beyond.

Despite the way the case was later presented, in the aftermath of the *Pioneer* letter the upper echelons of British Indian officialdom do seem to have feared that the Maharaja of Kashmir might try to have Hayward killed. He had to be stopped. Lord Mayo telegraphed London requesting that Sir Henry Rawlinson do something to bring the explorer to heel. Rawlinson himself must have been furious – not to mention deeply embarrassed – by what Hayward had done. He was, after all, a member of the

India Council before he was the vice-president of the RGS, and the Council were of one mind with the viceroy about how to handle the maharaja. But what could he do? Precisely because of the political dangers it had always been made clear to an almost unnecessary degree that Hayward was a private traveller, exploring entirely at his own risk. It was not within the RGS' powers to stop him if his insane desire compelled him to continue.

From the moment that the letter appeared in the *Pioneer* George Hayward's story becomes almost too horrible to watch. It is like seeing a fatal car crash unfold, agonisingly slow and hopelessly inevitable, or watching from a distance beyond which a shouted warning will not carry as a man walks blindly across a frozen lake towards the point where the ice is thinnest. The dark shadow that has lingered around him for so long now becomes a howling abyss; the awful becomes inevitable, but still he presses on. Still he is possessed of that insane desire, though the harsh mountain sunlight is now openly glittering on the cold steel.

Hayward was actually in Srinagar when the letter was published. The maharaja was predictably furious. There was panic in Hayward's camp. Locals were even more distrusting of the Kashmiri court than English visitors. Hayward's servants must have been convinced that disaster was imminent as rumours of plots and poison abounded; several of them deserted. But Hayward still continued with his preparations for that final push to the Pamirs, taking some cold comfort in the idea that the maharaja would be unlikely to murder him while he was actually in the capital city. He sent a train of baggage animals and supplies west towards Gilgit as soon as the passes he had crossed a month earlier were properly open, and told everyone who incredulously asked that yes, he was still going to the Pamirs.

For all the bravura he must have felt almost physically sick when he paused really to consider his situation. Lying awake in the mild Kashmiri nights, he must have thought of the letter in the *Pioneer*, of his name at the bottom, and cringed. On 21 May he wrote what must have been a very difficult letter to Sir Roderick Murchison at the RGS. He explained in detail the 'bad faith' of the Kashmiri Dogras, and stressed again his own 'friendship established with the Yassin people', and then, seeming to shuffle and blush like a mortified schoolboy, he came to the matter which could not be avoided:

> I regret, however, to tell you that a letter of mine representing the atrocities committed by the Maharaja of Kashmir's troops in the countries across the Indus, with an account of their massacre of the Yassin villages in 1863, and certain comments and opinions expressed thereon, has been published in the 'Pioneer' newspaper of May 9th The publication of this letter is most unfortunate; and likely to interfere very much with the objects I have in view. I extremely regret that the editor of the paper in question should have thought fit to publish this letter, and the publication of it has been entirely in opposition to my wishes and instructions, while certain comments in the letter were never for one moment intended to be published in the form in which they appear ... The resentment aroused amongst the maharaja's officials is very great, and it cannot be doubted they will in every way *secretly* strive to do me harm.

In spite of all this, 'in the interests of geography', Hayward felt compelled to continue. He would not stop; he would not turn back, but he had come to a decision that only makes him seem all the more sad and lonely:

> In order, however, to relieve the Royal Geographical Society from a shade of responsibility on my account, I deem it right to offer to sever all connection with the society during the expedition I am contemplating; and though the severance of a connection so auspiciously begun will be a source of profoundest regret to me,

I am aware that before I left London it was distinctly understood that this exploration was undertaken solely at my own risk and on my own responsibility.

Hayward was tendering his resignation without abandoning the job in hand. Yet remarkably he was still claiming that 'the prospect of success looks very fair indeed'. He expected to be on the Pamirs before midsummer. He signed off the letter with more of this forced optimism:

Forewarned in this case is forearmed, and, notwithstanding all there will be to contend with, I firmly believe that (D.V.) success will ultimately attend my efforts, and carry through the enterprise in safety to the end.

I remain, yours very sincerely,

George W. Hayward

It was his last ever letter to the society.

Warnings continued to come thick and fast to Hayward in Kashmir between insincere Dogra smiles. Englishmen he knew there begged him not to go, warned him to leave Kashmiri territory at once, servants were hysterical and official messages of negativity were delivered daily. But nothing would stop George Hayward. On 10 June, the day after Hayward's thirty-second birthday, Lord Mayo wrote to him a final stern warning. Kashmir, unlike the frontier, was a sovereign territory and the government could not officially ban him from going, but 'If you still resolve on prosecuting your journey it must be clearly understood that you do so on your own responsibility'. Hayward understood, and a few days later his unhappy little caravan left Srinagar for the last time and stepped into the wild.

Why did he do it? Why did George Hayward embark on a journey that was at best foolhardy and at worst suicidal? When all around him were begging him with absolute sincerity to desist, why did he carry on? Glib answers would be that he was crazy, that he was suicidal and that he was simply the most dedicated geographer ever known. The truth is more straightforward and more sad: he had no other choice. George Hayward had always been a nobody; he had no money and no home to return to. If he failed there was no family waiting to tell him that they would always love him, no matter what happened. All George Hayward had was the High Pamirs. Lying awake back in Srinagar, nauseously reflecting on his ill-considered letter to the *Pioneer*, he would have realised one thing very clearly: he had destroyed his own career. If the RGS had taken a huge chance on him at the beginning, they would never, ever again grant him another bursary and point him in the direction of another unexplored mountain range, and nor would anyone else, in spite of the Gold Medal (news of which he had received just before leaving Srinagar).

He had let the world know about the Madoori massacre, but he had also made it clear to any future employer that he was a total liability. Had Hayward been a moneyed aristocrat, able to fund his own explorations, none of this would have mattered; he could have shrugged, walked away from India and set sail for darkest Africa. But he wasn't and he couldn't. He knew that he would never again be able to travel safely in Kashmir; he knew that he was now a *persona non grata* with the Indian Government. Whether or not he thought that in reaching the Pamirs he could somehow, like a Hindu pilgrim bathing at the source of the Ganges, wash himself clean of all that sin, whether or not he had any plans for what he might then do, where he might then go, cannot be known. But George Hayward, the orphan from Leeds, had nowhere else to turn.

Another of Dr Leitner's Dardic proverbs is the story of the fox and the river:

> A fox one day fell into a river: as he swept past the shore he cried
> out – 'The water is carrying off the universe!' But the people on
> the banks just laughed and said, 'We can see only a fox who is
> drifting down the river'.

It was meant to be used to admonish those inclined to overstate
the severity of a situation, but for George Hayward, glancing back
one last time at the Vale of Kashmir then turning west, the river
really was sweeping away the universe.

The Deosai Plateau would have been beautiful in late June,
with rolling grasslands and clear brooks running between the low
hills. Small birds would have been singing and a few nomadic
herdsmen would have come up to summer camps from the
Skardu Valley with thickset sheepdogs to guard against the brown
bears that haunted the fringes of the plateau. Even the grim Astor
Valley would have been at its greenest, but none of this would
have lightened the mood around Hayward's unhappy camp. He
reached Gilgit at the beginning of July. His reception there must
have been decidedly frosty, but remarkably he had made it this far
without coming to grief. His mood must have lightened a little,
and when he headed west on about 9 July, away from the clutches
of the Dogras, and crossed the troubled frontier without incident,
he must have felt, almost, that all was well.

He reached Yasin on about the 13th. Whether his welcome was
as warm as it had been in March is not clear, but there seems
to have been some kind of confrontation while he was there.
He then set out uphill. On the evening of 17 July 1870 George
Hayward reached the little campground near Darkot. He was perhaps just two days' march from the foothills of the High Pamirs.

Notes

1   The titillating possibility that Hayward and Shaw may have
    been offered some feminine comfort by their Turkic cap-
    tors is worth considering. In a sternly disapproving footnote
    in the section of his translation of Marco Polo's *Travels* that
    deals with Eastern Turkestan, Sir Henry Yule points out that
    as way-stations where ships of the desert passed in the night,
    the morals of the caravan cities of Central Asia were 'much on
    a par with those in our own seaport towns'. Kashgar in par-
    ticular, he wrote, was 'noted in the East for its *chaukan*, young
    women with whom the traveller may readily form an alliance
    for the duration of his stay, be it long or short'. Unsurprisingly,
    however, the reports of Shaw and Hayward contain no scan-
    dalous admissions of dalliances with fragrant *chaukans*, and
    Hayward's favourable comments about the Turki women are
    the only faintly perfumed hint that we have that such things
    might have gone on.

2   The first confirmed slaughter by a European of a Marco Polo
    sheep came in 1874, during the second Forsyth Mission to
    Eastern Turkestan. After two failed attempts and some frost-
    bitten fingers, an English surveyor named Henry Trotter
    finally bagged the beast – high on the slopes of the Pamirs.

3   Talk of Aryans, Hindus and Mount Meru were all silly
    romanticising on Rawlinson's part. The Pamirs had merely
    been posited as a possible location for the sacred Mount
    Meru by some English scholars of Sanskrit. Most actual
    Indian Hindus would have pointed vaguely in the direc-
    tion of Tibet, and in any case, Mount Meru was a mythical
    concept so it hardly mattered. As for the 'Aryan nations',
    that much-mythologised master race of Indo-Europe cer-
    tainly seem to have sprung from somewhere in the vastness
    between Mongolia and Hungary, but that they started out

shivering under the eaves of the far from paradisiacal Roof
of the World seems rather unlikely.

4   Mayo did not complete his term as viceroy. In February 1872
    he made an approving official visit to the remote Andaman
    Islands out in the middle of the Bay of Bengal, the place to
    which the Raj sent many of its most troublesome prison-
    ers. Mayo strutted around beneath the palm trees, nodding
    approvingly at the strict conditions. The inmates were sup-
    posed politely to salute the viceroy, but one of them, a Pashtun
    named Sher Ali, was not only in possession of a profound
    sense of injustice at his imprisonment; he was also in posses-
    sion of a very sharp knife. In a spectacular security breach he
    was able to launch himself at Mayo and, with the guards per-
    haps a little torpid in the tropical heat, before anyone could
    stop him he had stabbed the viceroy to death.

9

STRANGE AND SUGGESTIVE

Outside on the street London was as damp, cold and smoggy as it had been eleven months earlier. The same horses snorted and stamped at the grimy air between the shafts of the same hackney cabs; the same flickering gaslights cast smears of orange light over the dripping railings and greasy pavements. But inside the hallowed halls of the Royal Geographical Society there was none of the eager anticipation and bubbling good cheer that had warmed the Fellows on the night of their mid-December meeting in 1869, when George Hayward's report of his first journey had been so eagerly read and so effusively praised. Now on 15 November 1870 there was a grim and even – by the standards of elderly gentlemen with venerable beards and letters after their names – an angry atmosphere.

Sir Henry Rawlinson rose to the lectern, his face set with indignation. 'The last time I had occasion to address you on the subject of Mr Hayward was under very different circumstances from the present,' he began. The circumstances – and Rawlinson's emotions – most certainly had been different: then, just six months earlier, he had been collecting the Founder's Gold Medal on Hayward's behalf and basking in the absent explorer's reflected glory.

Rawlinson reminded his listeners of that mild spring evening six months previously:

> I then described Mr Hayward as a young man in the full vigour
> of manhood, proud of his past honours, full of high hopes for
> the future, starting on his daring enterprise to explore the Pamir
> Steppes, resolved to achieve success, and with every prospect of
> that success before him.

Now there were none of the beaming faces that Rawlinson had looked out on from the same lectern on that evening; there were only pinched lips, stern frowns and the occasional agitated tug of a greying, scholarly beard.

'Now, all is changed,' the vice-president continued. 'Mr Hayward lies cold in death: not on the battlefield, not in Christian or hallowed soil, but under a heap of stones, on the bleak hillside, near the crests of the Indian Caucuses,[1] the victim of a barbarous and cold-blooded murder.' Such overblown language was standard for the time, but the sense of utter outrage was very genuine. It was hard, Rawlinson spluttered with undisguised emotion, 'to speak coolly of a subject of this sort'. Indeed it was, and for Rawlinson more so than anyone. After all, at that previous meeting he had gone to great lengths to point out that Hayward was his protégé, that he had dispatched the young traveller in the direction of the Pamirs. Now that mutilated body, lying under its pile of heathen, unhallowed rocks on that lonely Hindu Kush mountainside was creating serious diplomatic problems in India, and was – as many pointed out – a prime example of just why Englishmen ought not to be allowed to wander off into wild frontier regions. If agitated politicians in the India Office were from time to time asking just where this bothersome traveller, more of a nuisance in death than he had been even in life, had come from, Rawlinson must have found a few accusatory stares aimed in his direction.

Still, Rawlinson could hardly disown Hayward's rotting corpse. 'I know it has been said that Mr Hayward was wanting in discretion, in caution, in regard for his own personal safety,' he went on (to be honest that was probably just about the most restrained thing that was being said about him in official circles). 'All that may be admitted. Disregard for his personal safety was an essential point in his character, and it was one of his chief qualifications as an explorer in unknown and savage regions.' Rawlinson could not dispute that Hayward 'had his faults', but, he reminded the Fellows, the man was gone to the Great Beyond after all, and one ought not to speak ill of the dead. Hayward should be remembered not for his rashness but for his bravery, his skill as a surveyor and draughtsman, and above all, for his not inconsiderable achievements.

There was one other point that Rawlinson was very eager to press, for even as the Fellows had taken their seats and shuffled their papers one word above all others had hissed its way along the benches with bitter acrimony: 'Kashmir'.

Drawing himself up and swallowing any sense of governmental shame, Rawlinson admonished the gossips: 'I wish, in the first place, to correct an impression which the meeting might entertain of the complicity of the Kashmir Government in this affair. I can assure the meeting that, as far as I have means of judging, there is no foundation whatever for that impression.' A rumble of disquiet must have passed through the audience at this, but Rawlinson pressed on – he was now on official damage limitation duty. He raised the ghastly spectre of a certain letter in the Calcutta *Pioneer*: 'It is clear that Mr Hayward's letter, which was published, very unfortunately, I admit, had nothing whatever to do with the circumstances of his death.' The maharaja, Rawlinson declared, doing his best to ignore the mutterings from the benches, had been 'most loyal', and the very suggestion that there had been Kashmiri intrigue was nothing but malicious mischief-making. The Fellows, the journalists and the public could all forget entirely about the idea that the *Pioneer* letter had something to do with Hayward's demise: 'it is now quite clear that the two circumstances are entirely disconnected.'

Rawlinson was taking some serious liberties here. In November 1870 his 'means of judging' that the maharaja was entirely innocent were limited in the extreme. In addition, although there were equally impressive alternative theories, to suggest that there was 'no foundation' for even a suspicion of Kashmiri culpability was, quite frankly, to tell a lie.

Even the President of the RGS, Sir Roderick Murchison, who had no government role to conflict with his geographical duties, was far from assuaged by Rawlinson's frantic fire-fighting. When the vice-president was done he rose to his feet clutching a piece of paper. 'You have entirely exonerated the Government of Cashmere,' he rumbled, 'but there are persons, and I hold in my hand a letter from one, who still have their doubts about it.'

Such letters had been flying thick and fast; that was precisely the government's problem. All Rawlinson could do was repeat his same feeble assurances, beg the society to remember that Hayward had 'died in the path of duty' and that 'all honour is due to him', and to press, to push, to point out the one thing that was definitively known about the horrible affair: the identity of the man who had actually organised the murder. This man, Rawlinson assured the Fellows, was doomed for his dastardly deed; he was already in full flight across the mountains and 'the mark of Cain was on him'. His name, this vile criminal? Mir Wali of Yasin.

On 30 August, two and a half months before Rawlinson addressed the RGS, a Pundit named Hyder Shah had heard a terrible rumour at the roadside a day's march from Chitral. Shah was a Pashtun from Kohat, south of Peshawar. He was on a geographical spying mission for Montgomerie of the Great Trigonometrical Survey, his aim to scout out more of the ground that had been charted by the Mirza two years earlier. His code name in the GTS reports was simply the rank he had attained in the Bengal army – the Havildar, a non-commissioned native officer – and his

journey was mind-blowingly dangerous, even for a Muslim, even for a proud Pashtun. He had only just survived the horrendously risky crossing of the Lowari Pass from Dir into the Chitral Valley. The pass itself was neither particularly high nor particularly steep; that was not the problem. The danger came from the marauding bands of Kafirs, the wild pagans of the Hindu Kush, who infested the surrounding hills and preyed upon helpless travellers. The road across the pass was lined with bleak little piles of stones, each marked with a threadbare martyr's flag, snapping in the thin wind. They were the graves of those who had felt the sharp end of a Kafir dagger.

The Havildar had bribed the chief of Dir with a gold-embroidered scarf to provide him with an escort, but despite the presence of twenty-five armed men he had barely made it across, and in the village of Asreth, the first settlement on the Chitral side of the pass, the escort had had to fight a running battle through the night to ward off attack.

If the Havildar had felt some relief at crossing into the Kafir-free zone of Chitral, under the firm rule of the mehtar, he can hardly have been cheered by the story he was told at the miserable little hamlet of Brary. There, over cups of murky tea in some grubby, smoke-blackened roadside hovel, with the light of the guttering fire casting dark shadows across the bearded, piratical faces of his hosts, he heard a story that was already well known throughout the Western Himalayas. Six weeks earlier, some way north-east of Chitral, an Englishman had been murdered. The men in Brary said this unfortunate foreigner had been called 'Hawel'.

Murder in the mountains was as commonplace as marriage and hardly worth mentioning in normal circumstances – the graves on the Lowari road were beyond number after all. But Englishmen were entirely unknown west of Gilgit, so the incident had become a hot topic over tea at wayside halts. The story, according to the Havildar's informants, who seemed to relish the rumour as much as they enjoyed the greasy kebabs they were chewing, was that this foreigner had been beheaded – the standard Dardic death

– sometime in mid-July at a place called Ooshgoom (another name for Yasin – derived from that of its language, Burushaski) about a week's march from Chitral town. The Havildar must have guessed that this 'Hawel' could be none other than that troublesome traveller whose name was well known amongst explorers and geographers in India – George Hayward.

The Brary gossipmongers said that the foreigner's camp had been looted after his death and a certain quantity of gold coin – approximately the amount that one might accrue from government and RGS bursaries – had been carried off. Pistols, rifles, tent cloth and portable camp furniture had been distributed amongst mountain villages. It was said that the Englishman's servants had also been slaughtered, though a disputed strand of the story suggested that one had escaped, horribly wounded. When the Havildar demanded to know who had committed this awful crime he was told that the question hardly needed asking – everyone between here and Hunza knew that Mir Wali had ordered and organised the Englishman's death.

If the Havildar found all this rather unsettling (he was a British agent after all), the next piece of news must have disturbed him even more. He was told that this murderous Mir Wali had fled his homeland and was now skulking to the west in Badakhshan, the wild country on the upper reaches of the Oxus – the very place towards which the Havildar was now heading.

At about the same time that the Havildar heard of Hayward's death the first bloody reports were beginning to trickle out of the mountains; over the passes and along the courses of boulder-filled rivers; through the chilli-scented alleyways of the bazaars; between the knots of the threadbare Afghan carpets in the durbar halls of petty chieftains; and, finally, to the ears of British officials. Long before it arrived at its final destination the story was already addled with wild rumour and careless conjecture. Yet, in all the theories, accusations and counter-accusations that eventually emerged, there remained one constant, one thing that no one seriously disputed. What the Havildar heard at the Brary roadside on 30 August, unadorned by theory of motive,[2] was essentially the truth. George Hayward had been murdered by, not actually but certainly at the direct instigation of, his supposed friend Mir Wali. His servants too had been killed and all his possessions stolen.

The first port of call for all of the reports emerging from the high country was the British-ruled Punjab, and the man who collected them together, tried to make sense of them and then passed them on to his superiors, the viceroy and the Secretary of State for India, was the Lieutenant-Governor, Sir Henry Durand. When the Government of India first heard tales of Hayward's demise at the end of August, however, they tried to suppress the news. The attempt to enforce silence was never going to last long – India was a rumour mill, and idle talk over a *chota peg* at the club of an evening was de rigueur amongst petty officials and senior soldiers. However, even once news of the murder was officially made public the government placed a ban on any discussion of the matter – and particularly any theorising about motive or culprit – in the Indian press until after official investigations had been completed. The reason for this shutdown was obvious. Even had that scandalous letter not appeared in the Calcutta *Pioneer* back in May, the accusatory fingers of commentators and busybodies would largely have pointed in the direction of Srinagar.

It was also clear that the viceroy and the rest of the Indian Government had been more than half-expecting George Hayward to come to grief. Despite the official line – that which Sir Henry Rawlinson so determinedly pushed at the November meeting of the RGS – the idea that it had been that 'feudatory of the British crown' Ranbir Singh, Maharaja of Kashmir, who had done the deed was certainly being considered. Colonel Pollock, the British commissioner at Peshawar, had collected the very first hints that a traveller had come to grief somewhere in the mountains. As soon as he received confirmation he wrote directly to the viceroy to let him know the unfortunate news, and to give a few thoughts of his own on the matter:

> It was simply <u>a wicked</u> thing publishing that letter in the Pioneer. One would have supposed that <u>anyone capable of reading it</u> must have known how exceedingly prejudicial to the author its publication must be, both at once, and in the future.
>
> Risky enough to travel in those regions at all – doubly so as the known author of a forcibly written attack on Cashmere [Kashmir] misgovernment and annexations attended, or said to be so, with circumstances of extreme barbarity.

Pollock was clearly unfamiliar with the unscrupulous standards of newspaper journalists, but his outraged underscoring makes very clear the nature of his suspicions. The publication of 'that letter' would hardly have been 'exceedingly prejudicial' to Hayward's safety with the Dards of either Yasin or Chitral – or indeed with any of the other terrible tribes in Badakhshan and beyond. It was, however, as everyone realised, prejudicial in the extreme to his relationship with the Kashmir court. On hearing that Hayward was dead, Colonel Pollock seems to have jumped to the very obvious conclusion – that it was the maharaja who had done him in. Such suspicions were clearly widespread amongst British officials, and all the more reason to order a press blackout.

The viceroy, Lord Mayo, must have uttered some earthy Irish oaths when he heard the news: George Hayward had been a nuisance to the government in life, but he was an absolute nightmare in death. Though Mayo quite reasonably absolved himself from any sense of guilt about the explorer's demise – 'I have nothing to reproach myself as both in conversation and in letter I did all I could to dissuade him from going' – that was the least of his concerns. If the maharaja had actually murdered a British citizen then the entire government policy of having someone else, such as a loyal vassal, deal with the sensitive north-west corner of India would collapse. What could the government possibly do if that was what had happened? Would they have to arrest the Dogra royal? Bring him to trial? Such an unspeakable eventuality had not happened in over a century of British rule in India. Petty, insignificant down-country rajas had been dethroned for bad behaviour on occasion, but nothing on this scale: Ranbir Singh was just about the most important of all the Indian royals; he was worth a twenty-one-gun salute! What if he resisted? Would Britain have to invade Kashmir? And if they did, the British would have to deal with all those undefined borders and ugly mountain wars themselves. The prospect didn't bear thinking about. The viceroy's only comfort would have been in the knowledge that there were at least a couple of alternative suspects.

The various conflicting theories about Hayward's lonely, violent end that emerged from the Western Himalayas through the last months of 1870 and in the spring of 1871 can be filed neatly into three separate trays on the desk of any would-be investigator. The first could be marked 'Mir Wali did it, alone, for his own reasons'; the second 'Mir Wali did it, on the orders of the Mehtar of Chitral, for obscure reasons'; and the third 'Mir Wali did it, at the instigation of the Maharaja of Kashmir, for obvious reasons'. If that would-be investigator is genuinely professional and impartial he will immediately note a major stumbling block standing like an avalanche-cast boulder in the way of his sleuthing: a great deal of the information he has been given was provided, openly and with protestations of good faith, by two of the three prime suspects – the Mehtar of Chitral and the Maharaja of Kashmir, the rival royals brooding at either end of the Western Himalayas. In fact, the very first report of the murder, sent south to Colonel Pollock at Peshawar by the hand of a traveller named Meean Raht Shah, had come from the mehtar himself. This, then, will cause obvious problems, and is probably in large part the reason why 'truth' of a kind to satisfy anyone with an enquiring mind has never really emerged. But our honourable investigator has to begin somewhere. Better then to leave the politics for later and to start with what happened in the high Hindu Kush in the

aftermath of the dreadful event, and what actually happened on
the morning of 18 July 1870 itself.

Mir Wali did it; that much is clear. It was said that once Hayward
was buried under that pile of stones in the woods near Darkot,
and once all the spoils of his camp had been lugged back downhill
to the Yasin fort, Mir Wali 'became silent, said hardly a word to
anyone'. He may, of course, have been reflecting on the horror of
what he had done to his one-time friend, but it seems more likely
that he was pondering his own fate.

The Yasin chief tried to keep what had happened quiet, but of
course he had even less chance of success in this than the British
would have weeks later down on the plains. Everyone in the
valley knew about the Englishman's death. Also, according to the
early reports, Mir Wali had fallen out with his wazir (prime minister), a man named Rahmat who, it was claimed, had been even
greater a friend to Hayward during his first visit to Yasin than the
chief himself. Wazir Rahmat had tried to dissuade Mir Wali from
carrying out his plan. When he was ignored he sent word of what
had happened west across the Shandur Pass to Chitral.

The Mehtar of Chitral had a record of fuelling the sibling
rivalry of the Yasin brothers. He had already helped to topple
Mulk Aman in favour of Mir Wali, and now the Chitrali chieftain
seems to have decided to unleash the weapon he had been keeping in reserve for just such a moment. Little brother Pahlwan,
who had been governing Chitral's far north-east from the mud
fort at Mastuj, was ordered across the Shandur with a force of
500 men to topple Mir Wali. Mir Wali panicked and fled, bolting
north past the hillside where the bodies of Hayward's servants
were still rotting in the summer sunshine, and across the Darkot
Pass to seek shelter in the badlands of Badakhshan. Pahlwan, who
was barely 20 years old, took instant possession of that which had
already belonged to both his elder brothers – the throne of Yasin.

Just why the Mehtar of Chitral engineered these events is unclear. The straightforward suggestion – that improbably claimed by British officials later on – that he had done it to punish Mir Wali, his own son-in-law, seems rather unlikely. More convincing is the idea that he had instantly realised that, having murdered an Englishman, Mir Wali's days as ruler were numbered. If the Dogras marched up the valley from Gilgit on a mission of retribution – and if this time they didn't march back again once they had done with killing women and children – then the mehtar would lose all his malign influence over the country east of the Shandur Pass. Alternatively, he could have chased off the murderer simply to impress the British, who he had been quietly courting (letter carriers had been risking the Kafirs of the Lowari Pass on mail runs between Chitral and Peshawar for some time). And there was one final, sinister possibility, an idea certainly worth considering in light of later developments: the whole thing could have been an elaborate set-up; the mehtar could have had Mir Wali chased out of Yasin simply to cover his own bloody tracks, to allay any suspicions that it could have been he who ordered the murder.

In any case, Mir Wali was gone, and the mehtar had more influence in Yasin than ever before. The first full account of the murder that the British received actually came from Chitral. It was the report of a servant of Pahlwan who had accompanied the young chieftain on his pursuit of Mir Wali and had heard the details from the murderer's estranged prime minister, Wazir Rahmat. This report claimed that the motive for Hayward's death had been simple, petty and almost ridiculous – a dispute over the hire of porters:

They stated that when the sahib[3] came to Yassin on the first occasion, he gave liberal presents both to the Rajah [Mir Wali] and the people of Yassin territory, and everyone was pleased with him. But when he came the second time, he did not pay any attentions either to the Rajah or the people, and prepared to go away to Badakhshan. He asked for 25 porters, and was told in reply that porters were scarce in the country, the people of which were generally very respectable, and he could not be accommodated with so many porters. The sahib said sternly and in harsh language – 'Why do you get annoyed at being asked to furnish only so small a number of porters? When I return from Badakhshan I shall have a numerous party of Pathans [Pashtuns] with me, and a large number of porters will be required. How will you manage then?'

When the people heard these words they were exasperated. They said, – 'At present we are not the subjects of anyone, and we are spoken to in such harsh language. When the sahib returns with a force from Badakhshan, we shall have no homes left to live in.'

When Mir Wali heard of what the sahib had spoken, he assured the people and the elders that they need not distress themselves, as he had determined to get rid of the pest i.e., to kill him, and on no account let him live.

According to the report, Hayward was then traitorously dispatched from Yasin fort with all the porters he could wish for, but as soon as he had gone Mir Wali set in motion a carefully considered plot.

An armed posse headed up the valley after him under the charge of several of the henchmen and hangers-on of the ramshackle Yasin court, principal amongst them a man by the name of Shah Dil Iman who was, according to some reports, an illegitimate half-brother of Mir Wali. They kept their distance until Hayward reached Darkot and made his camp. They had meant to take him by surprise there, but Hayward had heard that trouble was brewing. That night the explorer sat awake in his lighted tent with his loaded weapons. His pursuers were apparently without firearms, and they waited until the morning, when the Englishman and his servants 'were overpowered by sleep', to attack. Hayward was dragged from his bed, begging and offering the men 'his own weight in gold and jewels if they spared his life'. However, 'the wretches were inexorable'. They took him away into the forest and killed him. They then destroyed the camp, killed four of Hayward's companions, and took the loot and the mortified munshi back to Mir Wali. Apparently the munshi was imprisoned in Yasin fort until Mir Wali and his little band of fugitives – which surely included those who had actually done the killing – fled at the approach of Pahlwan. They took the munshi with them, but only as far as Darkot. There, in the very same bloodstained place, he shared the fate of his employer. The delay in the murder of the munshi must have been the source of the rumour heard by the Havildar in Chitral that one man had survived the slaughter.

The idea that Mir Wali had had George Hayward murdered over the issue of porterage seems patently absurd, even given the generally lawless standards of Dardistan. However, many of the details, both of the death and of Hayward's last days in Yasin, were confirmed in the next report on the affair to emerge from the mountains, the most comprehensive of them all, and, as far as just about everyone ever since seems to have felt, the most trustworthy. This report is certainly impressive in its detail and its apparent thoroughness, but the widespread faith in its fairness is rather odd considering the background of the author.

The British authorities in India never deputed an official to go to Gilgit to investigate George Hayward's murder. This certainly seems odd now, and indeed, to many people it seemed just as odd at the time. Hayward may have been nothing more than a private citizen, but he was still an Englishman, and the violent death of any other Englishman anywhere else in India would have led to whole investigative committees being formed and – be sure – swift justice for the culprit. The excuse forwarded at the time was that the scene of Hayward's demise was simply too remote and very obviously far too dangerous for another Englishman to – quite literally – risk his neck there. This was yet another reason – if more were still required – why expeditions like Hayward's were to be frowned upon: the scant chance of retribution in the case of mishap. This might have convinced some people, but still, there was absolutely no reason why some capable and enquiring young soldier should not be sent to Gilgit to sniff around for gossip and first-hand accounts in the bazaar there. Gilgit was supposed to be the territory of a 'loyal feudatory', so what was the problem?

It was not that the British were not taking an interest in the case – far from it. The deceased George Hayward, under his heap of Hindu Kush rocks, was the subject of far more official attention than he had ever been when alive. Reports were being gathered from every corner of the Himalayas and forwarded to the India Office, and local rumours were being carefully sifted. This was all being done in conditions of strict secrecy, however, and it has to be considered that the glaring absence of any official British investigation on the ground had as much to do with an official terror of what unspeakable horrors such an enterprise might turn up – principally irrefutable evidence of Kashmiri culpability – as with understandable concerns about personal safety in Dardistan. Probably the British Indian Government would eventually have been forced by public grumbling to send someone to Gilgit, but long before things got that far their problem was solved: in mid-September, as soon as the news of Hayward's death was public knowledge, the dear, wise, loyal Maharaja of Kashmir offered to send his own man to the spot to find out what he could.

The very idea of one of the key suspects in a murder case sending his employee on a quasi-official mission to investigate the crime in question ought to have raised howls of protest. But the maharaja was not stupid, he had picked his man wisely and he knew exactly how to safeguard himself from British complaint. This was the heyday of the Raj after all, and race and religion counted for everything. When the maharaja announced his plan the government was delighted; all would be well; the truth would surely out; there was nothing to worry about. With infinite political judgement, the Maharaja of Kashmir had sent a tame Englishman to investigate the murder.

Frederick Drew was an interesting character. He was born in Southampton where his father ran an expensive private school.

After an education under the auspices of Drew senior, he trained as a geologist at the Royal School of Mines where he was, by all accounts, a star student. In 1862, at the age of 26, he had taken the post of state geologist to the Kashmiri court. His job was to assess and survey the mineral wealth of the Himalayan kingdom. He had been there ever since.

To the relief of those members of the British public who had taken an angry interest in the Hayward case, Drew seemed to be the very epitome of English decency and fair play – so much so that he eventually went home to become the science master at Eton. Such a man – such an Englishman no less – would surely never willingly take part in a cover-up. This may have been so, but there was something else important about Frederick Drew: he was a slavishly dedicated servant of the maharaja. Not too long after his involvement in the Hayward affair he was actually appointed Kashmiri governor of the highly sensitive border region of Ladakh, a position that the maharaja would only ever have given to one of his most trusted lackeys. When Drew published his own monumental book on Kashmir five years later he dedicated it in unnecessarily flowery terms to his employer, 'With the author's good wishes for the prosperity of his house and government'.

He simply could not countenance any ill words against the maharaja. In the part of his book dealing with Dardistan, Drew commended Dr Leitner's wonderful work with the languages, but he had to take issue with the doctor's accounts of the Kashmiri conquests of Dardistan:

> As to the 'History of the Wars with Kashmir,' given in the same work of Dr. Leitner's, as taken down from the statements of a native of Sazin, there are in this many exaggerations and inaccuracies – so many, indeed, are they, and so difficult is it to wash free from them the grains of truth that are mixed up, so confused is the whole tale, that the account is of but little value.

Naturally Drew would write this, for Leitner's account is full of tales of Kashmiri atrocities. He rather presumptuously states that Leitner himself would doubtless admit to the limited value of the account 'derived as it must be from the mouths of a few, who could not have been eye-witnesses of most that they told' (it is of course highly unlikely that Leitner, with his monumental self-assurance, would have made any such acknowledgement). Drew then, without irony, admits that his own account – all Dogra decency and restraint in the face of Dardic barbarity – comes from exactly the same kind of shaky second-hand sources, but declares it to be that 'which I conceive to be nearest the truth'. He also scoffed at the more lurid aspects of Hayward's by then infamous *Pioneer* letter (which Leitner had republished as an appendix in his most recent book). He grudgingly acknowledged that something nasty had probably happened at Madoori during the Dogra invasion, but came within a breath of justifying war crimes as 'so apt to the taking of a place by assault'.

Despite pouring scorn on Leitner and Hayward's accounts of Dogra atrocities, Drew was quite happy to pass on as truth any hearsay he happened upon about the brutality of the Dards. He even gave space to exactly the same myth of unspeakable cruelty that Hayward had attributed to the Dogras in Yasin, simply shifting it on to the person of Mir Wali's father, Gohar Aman: 'I believe it to be a fact that on one occasion at least he killed a young child by throwing it up and cutting it in the air with his sword.' Again, preposterously, given the snooty condemnation of Leitner's and Hayward's reports, Drew states that 'I cannot doubt the truth of this that I heard' before recounting some hoary, many-decades-old rumour of Gohar Aman beheading a village headman and leaving the body to be eaten by dogs. Drew's entire account of the history of the Gilgit region is riddled with 'I hear', 'I do not know exactly' and 'as near as I can make out'. Yet be sure, it is all engineered to reflect as badly as possible on the savage Dards, and as well as possible on the manly and magnificent Dogras.

It is a wonder that no one took issue with all this at the time, and thought, on the basis of Drew's ludicrously biased *The Jummoo and Kashmir Territories*, to raise concerns about the geologist's qualifications for investigating Hayward's death. But by the time the book was published in 1875 the 'truth' – Frederick Drew's truth no less – was so firmly established in the public consciousness that any element of mystery had long since been forgotten.

In September 1870 only the maharaja really knew how unlikely it was that his loyal little rock-tapper would produce any evidence that reflected badly on his own conduct. It was not that Drew would actually lie; it was just that as perhaps the most pro-Kashmiri Englishman in all India there were certain avenues of investigation that he would never even think to venture down.

However, ridiculous as Drew's appointment as detective-in-chief for the Hayward case was – and despite his glaring lack of qualifications for actually assessing the background of the murder, making sense of its causes and purpose, and identifying its ultimate mastermind – he seems to have made an admirably thorough attempt to investigate the actual circumstance of the horrible deed itself.

Drew had been peering under boulders in Baltistan in search of valuable minerals that might enrich the Kashmiri coffers when news of the murder and the subsequent royal order to investigate arrived. Like any dutiful servant he immediately downed his geologist's hammer and headed for Gilgit. For Drew, an employee of the same state, the welcome at the Dogra frontier would have been much warmer than Hayward's. Though he had far less chance than his unfortunate predecessor of actually going to Yasin – even had he wanted to – he certainly had no complaints about the hospitality of the garrison, and he mentioned no obfuscation or attempts to baffle his investigations.

He did whatever he could to piece together the last days and hours of Hayward's life, building a picture from several sources. He had local reports in Gilgit itself from which to establish the dates of the explorer's final march, and he had the statements of

Mir Wali's estranged prime minister, Wazir Rahmat (with whom Drew claimed to have been previously acquainted), delivered both as a letter and by the mouth of a Yasini agent sent to Gilgit. On hearing that an English investigator was in Dardistan, the Mehtar of Chitral too had rattled off a couple of missives full of whatever gory details he currently had to hand. Lastly, Drew actually managed to get an agent of his own into the Yasin Valley – even as far as the scene of the murder at Darkot itself.

'From these materials a connected view of the last events in Mr. Hayward's life can be made out, and one which, from the corroboration of the statements derived from various sources, deserves, I think, considerable confidence,' wrote Drew. To be fair, his account of the murder itself does indeed inspire considerable confidence.

According to Drew's report Hayward's return to Yasin got off to a bad start with an unfortunate faux pas. Mir Wali apparently rode out some way towards Gilgit to meet his friend, 'and, on coming within hail, got off his horse'. Hayward, however, did not repay the respectful compliment, 'but remained mounted till quite near'. Mir Wali was 'somewhat offended at this'. Drew, a gentleman to the core, was quite prepared to explain this incident away as Hayward either not seeing Mir Wali's approach or simply having no idea of correct protocol. In any case, it was hardly a beheading offence.

The incident smoothed over, Hayward pitched his tent near the Yasin fort. He was there, Drew reckoned, for two days, and during those two days Mir Wali came to visit him several times. There were none of the happy hunting trips of the previous March; the Yasin ruler got straight down to business. What, he wanted to know, had been the outcome of Hayward's attempts to speak on his behalf in India? The negative reply did not go down well: 'Mir Wali, it seems, had built much hope on Mr. Hayward having originally undertaken to represent his case, and was proportionally disappointed at nothing having resulted from it.' Still, once again, this was no reason to kill the guest. But then came the question of Hayward's plans for his onward journey.

According to Drew's informants the explorer was determined to follow the route he had spied out at the end of the winter – the direct road across the Darkot Pass. After all, four months earlier Mir Wali had been amongst the first to assure him of the excellence of this particular gateway to the Pamirs. Now, in mid-summer, the pass was open wide, and Hayward was surely eager to be on his way. However, during the spring word had come from the west that the Englishman was to be sent via Chitral. The mehtar had decided, it seems, that it really was time for this wandering foreigner to present himself to the pre-eminent potentate this side of the Pamirs and his son-in-law, despite his earlier pleading with Hayward to ignore Chitrali advances, now seemed forcefully to press the request. Hayward, of course, had no intention of complying with the mehtar's desire for a meeting. The Darkot Pass was there, almost within view, begging to be crossed; no hordes of Kirghiz bandits thronged its approaches; no government red tape was strewn across its lower slopes. If all that stood in the way was the wheedling letter of some petty fief more than 100 miles distant, George Hayward saw nothing that could stop him.

Mir Wali was not, it seems, pleased with his guest's stubbornness; there was an angry dispute:

> This argument between the two was conducted with a good deal of warmth. The accounts say – but I am unwilling to believe them – that Mr. Hayward called Mir Wali by a hard name that he was likely to resent. However, Mr. Hayward kept to his purpose (which was to go by as straight a road as possible to the Pamir), and Mir Wali gave in and provided coolies; and probably then only, when he saw the coveted goods going out of his reach, formed the design against Mr. Hayward's life.

So this was the conclusion of Frederick Drew, loyal servant of the Maharaja of Kashmir: George Hayward had been murdered by his former friend Mir Wali of Yasin in the aftermath of a fiery argument, with the sole motive being the plunder of the explorer's baggage. Indeed, this was soon to be the official line on the matter too – an explanation as politically convenient as it was unlikely.

The other pieces of the story all seem reasonable enough. The faux pas at the gates of Yasin is feasible – though, like Drew suggested, as a simple error rather than an arrogant snub. Hayward would unlikely have reacted warmly to a demand to turn away from the Pamirs yet again on a detour to Chitral, and given his past record of foot-stomping in Eastern Turkestan the idea of a heated confrontation is by no means far-fetched. The idea of an ugly and embarrassing dispute over payment and presents seems quite feasible too – plenty of foreign travellers in Asia in the decades since have encountered delightfully warm and apparently sincere hospitality, only to be presented with the bill when they come to leave.

Still, the idea that Mir Wali had Hayward murdered merely to get his hands on a few odds and ends of expedition equipment and what was, all things considered, a fairly modest sum of money, seems frankly absurd. The Yasin chief was, according to Drew, 'a known avaricious man', and he certainly had a history of family treachery. But he must have realised that killing the Englishman would almost certainly lead to the loss of his kingdom – and even his life. Surely even a moderately unhinged person would have paused to consider – several hundred square kilometres of territory and absolute authority of thousands of people weighed against, at most, £400 and a folding camp chair – and decided that it wasn't worth it.

The bitter argument and the 'hard name' have to be taken into account, and had Mir Wali in the heat of the moment drawn his sabre and run the foul-mouthed Englishman through on the spot it would have been quite in character. But he didn't. The plot that was actually put into action was meticulous and relied on patience and a cool head – and indeed it was not until a couple of days after Hayward left Yasin fort that the deed was done (according to Drew, thanks to deliberately prevaricating porters, it took

Hayward three days to cover the 19 miles to Darkot). If Mir Wali had simply been in a fit of affronted rage he would surely have had plenty of time to simmer down. The whole theory, impossible as it is to disprove after 140 years, seems decidedly unlikely.

Nevertheless, what had actually happened at Darkot in the sharp dawn light of that July morning? Frederick Drew was never going to visit the crime scene himself, even with the Mehtar of Chitral's nominally friendly puppet Pahlwan now in charge. After a certain amount of wheeling and dealing, however, he eventually obtained permission for a single Kashmiri foot soldier, a man named Gufar Khan, to visit the valley. Though Khan later complained that he had been kept hostage in the Yasin fort for several days while instructions about what to do with him were awaited from Chitral, he was allowed to visit Darkot itself, alone and unimpeded. He saw the spot where the killing was done, and he heard the story of exactly what had happened from the village headman, who had been there that very morning.

Gufar Khan was, like Frederick Drew, an employee of the maharaja – indeed, as soon as he got back to Srinagar he was promoted for his sterling work in Yasin. By the time the knots and tangles of the Hayward case have been unpicked all the way down to the hard, cold events of 18 July, however, politics and motives are irrelevant. The account of the Darkot headman, as collected by Gufar Khan, is stark and striking. It corroborates and expands the first description that came via Chitral, and is, in its unembellished matter-of-fact manner, eminently believable:

> The sahib came to Darkut [sic] in the afternoon [of the 17th], and encamped in a garden, close to which is the forest. Shah Dil Iman came the same evening with sixty men; he went to the house of one Rustam, who asked why he had come with so many people, to which he answered that he had orders to see the sahib safe across the Pass. There being some communication between these new comers and the coolies who were with the sahib, it reached even to his munshi's ears that there was cause for

apprehension, and he informed his master. That night the sahib did not eat any dinner, but only drank tea, and sat watching the whole night in his chair with his guns and pistols before him, and a pistol in his left hand while he wrote with the other. In the morning, after taking a cup of tea, he lay down for an hour or two's sleep. Shah Dil Iman having sent a man to see, and found that he was sleeping, took his men by a round to the ground in the forest above where the tent was, and then himself coming, asked the Khausaman [Hayward's cook] if he were asleep: on his being told that he was, Kukali [another of the Yasinis] entered the tent. One of the Pathan servants asked what he was about, and took up a stick to stop him, but others coming round and keeping the Pathan back, Kukali went into the tent and caught the sahib by the throat, and, more at that moment coming in, put a noosed rope around his neck, and, with the same rope, tied his hands behind him. The servants were all overpowered and bound at the same time. Then they brought the sahib, thus bound, away from the village into the forest for a distance of mile or a mile and a half; and as they were going he tried to induce them to spare his life by promises, first of what was in his boxes, – but that, they jeeringly said, was theirs already; then of a larger ransom to be obtained from the English country; and, lastly, he said he would write to the Bukshee [military paymaster] at Gilgit for money for them. This, however, they would not listen to. Then the sahib asked for his munshi to be brought, but he had been taken off in another direction, and could not quickly be found; then they took the ring off his finger, and then Shah Dil Iman drew his sword, on which the sahib repeated some words which seemed like a prayer, and Shah Dil Iman felled him with one blow. Then Kukali brought the sahib's own sword, and said he would like to try it; so he struck a blow with it on the sahib's body. It was 8 or 9 in the morning when the murder was committed.[4]

While all these grizzly details were being uncovered, what had become of the murderer himself? Where was Mir Wali?

The Pundit, Havildar Hyder Shah, who had first heard of Hayward's death at the end of August, spent five somewhat nervous days in Chitral after his terrifying crossing of the Lowari Pass. All the way north from Peshawar his cover story had been that he was going to the mehtar's country to buy the famed falcons of the Hindu Kush – much prized by Pashtun sportsmen. Now he had to come up with some other excuse for an onward journey into Badakhshan. He told the Chitrali chief that he was heading to Bokhara, in Uzbek country beyond the mountains, to recover a debt. This was an unfortunate story to have chosen, for the mehtar haughtily told him that he had no chance of going to Uzbekistan. The Afghan political climate was typically stormy in 1870, and Abdurrahman, a young pretender to the throne of his uncle, the Emir Sher Ali, was plotting treason from the northern shore of the Oxus. The emir had recently declared the borders of Badakhshan – an Afghan vassal state – closed to try to bring a halt to his nephew's traitorous meddling.

Despite this, and apparently without having explained himself, the Havildar left Chitral on 5 September. He passed once more into wild borderlands haunted by murdering Kafirs, and – as a man from the bone-dry hills of the lower frontier – saw real snow peaks for the first time (his report, with its talk of great 'cracks' in the frozen ground between the mountains, was the first evidence that British geographers ever received that there were glaciers in the Hindu Kush). Struggling over high passes, gasping in the thin air, the Havildar eventually reached Faizabad, the cold capital of Badakhshan.

Badakhshan was wild country. Pushed up into the north-east corner of Afghanistan where the River Oxus turns to the west from the outer buttress of the Pamirs and along the southern flank of the Tien Shan. It had borders with Tajik and Kirghiz country, with Chitral and with the terrifying wilderness of Kafiristan. It had long been nominally a part of Afghanistan – whenever the emir's remit extended beyond Kabul – but the rule of law there was rough and raw. While he was in Faizabad the Havildar saw with his own eyes what happened to those caught carrying seditious letters from the upstart prince Abdurrahman. A man was caught with just such a missive, and 'The unfortunate wretch was thrown from a lofty bridge down into the rapid stream of the Kokcha [River], and, though not killed on the spot, he died a few days later from injuries received by being dashed against the boulders which protrude from the water in every direction'.

Having witnessed what was apparently the 'favourite mode of execution in Badakhshan', the Havildar must have been somewhat relieved to discover that the mehtar had told the truth. All routes north and west from Faizabad were indeed closed, and he would have no option but to abandon his journey and return to the south. Turning back into the Hindu Kush, on 31 October at a mountain township called Zebak, the Havildar happened upon a royal conference: a meeting between Jehander Shah, the Afghan puppet prince of Badakhshan, and his more consequential eastern neighbour, the Mehtar of Chitral. Hanging around the fringes of this meeting was an unpleasant-looking man, surrounded by a mob of lean, bearded and thoroughly villainous characters in roll-edged flat caps. He was of course Mir Wali, and his companions were the rascals with whom he had fled Yasin.

Since fleeing across the Darkot Pass from the armed advance of his little brother Pahlwan almost three months earlier, Mir Wali and his band had been wandering the wilds of Badakhshan, forcing themselves upon the hospitality of local villagers and minor chieftains. Now he had decided to take advantage of the royal conference to throw himself on his father-in-law's mercy. Even though he had him kicked out of Yasin, the Mehtar of Chitral seems to have made his peace with Mir Wali – he granted him permission to return to Chitral.

As the Chitrali-Badakhshani talks broke up the Havildar found himself attached to Mir Wali's party. He was glad of the extra guns for protection against the Kafirs, but hardly pleased to be in such villainous company. He must have been looking forward to getting back amongst his own people – the honour codes of the Pashtuns may well have been blood-soaked, but at least they were rigid. The schizophrenic Dards, on the other hand – enemies one moment, bosom-buddies the next – were hardly people to inspire confidence in the traveller, and if the Havildar had been nervous of the mehtar he was downright disgusted by Mir Wali. He took a certain wicked satisfaction in seeing that the murderer had recently received a vicious kick from one of his own horses. The well-placed hoof had shattered Mir Wali's lower leg, and given his itinerant existence of recent weeks, the bone had never properly set; he 'was in great pain', the Havildar noted.

The return to Chitral, with winter rapidly descending on the high mountains, was hideous. Snow, Kafirs and unsavoury company combined to make it the worst journey of the Havildar's life – and if he had expected respite when he reached Chitral he was sorely disappointed. Indeed, it seemed like his luck had finally run out. Perhaps having taken note of the Havildar's apparently aimless wanderings in Badakhshan, or perhaps having heard a rumour of his fiddling with compasses under cover of darkness, the mehtar now suspected the truth – that the travelling Pashtun was a British agent. The terrified spy was summoned to the court and found himself before a deeply suspicious Chitrali chief. Seated alongside the mehtar, with whom he was now apparently on the best of terms, leering horribly, was Mir Wali.

The Havildar later admitted to his boss Montgomerie that he had thought his final hour had come. Still, he was a brave and cool-headed man, even by the usual formidable Pashtun standards. Without betraying his understandable terror he kept his hand firmly clenched around the revolver hidden in the folds of his robe. He was determined that when the moment came he would slay both the Dardic royals before they could overpower him. Fortunately such things never came to pass; the mehtar probably thought better of killing or imprisoning a British agent, and the Havildar, sweaty palm still clasped on his concealed weapon, was allowed out into the crisp winter sunshine with permission to return to Peshawar. As he steeled himself to run the Kafir gauntlet once more he took a certain pleasure in noting that Mir Wali's broken leg was still causing him excruciating agony. You could hear the fragmented bones scraping together when he walked.

The Havildar's report was perhaps the strongest evidence for the 'Mehtar did it' school of thought on the Hayward murder case. At first glance the fact that, after such a short interim, the Chitrali had welcomed his estranged son-in-law back into his court does seem highly suspicious. Just a couple of months earlier he had unleashed an army of 500, apparently with the intention not only of unseating Mir Wali, but also, if at all possible, of killing him. The idea that Mir Wali, handicap of an agonisingly broken leg notwithstanding, should even want to return to the favour of such a man seems equally odd.

The interpretation of these circumstances went like this: the mehtar had given instructions that Hayward must come through Chitral after his second visit to Yasin (entirely so that the Chitralis could get their avaricious hands on his goods). When the traveller stubbornly and rudely refused to comply the mehtar gave the order for him to be murdered, and his dutiful son-in-law carried it out. During the Havildar's nerve-wracking meeting in the Chitral court he had made a grim note of the fact that the mehtar was now in proud possession of one of George Hayward's breach-loading rifles. Pahlwan's excursion across the Shandur and Mir Wali's escape to Badakhshan had been nothing more than a charade, and now, with the right impression made, the murderer could return to being what he had always been – a loyal and dedicated lackey of his father-in-law with a prime position in the Chitrali court.

At first glance it is a convincing theory, but look more closely and the cracks begin to show. First of all there is the question of motive. From the very beginning the robbery line was pushed by everyone who dismissed the possibility of Kashmiri involvement. Robbery was certainly an accepted way of making a living – of making a killing even – in the Western Himalayas; those terrifying bands of Kafirs were bent on plunder after all. On his final journey George Hayward was better stocked and better funded than he had been on any of his earlier expeditions, and along the banks of the Oxus, on the slopes of the Pamirs, and beyond on the fringes of Russian territory there would have been plenty of wild tribesmen who would have covetously eyed his caravan and sharpened their daggers. But we are not dealing with mere wild tribesmen here; in the person of the Mehtar of Chitral we are dealing with the king of a country the size of Wales. He already had plenty of money from slave-trading and from levying tolls on travellers crossing the borders of his realm. Though the gift of a new breach-loader from a penitent son-in-law would certainly have been welcomed, the idea that the mehtar would have had Hayward killed simply to get hold of his relatively modest stock of money and possessions is rather hard to swallow.

The whole theory rests on the typically Victorian idea of the mehtar as a deranged barbarian devoid of reason; the avaricious Oriental archetype – dusky visage a vision of drooling greed as the prospect of a little gold and a few modern guns compels him to command murder. Staunch nineteenth-century Englishmen liked to view all their 'Asiatic despots' in such fashion, but in truth the Mehtar of Chitral, despite his rather dysfunctional family history, was a smooth operator and a wily politician not given to errors of judgement. What was more, he had already proven himself interested in friendly relations with the British – who he clearly understood to be the subcontinent's main players. Whether he had requested Hayward visit his court with a motive of greed or because he suspected the traveller had some official capacity and might be a useful ally, the idea that a refusal would prompt him to commit murder seems somewhat unlikely.

The second weakness in the case against the mehtar involves purely practical considerations. The theory runs that the mehtar ordered the crime after Hayward's refusal to detour through Chitrali territory. However, more than a hundred miles of mountains separate Yasin from Chitral. According to Drew's meticulous reconstruction of events Hayward was only camped out at the Yasin fort for two days. He departed shortly after his argument with Mir Wali; the murder plot was immediately put into action and he was killed three days later. Even today, given the unreliability of telephone lines in the Hindu Kush, the mehtar's modern descendants would have difficulty ordering a murder over that distance and within that timescale. In 1870, even allowing for the most fleet-footed of mail runners with a back-of-the-hand knowledge of the paths across the Shandur, a correspondence between Mir Wali and the mehtar, with time to put any order received into action inside five days, would have been simply impossible.

This, interestingly, was the very conclusion of investigator-in-chief Frederick Drew. The maharaja and the mehtar were sworn enemies, and Drew certainly would have had no reason not to consider the possibility that the murder was the doing of the Chitrali. But with his careful accounting for the last days of Hayward's life, he too saw no way that the mehtar could have instructed Mir Wali to act – unless the killing had been set up weeks in advance, and that idea, once again, ran into the brick wall of a missing motive.

Mir Wali's apparent return to favour in Chitral at the beginning of winter might strike most outsiders as odd, outrageous and hypocritical – but in the ul-Mulk royals of Chitral we are dealing with an odd, outrageous and hypocritical family. The fact that the same clan had already ruled the country for some two centuries gives a false impression of stability and order. The truth was otherwise, and the royal bloodline ran sideways, backwards, diagonally – anything but straight. Standard successions were rarely successful; the kings had multiple wives and multitudinous offspring. Even when an old mehtar died peacefully in his bed – rare enough as it was – there would be a veritable horde of rival claimants to the bloodstained throne. Fathers alternately feuded and conspired with sons, nephews with uncles, cousins with brothers. The ul-Mulks had kept Chitral in the family merely because there were so many of them.

That the mehtar should have let Mir Wali hobble back into favour is not so strange – he was married to the chief's daughter after all. And despite the Havildar's impression that the two were on the best of terms, the Yasini's reprieve turned out to be temporary. Before long he was turfed out of Chitral once more and spent the rest of his short life as an unhappy fugitive, limping over the passes with the mark of Cain upon him.

The British authorities seem never to have taken the possibility of Chitrali involvement in George Hayward's death very seriously. A guilty mehtar would have scarcely been more convenient than a guilty maharaja. Chitral was not treaty-bound to Britain, but it was by no means an insignificant state, and worse: it was absurdly inaccessible and surrounded by some of Asia's most violent and lawless country. If conclusive evidence that it was the mehtar who killed Hayward had emerged, punishing him would have been decidedly difficult. Chances are that this Oriental despot – with the blood of an Englishman on his hands – would have remained untouched and undisturbed, a monumental embarrassment to the Government of India, laughing at them from his Hindu Kush fastness.

Political inconvenience aside, of the three principal theories about the death of George Hayward, the case against the mehtar was always shakiest. But what about the alternative, the possibility that caused the sweatiest of British palms in India? Was there really anything beyond circumstances, the declarations of the dead man himself and a gut feeling to suggest that the Maharaja of Kashmir had been behind the crime?

On 3 October, two and a half months after Hayward's death – and with Frederick Drew's Kashmir-friendly investigations underway in Gilgit – a party of exhausted and embittered men came slouching down along the course of the icy stream between the stark brown hills of the Chang Chenmo, high in the Karakorams north of Pangong Lake. The leader of the group – and bitterest of them all – was the Punjab commissioner Douglas Forsyth. The other Europeans with him were the doctor, George Henderson, and, of course, Mr Eastern Turkestan himself, weak lungs somehow holding up for what was his fourth crossing of the Karakoram watershed, Robert Shaw. Forsyth had finally visited the country that had been his consuming passion for years; after endless lobbying during the inactive years of Lord Lawrence's passive viceregal rule he had at last been appointed leader of the first official mission to Eastern Turkestan. But any satisfaction he had taken in seeing the deserts and bazaars that he had visited so often in his dreams would have been cold comfort: the mission was a complete disaster.

The party had never even got as far as Kashgar, and they never met the self-made king, Yaqub Beg. The Turkis had done an excellent job of concealing the fact that their ruler was away, fighting a desperate war against the Chinese Muslims of Turfan on the far side of the Taklamakan Desert. It was only when they arrived at that notoriously dreary frontier post at Shahidulla that they learned the truth. All the gifts they carried went un-given, the treaties unsigned. At least they were not locked up for months on end and were able to retreat south before winter made the passes impossible for men less steely than George Hayward, but that was hardly a consolation. Now they were passing once more into the realm of the Kashmiris – people who had caused them no end of problems on the outward journey.

It was no secret that the maharaja did not look favourably on the idea of British friendship with Yaqub Beg. He liked to keep his wild border regions safe from the prying – and critical – eyes of outsiders (as was the case west of the Indus, he had already strayed far across his natural northern border on at least one occasion to build that fort at Shahidulla before the rise of Yaqub Beg). More importantly, he also kept a tight rein on trade through Ladakh, monopolising the valuable commerce in pashmina shawl wool from Tibet and levying crippling taxes on caravans from Yarkand; the idea of a British business agreement with Turkestan – an arrangement that might bypass Kashmiri customs officials – was to be resented.

Well versed in the art of subtle prevarication, the Kashmiris had covertly thrown all manner of obstacles in the way of Forsyth's outward journey earlier in the year. The Kashmiri governor of Ladakh had accompanied the mission as far as Chang Chenmo with snivellingly insincere wishes for success. He made repeated promises that the way across the mountains had been prepared for them and that food for the animals of Forsyth's enormous baggage train had been sent out and stockpiled at stages across the wastes of the Lingzi Thung. Forsyth already had Shaw's account from two years earlier to go by, and knew that such forward planning would be essential for a successful crossing of the high-altitude desert between Ladakh and Turkestan. Hayward had made it across without tent, fuel or food, but his party had been tiny and fast moving; Forsyth's was a veritable army, and for such a large expedition, even in the height of summer, the Lingzi Thung was a deathtrap. The governor of Ladakh knew this, and Forsyth knew that he knew it, so when the party descended on to the cold plateau and found that the promised heaps of raw barley were nowhere to be found, he was furious. The Kashmiri duplicity was nearly the end of Forsyth and his mission: almost 100 horses died in the three days that it took to stagger across the Lingzi Thung, and he had to abandon most of his baggage before pushing on to Shahidulla.

Now, returning empty-handed down the Chang Chenmo on 3 October in the bitter cold, the sight of a waiting Kashmiri escort, all insincere welcomes and smirking enquiries about the success of the mission, can hardly have cheered Douglas Forsyth. In other circumstances he might have roundly ignored the rumour that he heard the following morning from a loose-tongued member of the escort – by way of one of his own Kashmiri servants. However, given his understandable animosity towards the maharaja's officials and his lack of any other information on the affair, he found it starkly convincing. A day earlier Forsyth had received his first mail packet for months, and, amongst the other news from India, he had noted that George Hayward had been murdered in Yasin. There must have been a moment's uncomfortable silence, and a brief and chilly recollection of a singular prediction, when he passed this information on to Robert Shaw. Now this campsite rumour seemed to provide the explanation for the crime.

The story went like this: it was, as Hayward himself had always feared, the maharaja who had had him killed. Furious at the letter in the *Pioneer*, worried that further meddling in Dardistan would only lead to the uncovering of more atrocities and that precise British knowledge of the geography and politics of the region would be prejudicial to his expansionist ideals, the Dogra royal had decided that the explorer must die. While Hayward had been preparing for his final expedition right under the maharaja's nose in Srinagar, word had been sent to the Dogra officials in Gilgit to make suitable arrangements. The man they had looked to was the turncoat Dard, oldest of the three Yasin brothers, Kashmiri pensioner and Gilgit bungalow-dweller, Mulk Aman. For the considerable prize of 10,000 rupees – more than enough to buy off a younger brother once his sworn enemy – Mulk Aman had agreed to organise the evil. Once the deed was done he had been allowed to slip out of Gilgit into a well-moneyed exile somewhere in the mountains beyond.

Given his own experiences, Forsyth was quite happy to believe the Kashmir court capable of such a crime. He noted down the story and forwarded it to the government in the Punjab, where it was immediately filed away amongst the ever-growing mass of conflicting, contradictory and inconvenient rumours surrounding the murder of George Hayward. By October 1870 the government was well on the way to accepting – and promoting – the 'Mir Wali alone in the name of robbery' line.

Forsyth's story did seem rather unlikely. From the beginning no one had disputed that it had been Mir Wali who had arranged the actual killing; Mir Wali was surely no more likely to act on the instructions of the very brother he had kicked off the Yasin throne than on those of the man who was apparently trying to do the same to him – the Maharaja of Kashmir. Had the Kashmiri gossipmonger, whispering his wickedness in the wilds of Chang Chenmo, claimed that the viceroy himself had had George Hayward killed it would hardly have been more far-fetched – except that there was already startling corroboration with much of the story, corroboration that Forsyth, who had been incommunicado in Turkestan for several months, could have known nothing about.

Way back in early September, when the very first news of George Hayward's death had reached Colonel Pollock in Peshawar from the Mehtar of Chitral, the name of Mulk Aman, darkest of Dard horses, had been raised. Information had been so scant at the time that anything seemed possible, but even then Pollock and his superior, Lieutenant-Governor Henry Durand, thought that Mulk Aman was an unlikely culprit. Still, just to be on the safe side, a request was sent to Kashmir to place the oldest Yasin brother under house arrest in Gilgit. Though the British never knew until several months later, the request was never honoured; Mulk Aman had already fled and the loyal Dogras had been keeping this damning fact hidden from the British. By the time the news leaked out many weeks later, briefly raising all kinds of uncomfortable questions, Frederick Drew's report was ready; the maharaja immediately had it released. With its obvious thoroughness, its careful timescales and, above all, its Englishness, the thorny question of Mulk Aman was conveniently swept under the fine Kashmiri carpet. Drew himself had noted the disappearance from Gilgit of Mulk Aman – who was already long gone before he arrived there in September – but naturally had thought nothing more of it than to give the fact a passing mention.

With the emergence of Drew's report the British Government of India would have been quite happy to let matters rest; if its wad of meticulous detail could have been thrust like a jamming spanner into the cogs of the Himalayan rumour mill they would have been delighted. However, things don't work that way in High Asia – or in English drawing rooms for that matter – and problematic rumours continued to emerge from the mountains. First there was Forsyth's scandalous story, which fitted so neatly with the tales of Mulk Aman's disappearance; then, in the spring of 1871, more reports came down out of the Hindu Kush from the Mehtar of Chitral. These too held the Maharaja of Kashmir responsible and tossed Mulk Aman's name into the mix once more. Finally, unable to restrain himself from getting involved, there was the pronouncement of Dr Gottlieb Leitner Etc.

One of Leitner's Central Asian acolytes, a Yarkandi named Niaz Muhammad, had been dispatched to Dardistan to conduct his own investigation. Dr Leitner was an absolute magpie when it came to gathering information. He had no sense whatsoever of succinctness, and his book on Dardistan, *The Hunza and Nagar Handbook*, fitted into the hand of not even the gangliest of mortals. The handbook grew fatter with each new edition as Leitner tagged vast appendix on to vast appendix. In the end the appendices were longer than the main text itself. Leitner, of course, would never have allowed any professional editor to sharpen up his work; any detail, no matter how obscure, was worth printing. His Yarkandi investigator seems to have followed his master's example. Leitner described the report he produced as 'strange and suggestive'. It most certainly was. Niaz Muhammad seems simply to have gathered every conflicting rumour about Hayward's death, including the most far-fetched. Not wanting to leave anything out but at the same time not wanting to produce conflicting accounts, he seems to have blended them all together to create a story that is, quite frankly, ridiculous. In it the maharaja, Mulk Aman, Mir Wali – and the Mehtar of Chitral and Pahlwan – all lay aside their differences and for no obvious reason, communicating over hundreds of miles of mountain terrain, work together to kill George Hayward. Leitner's version of events was obviously absurd – although amongst its madness it did repeat the prickly possibility of Kashmiri culpability with Mulk Aman as agent. By the time it appeared no one was listening any more, and all it achieved was a further muddying of waters already more opaque than the mica-laden glacial streams of the mountains.

Could the maharaja really have done it? Could Mulk Aman have patched up his differences with his younger brother to plot the crime? From the start the Dogras were the only people with an instantly obvious motive for killing George Hayward – revenge for the *Pioneer* letter and concern that any kind of British exploration in Dardistan could only have negative consequences for Kashmiri interests. Mulk Aman was already on the Dogra payroll, and was clearly a man without scruple. Back in his days as ruler of Yasin he was known to have slaughtered various members of his own family. That he would arrange the death of some unknown foreigner is entirely possible – and his disappearance from Gilgit in the immediate aftermath of the crime, and the Dogra cover-up of the news, is certainly a striking coincidence. But what about Mir Wali? The idea of his conspiring with his former enemy Mulk Aman is certainly possible by the duplicitous standards of Dardistan. The Mehtar of Chitral had temporarily forgiven him, remember, and though he was then exiled south to Swat, in 1873 he returned once more to Yasin, declared a truce with Pahlwan and very briefly regained the throne. Clearly this was a family with serious issues.

Again there is the difficulty of the fact that Mir Wali must have known that there would be grave consequences for killing an Englishman, whether or not he knew that the ultimate command had come from Kashmir. Moreover, if he was prepared to lose his kingdom for the sake of George Hayward's loot and camp furniture – as was being accepted as the gospel truth by mid-1871 – then there is no reason whatsoever to scoff at the idea that he would do likewise for a share of 10,000 rupees.

There does remain a fourth interpretation of the death of George Hayward – a theory that seems never to have been raised at the time and that no one in the 140 years since seems to have considered either. The Dogra garrison at Gilgit lay at the very fringes of Kashmiri territory in a knot of huge mountains, cut through only with roaring gorges and howling passes. For some six months every year the main route of supply and communication between Srinagar and the chilly little township was definitively cut. There was always Hayward's line of approach along the Indus Gorge, but that was hardly practical. And while it was just about possible for the bravest and swiftest of runners to go the long way around through the mountains to the south, that country was not known as Yaghistan – the Land of the Ungovernable – for no reason. Clearly, for practicality's sake if nothing else, Gilgit was left to its own devices for much of the year.

On George Hayward's first journey into Dardistan the Dogras had been decidedly unhelpful, and it was entirely possible that the Gilgit commanders had received advance orders from the maharaja to try to baffle his advances on the Pamirs. However, there seems very little chance that that wicked plot to invade Yasin while Hayward was there – perhaps with the intention of precipitating the explorer's demise – could have been directly sanctioned from Srinagar. The maharaja could not have known in advance that Hayward's approach on Yasin would prove success-ful; in the depths of winter it would have taken months to send a message back to the Kashmiri capital and longer still to await a reply. Clearly the plot had been hatched in Gilgit alone; the com-manders of Kashmir's most westerly frontier were used to acting independently, and even to organising military excursions of sev-eral thousand men without waiting on the royal seal of approval.

If the Dogras of Gilgit had already cooked up one plot likely to prove fatal to George Hayward independently of their king,

could they not have organised a second, less blunt but more likely
to succeed? The three months between Hayward's departure from
Gilgit at the end of March 1870 and his final, fatal return were
scant time for extensive communication between Srinagar and
the frontier – even had the Burzil Pass not remained technically
closed until mid-May. It did, however, provide ample opportunity
to organise a plot that required nothing more than a stroll down
the muddy alleyway to a pensioner's bungalow within hailing
distance of the Gilgit fort, the exchange of a certain quantity of
rupees from the well-stocked Gilgit treasury (this was a pay office
that handled the salaries of thousands of soldiers) and the shut-
tling of some envoys back and forth between the town and the
valley of Yasin, just a few marches west.

Ultimately this can only ever be conjecture, but if the idea
of Mir Wali, no matter how thoroughly unpleasant a character
he may have been, acting alone out of ill-temper or avarice is
still hard to swallow, then the idea of a Dogra plot, conceived
independently in Gilgit, is at least convincing – in terms of the
practicalities of organising the murder if nothing else.

If the truth was obscure in the 1870s, it is only more so now.
George Hayward was dead; Mir Wali had had him killed: that is
as much as can be said with conviction. Unless some explosive
secret report detailing irrefutable evidence that the maharaja or
the mehtar ordered the killing one day emerges – covered in dust
and a little worm-eaten at the corners from an un-catalogued
file in an unmarked box, amid the forgotten odds and ends of
the India Office archives in the basement of the British Library –
then we will never be able to say more.

One thing is obvious, however. Despite briefly and queasily
considering the awful possibility, from a very early stage a decision
seems to have been reached amongst British officialdom in India
that the idea that the maharaja was behind George Hayward's

murder was too catastrophic to contemplate. Whether there really was any evidence to this effect was beside the point; it was the idea alone that was the problem. Kashmir was one of Britain's most important allied vassals, and a country central to the ever more frenzied play of the Great Game. If the consequences of having to bring the maharaja to justice for the murder of an Englishman would have been apocalyptic, then mere gossip to that effect was bad enough. It had to be brought to a halt. Frederick Drew's report had been a gift, and even before its final draft emerged the line it took was being pushed as hard as was possible, with Drew's gentlemanly credentials hammered home.

Back in London in that RGS meeting, Sir Henry Rawlinson, on India Office rather than geographical duty, had done everything he could to stamp out gossip implicating the maharaja. He and other officials continued to do so. Hayward's last letters – those which had been suppressed for their incendiary tone – were finally published in the society's journal in 1871, but not before someone, perhaps Rawlinson himself, had been through them, brutally marking out large sections of the lean, spidery handwriting with the word 'Omit'. These sections were, of course, those detailing both Kashmiri atrocities in Dardistan, and Kashmiri meddling in Hayward's own journeys – anything that would provide either more circumstantial evidence for Kashmiri involvement in the murder or that gave a generally poor impression of the Dogra court. No respect was given to the dead man in this cold-headed expurgation. The pencil of the unknown editor scratched decisively across the thin blue paper of Hayward's final letter to Colonel Showers, written from Srinagar in May.

Even the following passage was, inevitably, omitted:

You are very welcome to forward my two letters to Sir R. Murchison with the promise that nothing is omitted about the proceedings of the Kashmir maharaja in the countries across the Indus … I am determined that the public at home shall know exactly what our loyal feudatory is doing. You may perhaps think

I am prejudiced against the Dogras, and I confess to entertaining a
feeling of bitter enmity against the murderers of innocent women
and children.

Back in India too, anyone publicly suggesting the possibility that
the maharaja had killed George Hayward received the furious
opprobrium of officialdom – were they not aware that the truth
was already out, uncovered by a straight-backed, Christian, English
investigator? And little by little, purely through repetition, Frederick
Drew's interpretation – with all its uninvestigated avenues, not least
the disappearance of Mulk Aman – became the government's version of events, and then in turn was swallowed by the public. The
other lines of enquiry frayed and snapped; the unanswered questions were forgotten, and by 1873, when the journalist Andrew
Wilson – whose mind was usually as critical as it was sharp – visited
Kashmir there was only one truth and no reason to dispute it. The
lesson of the Hayward affair, Wilson wrote, was 'that one ought to
avoid Yassin rather than that it is dangerous to abuse the Kashmir
Government'. The case was closed.

Efforts instead were concentrated on quietly glorifying George
Hayward in exploring circles – efforts that culminated in the
syrupy bastardisation of his legend by Colonel Woodthorpe of the
Gilgit Mission and Sir Henry Newbolt of rhyming ridiculousness.
Half-hearted attempts were made – by way of polite requests to
the Mehtar of Chitral – to bring Mir Wali to justice. While occasional grumbling in newspaper columns that nothing decisive
was being done in this direction were assuaged by pointing out,
with the very example of George Hayward, just how dangerous
it was for Englishmen to venture into the Western Himalayas. We
wouldn't want another murder on our hands, would we?

Mulk Aman – the dark horse, the unanswered question –
remained unaccounted for, and was still loitering amongst the
violent tribesmen of Chilas years later. But Mir Wali did eventually meet a suitably bloody end, though not at the hands of the
British, and not – as various grumblers later pointed out – because

he had murdered George Hayward. After his second exile under
the violently fanatical auspices of the Akhund of Swat, he had
returned briefly to Yasin and was, highly suspiciously, reported
to be on good terms with his Dogra neighbours. However, the
typically tortuous nature of Dardic family relations resurfaced;
Mir Wali fell out of favour with the Mehtar of Chitral yet again
and once more Pahlwan was ordered off in pursuit. Finally, at
some unspecified location in the mountains, the murderer was
run to ground. The version of his death that seems generally to
have been accepted is wildly dramatic and more than a little far-
fetched. No wonder; it was collected by none other than the
fanciful Colonel Woodthorpe, the man who came up with the
melodramatic account of Hayward's murder that inspired the
poet Sir Henry Newbolt. He shamelessly cites his unnamed and
improbable informant, as the brother, no less, of a character that
had been one of Mir Wali's pursuers and had seen the denouement with his own eyes. Character is surely the appropriate
word; Woodthorpe would have had a thing or two to teach the
Hollywood scriptwriters of the coming century:

> One day [Mir Wali's pursuers] met him face to face on a narrow
> path leading round a precipice high above a foaming mountain
> stream. Escape was impossible, and the two men engaged in deadly
> conflict. Mir Wali shot his adversary, but in the same moment the
> latter ran Mir Wali through the heart, and both fell together dead
> into the torrent below.

An equally dramatic if somewhat more feasible version of events
– one apparently missed by most who have examined Hayward's
story – was collected in Yasin some years later. It has enough echoes
of Woodthorpe's wild imaginings to see from where he cooked up
his over-egged account, but is probably much closer to the truth:

> When the pursuers caught up to Mir Wali, they fired at him, hit-
> ting him in the thigh. He fell off his horse, and Pahlwan Bahadur[5]

ordered his men to cut his brother's throat. Two men ran forward to do so, but the wounded man drew his English pistol [possibly Hayward's] and shot them both. Two more came up, and these he killed with his sword. Bubuku, his Punyali[6] servant, a small man with a lion's heart, threw himself in front of his master to protect him, shouting to Pahlwan's men, 'Why do you kill your Raja?' Finally Mir Wali was slain, but Bubuku was spared.

This Bubuku, perhaps the last man who could have shed some light on the real motive for George Hayward's murder, died in his bed in Gakuch, a little way back towards Gilgit from Yasin, in 1922.

George Hayward was dead. He had never reached the Pamirs or traced the source of the Oxus. He had not even been successful in championing the cause of the Yasinis against their Dogra oppressors. In fact, his death was used in years to come as a stick with which to beat the Dards and as an excuse for their unreasonable treatment at the hands of both Kashmiri and, later, British invaders. In light of all this it would be nice to think that he could at least have been allowed to rest in peace. The lonely hillside at Darkot was as close as he ever got to the Pamirs; he would probably have approved of such a resting spot. But it was not to be. This was the height of the Victorian era, and more important even than truth and justice was a Christian burial. Frederick Drew was on the scene and he would use all his powers to do what he thought was right by the dead man.

Drew, who had unquestioningly assumed simple Dardic guilt from the very first, was genuinely upset by Hayward's murder. As far as loyal hangers-on of the Kashmiri court were concerned the Dards were just about the worst people on earth. That they had done such an unspeakable thing to an Englishman was bad enough; that Hayward's poor corpse was still lying in a shallow grave amongst these brutal sub-humans was simply too much.

The nearest authentically sanctified Christian cemetery was probably somewhere in the Punjab, but surely anything was better than an eternal rest in the Yasin Valley. Drew would do what he could in the circumstances. The irony of his actions – and the possibility that George Hayward would have bitterly resented them – naturally never occurred to him.

Gufar Khan, the Kashmiri sepoy who Drew sent to Yasin, had two tasks. Firstly, he was to uncover whatever he could about the murder (which he did admirably); secondly, he was to recover the Englishman's body and bring it back across the frontier. Pahlwan's people at the Yasin fort gave Khan a horse and he rode out alone, up the valley and along the stony track beside the river. He reached Darkot, just as Hayward had done three months earlier, as dark bruises of evening shadow were slipping across the hard brown mountainsides and the goatherds were bringing their bleating flocks down into the smoky villages. He went straight to the crime scene. Scouting around amongst the bushes he found five miserable little heaps of stones. The villagers who had brought him to the spot could not point out which of the graves held the body of George Hayward, but in the gathering dusk Gufar Khan spotted a pair of hands, 'crossed and bound together, the palms turned upwards', protruding from one of the cairns. Even so long after death, even in the failing light, there was something about the long, slender fingers that marked them out to the Kashmiri as those of a foreigner. Dropping to his knees and scrabbling to clear the stones, he uncovered the emaciated body. Three months in the cold, dry air of the mountains had seen more mummification than putrefaction, and Khan had no trouble recognising the fair, wiry hair and beard of an Englishman. The rope – sliced in two by the stroke of a jagged sword – was still around the severed neck. Calling the villagers to him, he had the grim clutch of dried skin and thin bones wrapped and carried to the house where he was lodging in the village.

In the morning, in the bright autumn sunlight, Gufar Khan came back to the hillside and uncovered the other bodies: 'Those who had been killed at the same time as their master had been much cut about, but the body of the munshi (who was killed later) had but one wound, in the back of the neck.' Khan searched but he could not find the remains of the fifth servant. Sweating at the work of digging in stony soil with only thin mountain air to breathe, and guessing roughly at the direction of Mecca, he gave the four Muslims as decent a burial as he could, and then, taking the macabre bundle with him, he rode back towards Kashmiri territory.

On the morning of 27 October 1870 George Hayward's corpse was buried in a garden not far from the fort in Gilgit. There can rarely have been a sorrier funeral. The apple trees would have long since shed their leaves, and the first dustings of snow would have already marked the bleak mountains beyond the town. The only mourners were Frederick Drew and Gufar Khan, and without a priest it was left to Drew himself with his pocket Bible to render the service in some sense Christian. As the stony soil was shovelled back into the hole, covering the thin, cloth-wrapped body for the last time, a detachment of Dogra troopers – the very men who Hayward held in such 'bitter enmity' – fired three volleys over his grave into the cold grey sky.

This was not to be George Hayward's final indignity, however. When Drew got back to the Kashmiri winter headquarters at Jammu he dried a righteous tear and sat down to pen a letter to Sir Roderick Murchison at the RGS. As far as anyone knew the RGS was the closest thing Hayward had to a family, and if Murchison so wished then Drew would see to it that the grave in Gilgit was marked with something more permanent than the hastily botched wooden cross that he had thrust into the ground at its head. Murchison thanked Drew for his kindness – of course, some suitable memorial to the brave young explorer whose death the world of geographical science was still so keenly mourning must be organised. Murchison drew up the inscription and mailed it back to India.

The following year, with the apple trees in bloom, a headstone of polished marble was placed over George Hayward's tomb in the wild, remote, brutalised town of Gilgit at the very core of the Western Himalayas. It read:

> Sacred to the memory of Lieut. G.W. Hayward, Medallist of the Royal Geographical Society of London, who was cruelly murdered at Darkot, July 18th, 1870, on his journey to explore the Pamir steppe. This monument is erected to a gallant officer and accomplished traveller by His Highness the Maharaja of Kashmir at the instance of the Royal Geographical Society of London.

It was the final line that was the cruellest.

George Hayward's epitaph had been paid for and installed by his nemesis Ranbir Singh, Maharaja of Kashmir.

Notes

1   This was simply another name for the tangled mass of mountains at the furthest limit of the Western Himalayas – one that has now fallen entirely out of use.

2   If the Havildar did have a theory about the reasons for Hayward's demise to report – and it seems unlikely that he didn't; Chitral and Badakhshan must have been rife with rumour by the beginning of September – it was suppressed in Montgomerie's official write-up of his journey. The account didn't emerge until long after the convenient 'truth' had already been established.

3   The term 'sahib' (pronounced saab) is often misunderstood simply to mean 'white man'; it was certainly misunderstood to mean so by many during the days of the Raj. In fact, it means nothing of the kind; it is simply a respectful form of address for anyone in a position of honour or power, and is still used as such in the Indian subcontinent today. But in the nineteenth century every blustering, sunburnt Englishman in

India, no matter how dishonourable, no matter how power-less, assumed that he was a sahib, and that he ought to be addressed as such. Very many of the subjugated subconti-nentals seem to have complied with this desire, and even in the use of the bastardised 'memsahib' (the correct feminine equivalent of 'sahib' should be 'sahiba').

4 Fifteen years after Hayward's murder an alternative ver-sion of events was collected in Yasin by Colonel R.G. Woodthorpe. He was a member of the Lockhart Mission to Gilgit, a British expedition of upstanding military gentle-men with walrus moustaches, plus-fours and stout walking sticks who scouted out the entire political, geographical and cultural arena of the Kashmir frontier. Woodthorpe's account, allegedly collected from an eyewitness, is ludi-crously overblown. It has a solitary, weary man sitting out a lonely vigil, the first rays of dawn appearing over eternal snows, and then, most ridiculously of all, the condemned Hayward granted a final wish to look out on the world for a few moments alone, to make a prayer and to return with the serene words 'I am ready': 'His prayer is granted; he is unbound and, in the words of our informant, as he stands up there, "tall against the sky, with the rising sun lighting up his fair hair as a glory, he is beautiful to look upon".'

Unless there happened to be a very peculiar Yasini with a penchant for the worst kind of romantic English novels, and more than a few symptoms of manic Christianity, it is safe to assume that it was Woodthorpe himself who was taking the most outrageous liberties with a legend already well estab-lished (incredibly, this deluge of purple prose was originally printed in a highly confidential and very serious government report). His account can, without hesitation, be laughed right out of the Hindu Kush with its tail between its legs.

Someone did take this absurd romanticism seriously, how-ever, and on reading the account he stifled a quiver, stiffened his delicate upper lip, saluted the Union Jack and took up his pen – he was, of course, the poet Sir Henry Newbolt.

5   The third Yasin brother's real name was Muhi-ud-Din, but he was usually known as Pahlwan, often with the heroic 'Bahadur' appellation attached. He also had a nickname – 'the Wrestler' – thanks to his reputation as something of a bruiser.

6   A native of Punial, the little country between Yasin and Gilgit.

10

HAYWARD'S CURSE

On a bright October morning I set out walking uphill along the Yasin Valley towards Darkot. It was a decade since my father and I headed west from Gilgit on the morning of the Musharraf coup, and more than 139 years since George Hayward started on his own final, fateful journey in the same direction.

The valley was a blaze of reds and golds and the light was sharper than glass. In a few weeks everything would turn grey and snow would fall, but for now there was only the gentle warmth of an Indian summer. What had been a rough path in 1870 – and a dirt track in 1999 – was now a thin strip of cracked blue tarmac, but there was no traffic. I quickly fell into stride in the yellow dust of the roadside. My backpack felt lighter than air and I enjoyed the sensation of my own limbs moving inside the loose cotton of my Pakistani *shalwaar kamis*. The Yasin Valley was more beautiful than I had ever imagined.

Behind me, hidden in a nail-bed of flaming poplar trees, was the main village where one tower of Gohar Aman's fort, the place where Mir Wali had received George Hayward, still stood. It was an uneven cube of packed mud, river-smoothed stones and lengths of buckled timber amidst pollard willows the colour of a golden oriole's plumage. The previous morning I had sat beneath the walls of the fort and a villager in a flat, roll-edged cap had given me a pomegranate. When he cut it open with a blunt pen-knife the seeds had shone like rubies in the sunlight.

I had been following George Hayward's trail for a year. On dreary winter mornings I had risen long before dawn to catch the first bus into London, lolling through the sick-sleep of the motorway as bloodless February daybreaks leached across sodden fields. Still only half-awake, I would walk diagonally across central London from Victoria coach station, through streets of overbearing red and white houses, past the conspiratorial huddle of exotic embassies at Belgrave Square, onwards past the shining shop-fronts of Knightsbridge and finally beneath the towering facades of the nineteenth-century museums. Overhead the blank, pearly sky would be full of the hollow roar of aeroplanes, banking in over the city and bowling for Heathrow. At the head of Exhibition Road, past the west wall of the Victoria and Albert Museum – still scarred by the shrapnel of a Second World War bomb – I would duck through the swing doors of the Royal Geographical Society, fill in my details for a visitor's pass at the desk, and trot down the short spiral of stairs to the basement. Inside the reading room a pair of white gloves and a stack of files full of sheets of brittle, slightly greasy blue paper covered with close-packed handwriting would be waiting for me. It would be dark again by the time I finished, collecting my bag from the lockers at the door and stepping out on to the chilly street to lose myself in the rush of commuters with my eyes aching from hours poring over the manuscripts.

Other days when my bus rolled into Victoria I would walk due north instead, towards King's Cross and the British Library, where they now hold the records of the old India Office. The reading room there had none of the obscure scholarly calm of the RGS basement. It was a grand, high-ceilinged place, but it had the frantic air and suppressed noise of a works canteen. You requested your manuscripts on a computer and found a desk amongst elderly men in tweed jackets researching military grandfathers and small, serious South Asian lady academics going through the records of irrigation in the Punjab in the 1920s. Here I fumbled with reels of microfilm or relished the childish pleasure of opening a box that contained a government report still marked 'top secret'.

I had tracked down obscure nineteenth-century travelogues from the catalogues of second-hand booksellers; I had scanned maps made when there were still glaring smears of unknown white space on the surface of the globe – then held them against the bright colours of modern cartography. I had learnt to adjust my eyes to the idiosyncrasies of Victorian handwriting, deciphering the ostentatious bubble-script of viceroys, the puckered staccato of provincial administrators and, above all, the erratic, frantic scrawl of George Hayward himself. I had leafed through his letters and reports – the original versions – and seen where he had furiously scribbled out an error or dropped a blob of ink on to the page. The paper was thin and torn at the edges and I had handled it carefully. The slant of the writing, the way the words bunched up early on and then swelled bigger and bigger as the end of the page approached showed how urgently he had written. As I picked over the sentences I could almost hear the manic scratch of the pen, almost see the lean, bearded figure hunched over the desk before a high window in streaming white Indian sunlight, or balancing the writing pad on a wobbling camp table in a high world of howling wind and driving snow.

I pieced it all together; I took pleasure in small discoveries or wasted hours ironing out some small but befuddling inconsistency, some contradiction between a handwritten original and the published version in the Royal Geographical Society's journal. Then, when the story was all laid out before me from the sketchy start to the dark denouement, I had flown to India to pick up the trail on the ground.

I had tried, wherever possible, to see the places that Hayward had seen. In Kashmir I had stood beside lakesides that he had painted

– and did my best to ignore the Indian soldiers, loitering with machine guns in the wheat fields. I had crossed the Zoji La in a blizzard in a rattling government bus, and pictured Hayward's small party picking through the same snowdrifts in 1868 en route for Turkestan, and a year later to tackle the Upper Indus on the way to Gilgit. I saw the white walls of the monasteries where he had slept in Ladakh, and across the Chang La Pass, beyond the turquoise head of the Pangong Lake, a soldier on a motorbike had turned me back on the road to Chang Chenmo, Shahidulla and Yarkand.

Many weeks later, 200 miles to the north in the same mountains, another soldier, Chinese this time, had turned me back from the valley of the Upper Yarkand in the hard brown hills of the Kun Lun. But I had still scrambled up a high ridge and, beyond the ribbed and scored valley of the Tiznaf – one watershed north of the Yarkand – I had looked out on 'an interminable mass of mountains'. Then I retreated to the caravan towns of Xinjiang in search of the little that the People's Republic of China had left of old Turkestan.

In Karghilik, Yarkand and Kashgar there were banks and boulevards; and bulldozers grunting into the smooth, creamy mud walls of the old Uighur quarters. But in the irrigated countryside there were still long stands of poplars, vine trellises, pomegranate orchards and unpaved lanes knee-deep in soft yellow dust. In the stretches of stony ground beyond, twin-humped Bactrian camels still stalked, dark silhouettes against the desert. In the little town of Yanghissar the royal caravanserai from where Hayward had taken in the view was no more – the place was now all knife shops and police stations. But from the top of a muddy escarpment, between the streets and the graveyards, 'the magnificent view of the lofty Kizil Yart range of the Pamir' had not changed. An hour west in the centre of Kashgar an enormous statue of Chairman Mao stood facing south towards the distant white line of the Pamirs, saluting the empty Central Asian sky. South of the river the garrison where Hayward was held was a garrison once more, although off-limits to wandering foreigners.

Then there was Pakistan. The Indus Gorge between Skardu and Gilgit was traced by a tenuous tarmac road, but the mountain walls were still sheer, and showers of rocks from above still stopped the traffic. Roads in this part of the world were still full of stones. In Gilgit – now a ramshackle city of wild polo matches and endless cups of tea, still locked in its bowl of grey-brown hills – I had paid my respects at Hayward's grave, then headed west in a minibus full of men making small journeys, a bag of bruised grapes, an axehead to be sharpened in the bazaar. Beautiful women with angry eyes and purple headscarves stood at the roadsides and the poplar trees were upwards brushstrokes of copper-gold.

And now, finally, I was in the Yasin Valley a day's walk from Darkot. Ahead the road snaked on beneath snow-dusted slopes and the valley narrowed between blue buttresses. There was no wind, and the high ridges were jagged brown blades slicing at a sky the colour of lapis lazuli. Breathing was like drinking cool, clean water from a mountain spring and the huge silence was underpinned by the hiss of the river. The road cleaved to the western slopes of the valley. Away to the right, where the opposite mountain wall splintered beneath the Asumbar Pass to Ishkoman, I could see the warty outcrop of Madoori, the scene of the Dogra massacre that had so angered Hayward, and the place, perhaps, that had compelled him definitively towards his brutal demise.

The previous evening, with a cold wind blowing down the valley from the Pamirs and the sun falling away towards Chitral, I had scrambled up to the top of that same hill, a schoolboy named Arshad from a nearby village leading the way over the boulders, and a teacher named Ghayas Ali following behind. There were no skeletons now and even the walls of the fort had long since vanished. But sitting there, shivering in the chilly sunset, Ghayas had explained how people in the valley still told stories of the massacre, of how a secret tunnel once led from the village up through solid rock to the fort and how during the Dogra attack of 1863 a local turncoat had sold the secret to the invaders for the empty promise of the throne of Yasin. This must have been the same tale of treachery that Hayward had heard that dripping morning in late winter when he counted 147 skulls amongst these same stones.

Things happen very quickly and history never stops. When Hayward came to Madoori the skulls had already been bleaching in the mountain sunlight for seven years. Gohar Aman, the infamous sire of the Yasin brothers, had been dead for a decade; before long both Hayward and Mir Wali would be corpses too. At the end of the twentieth century I had passed just a few miles to the south and known nothing of this place or the people associated with it, while in the decade since big things – things far bigger and more momentous than the lonely death of a wanderer – had happened in the region. In 140 years tens of thousands of children had been born in the Yasin Valley. Many of them would have died young; while those that grew would have seen their mountain fastness lose its independence to be ruled by Chitral, by Kashmir, by Britain and be governed by Pakistan and claimed by India. A flimsy electricity cable and a thin ribbon of road had snaked up the valley and the walls of the Madoori fort had crumbled to dust.

Sitting there at the scene of the massacre as the hillsides turned purple and the cold dusk fell over the valley, pursuing George Hayward had seemed for a moment absurd and petty, yet somehow – and I knew not why – all the more important. When I woke in the morning the road to Darkot was open and going there would mean something.

The tarmac gave out at the village of Hundur, where children with blonde hair smiled in the sunlight. The valley levelled and narrowed. To the west hung the blunt nose of a glacier and the river was a narrow channel between the boulders. A man with a red moustache and a rusty shovel over his shoulder passed me, whistling through his teeth and squinting at the hillsides. The road was full of stones. At midday men in pale clothes called me into a garden. They bade me sit beneath bow-backed apricot trees, spread a dirty blanket and fed me coarse bread and pounded barley; they then gave me apples to carry when I went on my way. Into the afternoon grey cloud spilled over the ridges and the long breeze from the north shifted down the valley. The track – on the east bank of the river now – was rougher underfoot. Ahead I could see a skirt of grey mountain, a cluster of houses and the point where the valley broke west towards Chitral, east towards the Punji Pass and north towards another, higher cleft in the mountains – one that would lead you, in perhaps two long marches across the forbidden Afghan frontier, to the High Pamirs.

I walked into Darkot in a whorl of wind-cast willow leaves.

In July 1933 another traveller arrived in Darkot. Despite his Germanic name Colonel Reginald Schomberg was British, and his bigotry knew no bounds. His book, *Between the Oxus and the Indus*, is best read today for its comedy value, for Schomberg was completely immune to the hospitable charms of the Dards. Though the hard mountain scenery compelled him to passages of crisp, admiring prose, the local people were 'a blot on the landscape'. The inhabitants of Ishkoman were 'absurd pigmies'; while those of Nagar were 'stupid, dirty, and but indifferent imitations of monkeys'; all of them were unspeakably lazy. The only people of the region for whom he had any respect at all were the Hunzakuts: 'a race of men amongst a rabble of hill-apes' and 'an oasis of manliness in a desert of trousered women'. But even in their case he couldn't help but declare that they were 'much declined' since their days of slave-trading and caravan raiding. About the Yasinis Schomberg was veritably schizophrenic, talking one moment of 'a very smiling country and a very decent folk' before bemoaning their degeneracy in the next breath.

Sneering, snorting and stealing from apricot orchards, Schomberg made his way to Darkot in the company of a long-suffering Kashmiri cook. Once there he reined in his con-demnatory disgust and condescended to question the villagers about the infamous fate of George Hayward. They gave him shaky explanations of motive (Schomberg himself concluded that the crime was simply a natural manifestation of the degeneracy of the Darkotis – who were given to 'quarrelling violently'), but also, with the event still just within living memory, an account of the murder itself that closely matched the story collected by the investigating Kashmiri lickspittle Frederick Drew. Demonstrating that his ire was not entirely reserved for Asiatics, Schomberg poured scorn on the flowery fantasies of Colonel Woodthorpe and Sir Henry Newbolt – the 'Laspur Hills', which Newbolt so lavishly evoked in *He Fell Among Thieves*, could not even be seen from Darkot, he huffed.

The Darkotis told Schomberg that some of the loot of Hayward's camp was still squirreled away in cracked wooden trunks and beneath piles of flea-ridden blankets in the hovels of the village – a pistol, a saddle and a telescope. The villagers also told the traveller of the ill luck that had hung over the valley in the decades since Hayward was slain. Ibex, the emblematic long-horned wild goats of the cliffs and high pastures, had once been plentiful around the villages. Old men told stories of harvest days in the long light of late summer when they had stopped their scything to see ibex watching them with fearless interest, a stone's throw away across the stubble. But with Hayward's blood spilt on the hard ground the ibex had fled from Yasin, beyond the passes to higher, wilder country. Hayward's death, they whispered, had brought down a curse on the valley.

Schomberg called all this 'picturesque exaggeration', but had he been capable of empathising with the Dards he might have seen that talk of a curse carried weight, and that the ill luck of the mountains extended far beyond the disappearance of the ibex.

By the time Schomberg came to Dardistan Hayward's bones had been resting beneath the maharaja's epitaph in that Gilgit orchard for sixty-three years. Around him the town had grown and his grave had provided the seed for a tiny Christian cemetery. He shared the stony soil with staunch soldiers who had slipped on the cliffs while in pursuit of ibex, with military men struck down by fever, and with an alarming number of colonial administrators who, when attempting to cross the Indus in full flood, discovered too late that the river really was capable of sweeping away the universe.[1]

In 1933 Gilgit was the headquarters of an agency, a parcel of de facto British territory existing by a quiet and slightly tetchy gentlemen's agreement within a Kashmiri province. The first British agent, John Biddulph, had been installed in the town in 1877, just seven years after Hayward's death. After ignoring the explorer's furious complaints at the state of affairs on the Kashmiri frontier, the British had quickly realised that he was – to some extent – right. The Great Game was moving into its fevered final stages. The Russians were now skirting the fringes of the Pamirs and edging dangerously close to Afghanistan and Chitral, and the first Muscovite explorers – all extravagant hats and sable-lined trenchcoats – were beginning to slip over the passes at the western edge of the Asian mountain system. In light of all this, the loyalty of the Maharaja of Kashmir, so loudly proclaimed in the aftermath of the Hayward murder, was now being openly questioned. If the tsarists were at the back door, was the maharaja really the man to be trusted with the keys? The Dogra royal couldn't actually be dethroned, but his actions in the vicinity of Gilgit certainly needed to be monitored.

Not that any of this boded well for the people of Yasin. When Biddulph came trotting into Gilgit one of his principal aims was to engineer affairs to ensure that Yasin, a lawless void through which it was feared a Russian army could descend, was placed under firm Kashmiri control. There were British plans – to which Biddulph was party – to supply the weaponry needed for the Dogras to make a final, definitive attack on the valley. Pahlwan was still clinging to the slippery Yasin throne when Biddulph was in Gilgit. Already well versed in the traitorous politics of the mountains despite being only in his mid-twenties, he actually appealed directly to the colonial agent – and entertained him hospitably in the valley as the first British visitor since George Hayward – with a proposal for a direct treaty with Britain, negating the need for a Dogra invasion and all the atrocities it would entail.

By this time, however, the embryonic Gilgit Agency was on its last legs and Biddulph was itching to abandon his lonely post. The problem, just as Hayward had found, was the Kashmiri Dogras. Jealous as always of meddling outsiders, the commanders of Gilgit had, Biddulph was certain, been manoeuvring against him. As the only Englishman in the outer reaches of the Western Himalayas a certain degree of paranoia had begun to creep in: he claimed that the Kashmiris were plotting to kill him. Uncomfortable echoes of Hayward were doubtless detected in the government chambers of Punjab and Calcutta. Biddulph was recalled.

But Gilgit was far from forgotten. Indeed, the British were beginning to consider the possibility of getting stuck in there themselves; leaving management of such sensitive territory to the Kashmiri Dogras was, it seemed, a liability. Recent events had only made that all the more obvious. In 1880 Pahlwan led a ludicrously ill-considered attack on Kashmiri Gilgit – at the Machiavellian instigation of the Mehtar of Chitral, it was claimed. The invasion failed; Pahlwan ended up on the run in the ungovernable hills around the Middle Indus, and in the ultimate denouement of the bloody saga of the fratricidal Yasin siblings, he was killed by his shadowy older brother, Mulk Aman. The upshot of this was exactly what the mehtar was said to have planned all along: after meddling in the valley for decades he had finally made Yasin his own. The cursed throne was occupied by one of his own multitude of unruly offspring, a hell-raising playboy named Nizam ul-Mulk, renowned for his love of debauched parties and fondness for the company of delectable dancing boys.

Fifteen years after Hayward's death, in 1885, the British returned to Gilgit with stout walking sticks and scientific equipment. This was the mission of William Lockhart, later to become commander-in-chief of all India. Lockhart was not there to open an agency, but to scout out the region in detail and to pass a verdict on the political state of affairs in the high mountains. His conclusion was that leaving Dardistan to the Kashmiris was intolerable. In 1888, on Lockhart's recommendation, the Gilgit Agency was reopened – this time with ample guns and money under the command of the redoubtable Algernon Durand. Within a few years the British Gilgit Agency was a well-armed little garrison and, though the region was still supposedly Kashmiri territory, Durand was soon appointing regional governors and even assuming unofficial command of the Dogra troops.

By the early 1890s there was a golf course in Gilgit. Between breakfast and a quick round on the links the British stationed there plotted heavy-handed meddling in the affairs of the surrounding valleys. In the chilly tail end of 1891 Hunza and Nagar were attacked – on the grounds of little more than impertinent intransigence. After a stout defence the fastness was undone; the one-time cradle of the Kunjuti bandits was overturned and a cable was wired to Kashmir: Hunza 'now belongs to the British Government'.

The following year Chilas was roughly annexed for the Crown too. Only one puzzle-piece remained – Chitral – and an opportunity had just arisen there. In 1892, after ruling his Hindu Kush kingdom for a quarter of a century, Aman ul-Mulk, the mighty Mehtar of Chitral, died. The British leapt into the bloody succession dispute with gusto, backing none other than the ghastly playboy prince then governing Yasin. Nizam ul-Mulk did end up briefly in British-prescribed control of Chitral – but not for long. In 1895 he went the way of most Chitrali princes – shot in the back by a traitorous younger brother.

The British sent an expeditionary force across the Shandur Pass in response – a force which ended up besieged in the Chitral fort for over a month. But although it was the British who spent that month cowering under fire, eating their horses and succumbing to dysentery, the Siege of Chitral was in truth the last stand of independent Dardistan. The besieged soldiers were ultimately relieved, and a new tame ul-Mulk prince – answerable to a British

Resident – was placed on the throne.[2] The whole of Chitral proper was tagged on to the Pashtun North-West Frontier, while the country east of the Shandur was hived off and finally thrown under the command of Gilgit. A British political officer was installed in Yasin.

Ungovernable Dardistan was governed; Hayward's pleas for the claims of its rightful owners were disavowed and the only voice of protest, howling irrelevantly from the distant wilderness, was Dr Gottlieb Leitner Etc. And no one was listening to him.

Meanwhile, to the north and west history had been rocketing forward too. Though their dynasty was going to pieces at the centre, the Manchus were back in Eastern Turkestan with a vengeance, while beyond Kashgar the Russians were chomping into the Pamirs. In 1890 Francis Younghusband, the magnificently moustached nephew of tea-planting Robert Shaw, made it to the High Pamirs and reached Karakul Lake, the icy sheet of white water that had lain at the core of Hayward's all-consuming insane desire. Karakul was not after all, it was generally conceded, the true source of the Oxus. Even today there has been no definitive identification of the ultimate wellspring,[3] but by the time Younghusband arrived on the Roof of the World the political significance that had given such import to these mysterious watercourses was soon to be an irrelevance anyway: by the mid-1890s the Russians had annexed the whole of the Pamirs.

In 1907 an Anglo-Russian convention was signed; with a little grumbling from the benches, the Great Game had been declared a draw. Borders were defined and spheres of influence decided. Tibet would be left to its fate; Afghanistan would be a British-influenced buffer zone. The Russian Threat was no more and events would shortly unfold back in Europe that would make the previous century of fretting about unguarded passes and mountain rebellions seem like a joke. But it was too late for the high mountains around Gilgit.

As the Gilgit graveyard grew around Hayward's tomb through the early decades of the twentieth century the strange dual system of actual British governance coupled to pretence of Kashmiri control continued. The bigoted Colonel Schomberg declared it 'an embarrassing arrangement'. It was, and in 1935 the fourth and final Maharaja of Kashmir signed the Gilgit region over to the British on a lease of sixty years. Sixty years is a long time, and though there were plenty of pompous heads buried deep in the colonial sand, those with a little more savvy could already have predicted that the British would be gone from the subcontinent long before the lease was out. In fact, they lasted only another twelve years.

As a nominally independent British vassal, Kashmir, like all the other princely states, had to choose between accession to India or Pakistan in 1947. With its large Muslim majority and cultural, economic and geographical ties into what would become the new Islamic state, logic suggested Pakistan. Indeed the K in the acronym that made up Pakistan stood for Kashmir.[4] But as a Hindu, Maharaja Hari Singh had shied away from the prospect. Some claim that he was trying to engineer true independence for his country; more likely he was merely in the grip of regal delusions. Just one month before the British departed India for good he was reportedly convinced that it was all a joke and that they would never really leave.[5]

As Nehru's 'tryst with destiny', the midnight hour of 15 August 1947, came and went and the Union Jack fluttered impotently one final time down the flagpole, the maharaja vacillated. It was only when a raggedy mob of Pashtuns from the North-West Frontier, raiders bent on rape and pillage, poured into his state and headed for Srinagar that the maharaja panicked and turned to India. On condition of his accession, the army of the new Indian republic invaded Kashmir to save it from the raiders.

Meanwhile, to the west in Gilgit the British had unilaterally decided that the 1935 lease was now null and void and had handed the territory back to the maharaja – a move that the Pakistanis would claim, with some reason, demonstrated the pro-Indian bias of the final British administration. However, the people of what had once been Dardistan would have nothing of treaties and leases agreed between invading foreigners. For the locally recruited Gilgit Scouts the idea of absorption into the armies of either Kashmir or India was anathema. They rebelled, raised a Pakistani flag over the Gilgit garrison, and hammered east over the passes to – in their eyes, and to be fair, in those of most of the residents – liberate Baltistan.

The newly independent India and Pakistan went straight to war, and Kashmir ended up divided between them, a snaking, crackling Line of Control marking the boundary. Dard country was, for the first time in almost a century, entirely free from Kashmir. But the damage had, it seemed, been done.

At the end of the first decade of the twenty-first century none of the countries through which George Hayward had blazed his wild trails were happy lands. As I picked my way through High Asia in Hayward's footsteps it sometimes seemed like the fleeing ibex had carried his curse across the high passes, following hidden tracks along the mountainsides, infecting other valleys with unhappiness to come, and then bearing it from the boundaries of the Western Himalayas and out into the flatlands beyond.

In Kashmir itself there had been machine gun-toting soldiers, stepping suddenly from the field edges or shifting in the shadows of the orchards. On a soft-edged summer afternoon I had drifted on Srinagar's Dal Lake in a brightly painted *shikara* – a Kashmiri gondola. It was warm and still and a few young men and boys were thrashing around over the green weed in an ungainly fashion, with inflated inner tubes for floatation. One of them splashed near to me, grinning and shivering.

'Is it cold?' I had asked.

'Not too cold. Actually I can't swim without this thing,' he laughed. His shoulders and upper arms were very white, but his forearms were tanned. His name was Imran. He was Kashmiri, from Srinagar, though he had only just returned home after two years working in a call centre near Delhi.

We passed the time of day, and then, as the *shikara* drifted away leaving Imran flailing and flapping in its wake, he called out, apropos of nothing, 'You know, the Indians treat us like dogs'. To the south the white ghost of the Pir Panjal range levitated over the valley. 'Really,' said Imran, 'they treat us like dogs, the soldiers and the police, the whole country.' The *shikara* was turning over the smooth water and the peaks were swivelling beyond the lake. Imran, shivering and thrashing, was drifting out of earshot.

'So what do Kashmiris really want?' I called out. 'Pakistan?'

'Not Pakistan, not India. They both treat us like dogs.' The last, hopelessly hopeful word I heard before he splashed away behind was 'Independence …'

Elsewhere, in Mughal gardens and overhanging alleyways, Imran's countrymen expressed the same sentiments with erudition and firm handshakes. Kashmir was calm at the time, but within days of my leaving across the Zoji La the valley erupted into stone-hurling, car-torching protests over the alleged rape and murder of two local women by Indian soldiers.

Across the passes in Ladakh there was no violence, but border disputes and revolutions had slammed the back door to Eastern Turkestan shut. It was half a century since the last caravans from Yarkand had struggled down from the Karakoram Pass. And if many Kashmiris resented Indian rule, then many Ladakhis resented being governed from Kashmir – a legacy of the expansionism of the first maharaja, Gulab Singh. They were neither Kashmiri nor Muslim; they held no share in the conflict or the violence; they wanted to be ruled directly from Delhi. But, they hissed, their wish would never be granted: the inclusion of non-Muslim Ladakh in the equation was a key justification for India's dogged refusal to let the Himalayan state slip from its grasp.

There was unhappiness 200 miles to the north too, in Xinjiang – what had once been Yaqub Beg's Turkestan. Twice more, during the post-imperial chaos of the first half of the twentieth century, an independent state had briefly been declared in the towns of the Taklamakan, but under the rule of the People's Republic, Eastern Turkestan was merely western China. The Uighurs, descendants of Robert Shaw's fine Turki fellows, were, whether they liked it or not, just another minority under heaven, though they had less chance of finding a job than a Han Chinese immigrant, and if they wanted to work for the government – as a teacher, a clerk or even a bus conductor – then the men must shave their beards and the women discard their headscarves. In the months before I arrived violent anti-government protests had broken out in Urumqi, the modern capital. The internet had been shut down across the state and it was impossible to make an international phone call. In terms of communication Eastern Turkestan was as closed to the outside world as it had been in the late 1860s. Army trucks bearing anti-separatist slogans were rolling on the streets.

English-speaking Uighurs whispered their disquiet in hushed, paranoid tones. In Karghilik a beautiful girl with amber eyes and a silver-embroidered headscarf said to me, quietly, sadly, but very firmly over cups of saffron tea:

> I would like to tell you about what has really happened here; there are many things that you should know about what they have done. But now we do not know where they are, or what they are listening to, so I cannot talk about these things. I am sorry.

They – the Chinese Government – were building a railway line along the southern edge of the desert to Hotan. One stop down the line in Yarkand another young Uighur, met at a kebab stall, had hissed angrily, 'When this railway is ready we will be finished; Xinjiang will be all Chinese.'

The paranoia carried in the unspoken parts of conversations – the same paranoia that had affected Shaw and Hayward in the same cities a century and a half earlier – was infectious. When the notebook in which I had jotted down what Uighurs had whispered and translations of the bullying government slogans spray-painted on old city walls disappeared from my Kashgar hotel room I was only too happy to travel onwards to Pakistan.

But there too things were bad. The newspapers hardly bore reading. Almost every day suicide bombs were crackling in a belt of bloodshed across the belly of the country – from Peshawar to Islamabad to Lahore and back. In Pashtun Waziristan the army were fighting a civil war against the Taliban. Gilgit and the mountains were quiet, but there was anger in the bazaars. Dardistan had thrown its lot in with Pakistan in 1947, but the Islamic republic had never granted the region provincial status. Gilgit, Hunza, Yasin and Baltistan had no representation in Islamabad; until recently they had almost no representation at all.

In a cloth merchant's shop in Gilgit, over cup after cup of sweet tea, two traders from Hunza – their names were Shaukat and Ali – voiced the anger of their country. What started as mild and faintly humorous complaints about the Sunni Islamists – 'the beards' – who were ruining down-country Pakistan, turned into furious rancour, not just against the beards, but against all of Pakistan. Somehow preserving the dignified idiom of South Asia, and somehow still insisting on calling me 'sir', Shaukat and Ali were soon thumping the counter and trembling with emotion.

'What has Pakistan ever done for us, sir?' Shaukat said, his voice cracking. 'Tell me – what have these Pakistani bastards ever done for us?'

Even in the burnished autumn calm of Yasin, a world away now from politics and violence, the local Ismaelis had snarled vitriol against the Sunnis. Sunni Pakistan cared nothing for them, they said; all that was good in the valley – the healthcare, the education and even the attitudes – came from Ismaeliism and the Aga Khan.

I had carried all this with me as I walked up the valley towards Darkot, and by the time I passed through the falling leaves and into the village I knew why Hayward was important.

In the decade that he had played on my imagination and in the year that I had traced him closely he had always struck me only as an individualist. Indeed, what had first drawn me to him was how isolated he had seemed in the Victorian scene. He had been a rebel and a renegade, moving against the stream of Himalayan history. Politics, colonialism and the play of the Great Game seemed to have been an irrelevance to George Hayward – and at first they had seemed an irrelevance to me when I considered his tale. He had beaten his own path through the mountains; nothing and no one else mattered.

That, I now saw, was all true – but there was something else. Though he was, of course, of his time and though he always framed his bitter complaints against Kashmiri actions around Gilgit in terms of the interests of the British Empire, Hayward, with his instability, his anger and his insane desire, had rejected the cold pragmatism that leads to small people and small countries being trampled. Whoever it was that really had him killed, George Hayward had died, I now believed, in the name of the people of Yasin, not in the name of the bleak, howling and inanimate High Pamirs. If a curse really had fallen across Kashmir, Ladakh, Eastern Turkestan and Dardistan then George Hayward's ghost, loitering in a Gilgit graveyard, would be full of righteous rage. Across the region in the modern era, national interests and the spectre of terrorism – the Russian Threat of the twenty-first century – are loudly proclaimed as bombs fall on village houses, as old cities are destroyed and as young men are arrested for daring to protest. Hayward would have rejected all that.

In a letter to Colonel Showers, written in February 1870 on the road from Gilgit, before he had even reached Yasin, before he had even seen the skulls on the Madoori hillside, George Hayward had, in one simple sentence, expressed a profound sense of humanity that seemed so often to be lacking – then and now: 'Apart from any religious fanaticism the tribes are simply men who are simply fighting for their homesteads.'

The police in Yasin Village – long, lean, handsome men with cropped beards and dark jerseys – had told me to report to their post in Darkot, but when I got there a gaggle of fair-haired schoolboys told me that the policemen had already left the village for the winter. For a moment they didn't know what to do with me, and then a name came forth –'We'll take you to Mohamed Murad' – and giggling, slightly hysterical, they led me through rough lanes under a heavy grey sky. The bright blue of the morning had all gone now.

Darkot lay beneath a great slope of pale scree. The village – small, rock-walled houses with crooked doorways and flat roofs – sprawled between stony fields and threadbare hems of poplar trees. To the west a great broken bowl of rock opened with the slug of a dirty-white glacier in its belly, a jagged guillotine ridge dark against the cloud above, and a spiny mountain rising beyond, hung about with skeins of mist like drapes of damp cobwebs. The cold, dank name of the peak, I later learned, was Dullichish – the Unhappy Mountain. No one had ever reached the summit. To the north a valley bent away towards the Darkot Pass, and to the east, over a bank of red-brown glacial rock, was the way to the Upper Ishkoman Valley.

The schoolboys led me to the room – a cube of rough stone in a little garden of cabbages and apple trees – where Mohamed Murad, the local schoolmaster, was sleeping. They knocked at the door and then retreated. With a grunt and a scratch of a tousled head Murad swung himself out from under a pile of blankets, clutched an old transistor radio to his chest and, fiddling with the dial, welcomed me. He was completely unperturbed by my unexpected arrival, though he later told me that I was the first foreigner to visit Darkot for more than a year.

In a few moments a cloth, a flask of salty tea and a plate of bread had come from somewhere and we were sitting against piles of cushions in the gloom of the little house. Outside the light was thinning and the clouds were sinking on to the valley. Murad had a certain endearing eccentricity and shabbiness about him – with uncombed hair and crinkled clothes. As we talked he reached reflexively for the dial of the transistor, twiddling it from far-off Urdu voices to the lean twang of Gilgiti music, from shrieking Bollywood strings to the startling sound of the BBC, crackling in the heart of the Hindu Kush.

He was the head teacher of the government school in the village, but long ago, before the war in Afghanistan and the troubles in Pakistan had destroyed tourism, he had lived in Gilgit in the summer and worked as a trekking guide. He had crossed all the high passes of the region with parties of European hikers in the days before 'Pakistan' was a scary word.

'Really I would like to be a guide again, but what can we do? There are no tourists.' There was a certain wry melancholy about him, and a gentle kindness too.

'So why have you come to Darkot?' he asked.

I had walked some 20 miles along the valley – for once and once only covering the ground faster than George Hayward, who, with the delaying tactics of his Yasini porters, had taken three days over the same road – but for some reason I was not in the least bit tired. And sitting on the worn carpet of Murad's room while the sky outside grew darker and heavier, an impatience overcame me. I was, I was sure, just a short walk from the very end of my journey – the point beyond which I could follow George Hayward no further.

In the 1930s the spluttering Schomberg had reported being shown the spot where the explorer died. It lay, he wrote, a little way east of the village near the path to the Punji Pass. So well fixed in local folklore was the event that they had given the place a name – Feringhi Bar, the Foreigner's Valley. Schomberg had sneeringly complained that the people of Dardistan were dropping their old customs one by one with each passing season, but surely a story fixed in the landscape with a place name would always endure.

I went straight to the point: I had come to Darkot because of George Hayward; I wanted to see Feringhi Bar, the place where he was killed.

'Of course,' said Murad, touching the dials of the transistor, 'it's not far from here. I can show you.' But he made no move to leave.

There was an hour until somewhere, hidden behind clouds and ridges, the sun would set. I had been travelling – in paper and on the ground – towards this place for more than a year; what was a small delay? Would it matter if I waited until morning to see the spot? But here, in this high, lost village, it seemed as if the urgency that had compelled Hayward himself through double marches and evening departures had infected me. I couldn't wait.

'Can we go now?' I asked, a little too keenly.

Murad smiled and unstopped the flask. 'Relax – it's not far; have another cup of tea first.'

Afterwards we picked our way across the stony stubble fields, up the gentle rise to the east. To the right the road back to the lower valley passed between two great black fists of up-thrown rock. Darkot was a harder, colder place than the other villages of Yasin. The fields here were thinner and rockier, and ahead the ground was a mess of grey alluvium, stream-scored and untilled.

Murad nursed his radio as we walked, gently touching it like a small animal – or a baby. Wiry Chitrali music, played on thin-necked instruments, came through the static and danced in the damp silence of Darkot.

'I like the radio very much,' he said, 'you can learn so much information from it.'

Murad's unkempt eccentricity belied his status. He was not only the village schoolmaster; he was also the chairman of Darkot's *Jamat Khana* – the prayer-house and community hall that passes for a mosque in Ismaeli Islam – and his family was one of the most important in the valley. As we walked old men came up to him to shake his hand and, in the heavy, gritty tones of the Burushaski language, to ask him advice on politics, finance and family affairs. Murad gave his replies without haughtiness or affectation, smiling and fiddling with the radio.

At a little shop, standing alone halfway up the alluvial fan, we met another schoolteacher, Abdul Rashid. Abdul Rashid was

Murad's counterpart, the headmaster not of the government school but of that funded by the Aga Khan Foundation. He was a very different man from Murad. His hair was combed and his moustache trimmed to sharp edges. His *shalwaar kamis* was neatly pressed. He held himself very upright and called me 'sir'. But the two men slipped easily into each other's company, without any sense of rivalry or seniority.

'You are going to Feringhi Bar?' asked Abdul Rashid.

'Yes. You know the place?'

'Certainly sir; actually my family own that land.'

Grinning, Murad clasped his counterpart's shoulder with the hand that was not holding the radio. 'A-ha!' he roared. 'This man is the criminal! This man is the murderer!'

We came to a fence of thorns, crooked around a pocket of level land under the trail-chased brown slopes that rose to the east. Abdul Rashid slipped the catch from a wooden gate and we stepped inside, picking over the roughly tilled soil.

'This is it?' I could suddenly feel my heart beating very rapidly.

'Over there.' A small farmhouse stood to the left; Abdul Rashid had pointed just beyond it where a cluster of willow trees stood at the foot of the hillside on the edge of the fallow land. I had never expected them to be so specific.

The air was soft and slightly clammy. The place lay on a little oval plateau looking out across the village and the glacier to the cloud-skirted Unhappy Mountain.

'Here?'

'No – here, right?'

Murad and Abdul Rashid were quibbling over mere metres, and suddenly another man had appeared from the farmhouse. His name was Badal Beg; he was a retired soldier and now a small-holder, the custodian of Feringhi Bar. He was also Abdul Rashid's uncle, and he decided it: 'Here!'

It was a patch of goat-cropped grass beneath a buckled apricot tree with the mountains all around. Suddenly I didn't know what I was supposed to do: sit, meditate, weep, pray, re-enact the scene?

But Badal Beg knew exactly what to do; after all, I was a guest in Dardistan. By now a small mob of wide-eyed children and youths had appeared out of the evening, and so had a blanket, a flask and a plate of freshly fried flatbreads. At Feringhi Bar, the exact place where George Hayward's unhappy journey had finally ended, the place where his insane desire had carried him to its ultimate destination – the waiting cold steel – I sat down with two charming schoolteachers, an old soldier and a crackling transistor radio to enjoy an impromptu picnic. Nothing could have been better.

As we munched on the hot, greasy strips of fried bread and slurped at the tea – sugary not salty this time – the men told me what they knew about the murder.

Abdul Rashid said that old people in the village – who had learnt the story from their own grandparents who had been alive at the time – claimed that Mir Wali had sent men to steal the explorer's baggage.

'The campsite was over there' – he pointed back to a stand of poplars behind the village:

> They came to take him, but people say he had a gun and they were scared so they only caught him in the morning when he was sleeping. Then they brought him here. At that time this was all jungle. There were more trees than now. Conditions were a little different, but this is the place where they killed him, with a sword I think …

'Right,' said Murad in a gentle, reassuring kind of way.

'And do local people have any ideas about why Mir Wali had him killed?' I asked. 'They were supposed to be friends.'

Abdul Rashid held a piece of bread delicately. Murad's radio was still playing Chitrali music. 'People say that this Mr Hayward was bringing a lot of jewels with him. Also he had a very special ring. They took the ring when they killed him.' That at least – the stolen ring – had been in the original account collected by Frederick Drew.

'Mir Wali was not an Ismaeli, you know,' Murad interjected. 'He was a Sunni, Chitrali originally I think.'

Abdul Rashid wagged a finger, 'That's right! A close-minded, negative person!' And the conversation fell to the merits of Ismaeliism.

'But don't people here have some other explanation for why Mir Wali killed Hayward?' I interrupted. 'They really say it was just a robbery?'

Abdul Rashid shook his head. 'You see, in this village people are simple and uneducated. They do not think too deeply about things; for them the idea that it was robbery is enough.'

'Right,' said Murad.

'And Mir Wali was a negative person; he was not Ismaeli …'

So, sitting cross-legged on the blanket under the apricot tree, Badal Beg refilling my tea cup every time I put it down, I told them everything I knew about George Hayward, all the places I had seen and all the things I had read, how Hayward had first come to the valley and learnt of the Madoori massacre – 'Ah, yes! Madoori!' a mumble of ascent went around – and about the theories surrounding his death. As I talked I saw grins and whispers amongst the children. 'They are saying that you know a lot of information about Mr Hayward,' said Murad.

When I was done Abdul Rashid nodded deeply for a moment, then said, brightly, 'I like this idea about the Dogras being responsible.'

'It's only a theory,' I said, hurriedly, feeling a little guilty.

'No, no! I like this theory!'

'Right,' said Murad.

It was dusk now, and the mountains were turning from red-brown slopes to blue-black walls and the still air held a hint of thin rain. The clouds were pulling their damp, cobwebby curtain across the glacier and the Unhappy Mountain. But the teacups were still being refilled.

What, I wanted to know, about stories of a curse? Was it true that after Hayward's death the ibex had disappeared from the valley?

'You know,' said Abdul Rashid, 'there is one story …' A few years after the murder, when it was still the talk of the valley and when the dynastic upheavals it had unleashed were still shaking occupants out of the Yasin throne on an annual basis, a wandering Pir from the Pamirs – an Ismaeli holy man who drifted through the mountains touting charms and prophesies – had dropped down the glacier-cut slopes from the Darkot Pass. Wild and bearded but giving off the unmistakable aura of austere holiness – and the slight threat that it implies – the villagers housed him, fed him, begged his charms and listened to his sermons. When the Pir asked about recent events in the village of course the story of the murdered foreigner was paramount. The Pir knew nothing of *feringhis* and nothing of the British Empire or the Great Game. But tugging his raggedy beard and fingering his beads he had prophesied a punishment for the crime. Within a century a disaster would befall Darkot, he said.

'And in 1978 there was a huge flood,' said Abdul Rashid. 'There used to be a big rock right here, behind Feringhi Bar, but it was washed away. All the fields on this side of the village were destroyed. You saw when we walked up? The soil is no good for farming now; we lost a lot of good land.'

I nodded. 'In 1978 you say?'

Abdul Rashid could see what I was thinking. 'This Pir came maybe eight years after Mr Hayward was killed,' he added quickly.

'Right,' said Murad.

The light was almost gone now, and it was cold. The tea was finally exhausted and Badal Beg began to fold up the blanket. As we stood up and stretched our limbs stiffly, and as Murad turned the volume back up on his radio, Abdul Rashid said, 'I think it was a bad thing for Yasin that Mr Hayward died. Not only the curse and the flood, I mean':

You know, our culture here is not really the same as Pakistan. We are Ismaeli people, but we are also Central Asian people. Our real connections are not with Kashmir or Punjab. We have more in common with Tajikistan, or even Iran, especially now, with all these Taliban and bombs in Pakistan.

Maybe if Mr Hayward had been successful in his journey, if he had gone across the Darkot Pass into Tajik country, then this connection would have been stronger; the world would have known about our link with those places. Maybe they would have made a road that way. Maybe we wouldn't be in Pakistan now.

There was nothing more to say. We all shook hands. The children vanished as suddenly as they had appeared; Badal Beg, blanket and flask under his arm, went back to the farmhouse where the warm glow of a cooking fire showed in the open doorway. Abdul Rashid took a beetling goat path up the hillside to his own home in the nearby hamlet of Gartens, the white of his *shalwaar kamis* fading as he went. Murad and I walked back down to the village, the transistor radio crackling in the darkness.

Notes

1   After the British left the subcontinent in 1947 the Gilgit graveyard was not entirely abandoned. Though the flowerbeds grew thick with weeds, the apricot and apple trees went unpruned and beyond the surrounding brick wall a small city grew, from time to time some other adventurous foreigner was interred there. These post-colonial travellers were perhaps better companions in death for George Hayward than the straight-backed soldiers of the earlier era – they were all mountaineers, killed in falls on the high peaks.

One final, small mystery attached itself to Hayward: in the 1960s the maharaja's marble tablet still marked his grave, but in the 1970s Edward Noack, an American Fellow of the RGS and a frequent traveller in the mountains, discovered on his customary visit to the graveyard to pay his respects that the headstone had vanished. Quite who might have stolen George Hayward's epitaph, and why, is an enigma, though one cynical Gilgiti suggested to me that it might merely have made a good foundation stone for some nearby concrete chai shop. Noack was horrified to find that Hayward, already long since condemned to obscurity, no longer even had a marked grave. At Noack's instigation a replacement headstone was installed in 1980.

2   The Siege of Chitral and its relief formed one of the earliest global news events. By the 1890s telegraph wires connected Asia with Europe and beyond, and new cables followed the routes of advancing armies even through the wild hills of the North-West Frontier. Newspaper reporters were able to file their copy from places that just a few decades earlier had been unmarked on any map. And the age of the high-profile war correspondent had already begun: Sir Francis Younghusband, whose star as a veteran Great Gamer was then burning brightly, was on hand for *The Times* of London.

3   One of the possible sources of the Oxus pointed out by modern geographers is, ironically, Lake Sir-i-Kol, the muddy puddle first identified by the incongruous navy man John Wood, way back in 1838.

4   The name and concept of a separate homeland for the Muslims of the subcontinent was cooked up by Indian Muslim students in Britain in the early twentieth century – while sitting on the top deck of a London bus, according to one legend. The P stands for Punjab, the A for 'Afghania' (the Pashtun borderlands of the North-West Frontier) and the K for Kashmir. The 'istan' is roughly apportioned between Sind and Baluchistan, and the whole conveniently adds up to the Persian for 'Land of the Pure'. There was, as Bengali nationalists bitterly pointed out before the eastern wing of the bifurcated Muslim state broke away to form Bangladesh, no B in Pakistan.

5   While the first two scions of the Dogra dynasty – founder
     Gulab Singh and his son Ranbir, the man who loomed
     malignantly over George Hayward's journeys – were formi-
     dable and ruthless, by the third generation decline had set
     in. Maharaja number three, Partab Singh, was a man with a
     wonky turban, an aura of unreliability and a brother who died
     of syphilis. He was succeeded by his nephew, Hari. This last
     King of Kashmir, the vacillator who presided over the mess
     of accession to India, carried about him the same whiff of
     scandal that had lingered around his uncle and father.

     As a young man, gallivanting through Europe, he had
     stumbled into a sordid honey trap laid by his own traitorous
     English aide-de-camp. The youthful prince was caught *in fla-
     grante delicto* in a Paris hotel room with a much older married
     woman – hired for the purpose – and promptly blackmailed
     for £125,000. He paid up but later took the case to court
     in England, where the sensitive judge allowed him to give
     anonymous evidence under the pseudonym 'Mr A'. However,
     the identity of the claimant was an open secret, and the world
     press showed no respect for royal sensibilities. Hari Singh was
     soon a laughing stock in teashops all over India.

CHAPTER NOTES

1. Death in the Morning

There are various accounts of George Hayward's death, some contradictory, some ridiculous. But the version that inspires most confidence is that collected by the Kashmiri sepoy Gufar Khan, working for the English Geologist Frederick Drew who investigated the crime in Gilgit in the autumn of 1870. The elements contained in this report – and for the colour, my own experiences hiking along the Yasin Valley 139 years later – are the basis of this opening chapter. The original transcript of Khan's account was in Drew's initial confidential report on the murder, forwarded to the British authorities by the Maharaja of Kashmir. A handwritten copy appears in the archives of the Royal Geographical Society, and it is also printed in the *Proceedings of the Royal Geographical Society of London*, Vol. 15, No 2 (1870–71).

2. Into the Wild

There is a delightful treasure trove of general literature on the Great Game, both contemporary and more recent. The most readable overview of the whole phenomenon is Peter Hopkirk's wonderful *The Great Game*, while Karl Meyer and Shareen Brysac's *Tournament of Shadows* provides a somewhat more scholarly, but still very readable account. For an account that focuses very specifically on the oddball characters who played the Game – and which introduces our own George Hayward – John Keay's superbly well-written *The Explorers of the Western Himalayas 1820–95*, originally published in two volumes as *When Men and Mountains Meet* and *The Gilgit Game*, is essential reading.

3. From Forest to the Frontier

Given the wild drama of the last two years of Hayward's life, and the abundant sources for that period, plenty of past writers have been perfectly happy to take the fact that he joined an Irish regiment as evidence that he was Irish himself, and then to crack on with the meaty matters of his time in the mountains. I am quite willing to concede that I would probably have done the same. However, the truth of his Yorkshire birth and the details of his education were finally revealed in 1998 in a fine paper in Vol. 29, No 2, of *Asian Affairs*, the journal of the Royal Society for Asian Affairs, after research by Charles Timmis. It is to his paper, 'George Hayward: his Central Asian explorations, his murder, his legacy', that I owe the scant but tantalising titbits about Hayward's early life.

There are far too many accounts of life in India under the British Raj to list here, but William Dalrymple's magisterial *White Mughals* gives an excellent explanation of the way the cultural cross-over of the early years had hardened to something approaching apartheid by Hayward's era.

Alexander Gardner's original papers – with their rumours of an accompanying curse – seem to have vanished, but in 1898 they were edited and put together in the form of *Soldier and Traveller: Memoirs of Alexander Gardner* by Major Hugh Pearse. Even in expurgated form they are a mind-boggling mess, and ploughing through them will leave you with no more conviction about the veracity – or otherwise – of his tale than you had when you started.

Gardner also crops up here, there and everywhere, like some kind of Himalayan Artful Dodger, in books, reports and travelogues from the mid-nineteenth century to the present day. The most accessible overview of his life is in John Keay's *When Men and Mountains Meet*. For a glimpse of contemporary perspectives on the man I turned to Andrew Wilson's *Abode of Snow*, while for more titbits, and a fine account of life amongst Ranjit Singh's foreign legion, Ben Macintyre's *Josiah the Great* was useful.

4. A Most Unsettling Companion – 6. The Way they Treat their Guests in Turkestan

The main sources for the chapters detailing the journeys of George Hayward and Robert Shaw into Eastern Turkestan are their own letters and accounts. Shaw's *Visits to High Tartary, Yarkand and Kashgar* is largely made up of polished excerpts from his own diary and letters, and it provides a very readable – and often unintentionally hilarious – account of a Victorian bigot in high-Asian action. He is in slightly more serious mode in his report in the RGS *Journal*. Hayward's report is in the RGS archives in its handwritten original, and is published in full in the society's *Journal* of 1869. Various letters from the two men also appear in the RGS archives; most of Hayward's also appear in print in the *Proceedings* and the *Journal* of 1869. The censorship that would creep in later is less of an issue here.

A photocopy of an unpublished journal-cum-first-draft report that Hayward wrote of the early part of his Turkestan journey is also in the RGS archives, and was very useful.

I picked up some nuggets about Robert Shaw – not least the location of his death – from Patrick French's excellent modern biography of Shaw's exploring nephew, *Younghusband*, and besides details in Hayward and Shaw's own writing, *Wild West China* by Christian Tyler filled in a few gaps on the turbulent history of Eastern Turkestan. The title for Chapter Four was taken from John Keay's *The Gilgit Game*.

On the Pundits, the most serious and complete account is in *The Pundits*, by Derek Waller, which details the Mirza's story. An account intended for a more general audience is Jules Stewart's very readable *Spying for the Raj*. Montgomerie's transcript of the Mirza's own report of his journey is the RGS *Journal* of 1871.

7. The Road is Full of Stones – 8. Speak, or Die Bursting with Rage

Again these two chapters rely heavily on sources in the RGS archives, mainly Hayward's own letters, route tables and maps. Although these were published in the *Journal* and the *Proceedings* of 1871, some vital passages were censored, so the originals count for something here.

Details of the kind of grumblings often heard about Kashmiri rule in the late nineteenth century were found in Andrew Wilson's *Abode of Snow* and the later *Where Three Empires Meet*, by E.F. Knight.

Trying to make sense of the history of Dardistan – now known as Gilgit-Baltistan – is tough: the area was as politically contentious and the commentators as partisan 140 years ago as they are today. For the most part it was an attempt to strike a balance between the information in Frederick Drew's laughably anti-Dard *The Jummoo and Kashmir Territories*, and what amounts to an unabashed love song to the Dards: Gottlieb Leitner Etc.'s *The Languages and Races of Dardistan*, *The Hunza and Nagar Handbook* and *Dardistan in 1886, 1883 and 1893*. Reginald Schomberg's otherwise almost inconceivably bigoted *Between the Oxus and the Indus* actually manages to provide a relatively neat overview, and Dr Ahmad Dani's modern *History of the Northern Areas of Pakistan* gives the post-colonial version of events.

9. Strange and Suggestive

Perhaps fittingly, the details of Hayward's demise are sketchy and indistinct, and to be tracked down in fragments here and there. Key sources were various letters and reports in the India Office archives (now held in the British Library), and letters and reports forwarded to the RGS and now in their archives (and some published in their *Proceedings*). The Havildar's report is in the *Proceedings* Vol. 16. Several India Office sources quoted by John Keay when he was researching *The Gilgit Game* in the 1970s seem to have vanished in the age of digitalised archives so I gleaned a couple of otherwise unavailable nuggets from him. Various contemporary sources that cover the event include Frederick Drew's original report, as well as his published *The Jummoo and Kashmir Territories*, in which, after slandering the Dards and doing his best to undermine Hayward's credibility as a witness, he gets all teary-eyed on the dead man's behalf. Dr Leitner's multitudinous ramblings mention the case here and there, and, of course, there are the flowery imaginings of Colonel Woodthorpe which appear in the otherwise very serious report of the Lockhart Mission to Gilgit, which can be found in the India Office Records.

10. Hayward's Curse

The bigoted Col Schomberg and the markedly less bigoted Dr Dani provide the main sources for the post-Hayward history of Dardistan in *Between the Oxus and the Indus* and *History of the Northern Areas of Pakistan*, respectively. Peter Hopkirk's eponymous *The Great Game* deals with its final closing stages, whilst all manner of books address the Kashmir issue.

For the rest, you'll have to pack your bags and head for the Yasin Valley – which I highly recommend: you'll find few more beautiful places and few better people anywhere on earth.

BIBLIOGRAPHY

Dani, Ahmad, *History of the Northern Areas of Pakistan* (Lahore: 1989)

French, Patrick, *Younghusband: The Last Great Imperial Adventurer* (London: 1994)

Hopkirk, Peter, *Foreign Devils on the Silk Road* (London: 1980)

———, *The Great Game* (London: 1990)

Keay, John, *When Men and Mountains Meet* (London: 1977)

———, *The Gilgit Game* (London: 1979)

———, *The Great Arc* (London: 2000)

Knight, E.F., *Where Three Empires Meet* (London: 1894)

Leitner, Gottlieb, *The Languages and Races of Dardistan* (Lahore: 1889)

———, *The Hunza and Nagyr Handbook* (Woking: 1893)

———, *Dardistan in 1866, 1886 and 1893* (Woking: 1893)

Macintyre, Ben, *Josiah the Great: The True Story of the Man who Would be King* (London: 2004)

Meyer, Karl & Brysac, Shareen, *The Tournament of Shadows* (London: 2001)

Pearse, Hugh (ed.), *Soldier and Traveller: Memoirs of Alexander Gardiner* (London: 1898)

Schomberg, Reginald, *Between the Oxus and the Indus* (London: 1935)

Shaw, Robert, *Visits to High Tartary, Yarkand and Kashgar* (London: 1871)

Timmis, Charles, 'George Hayward: his Central Asian explorations, his murder, his legacy', *Asian Affairs*, Vol. 29, Issue 2 (London: 1998)

Tyler, Christian, *Wild West China*, (London: 2003)

Waller, Derek, *The Pundits: British Exploration of Tibet and Central Asia* (Lexington: 1990)

Wilson, Andrew, *Abode of Snow* (London: 1875)

ACKNOWLEDGEMENTS

First thanks are due to my agent, Robert Dudley, for his sterling efforts, and to Simon Hamlet at The History Press for commissioning the book. Thanks also to Lindsey Smith and Christine McMorris at The History Press for the editing.

Thanks to the staff and archivists of the Royal Geographical Society's Reading Room, for showing great patience at obscure requests, and especially to Sarah Strong. The same thanks are due to the staff of the Asian and African Studies Reading Room at the British Library, whose public can be even more trying.

Sincere thanks to the doyen of Great Game writers, Peter Hopkirk, for allowing access to a copy of Hayward's Turkestan journal previously in his possession, and for being kind enough to take an interest in the project (and thanks too to Kathleen Hopkirk for the emails).

The greatest debt of gratitude is owed in the lands through which Hayward travelled. Thanks to various Kashmiri truck drivers and Indian tourists who gave rides to a bedraggled hitchhiker in Ladakh. On the other side of the Karakoram thanks to – amongst others – Abdul Wahab in Kashgar, and to Abdul Latif for company and driving skills on the doomed attempt to reach the valley of the Upper

Yarkand. In Pakistan thanks always to Yaqoob and Habib and everyone at the Madina Guesthouse in Gilgit for hospitality and help over the years, and thanks to the incomparable Mr Beg for tall tales of Partition and the Gilgit Uprising.

Heartfelt thanks to everyone who treated me so kindly in Yasin, especially the valley's magnificent schoolteachers: Ghayas Ali in Sandhi, and Mohamed Murad and Abdul Rashid in Darkot.

Finally, the biggest thanks of all to my family for everything, especially to my father, Des, for taking me to Pakistan the first time and for filling my head with stories.

INDEX